THE GARLAND OF LETTERS

STUDIES IN THE MANTRA-S'ĀSTRA

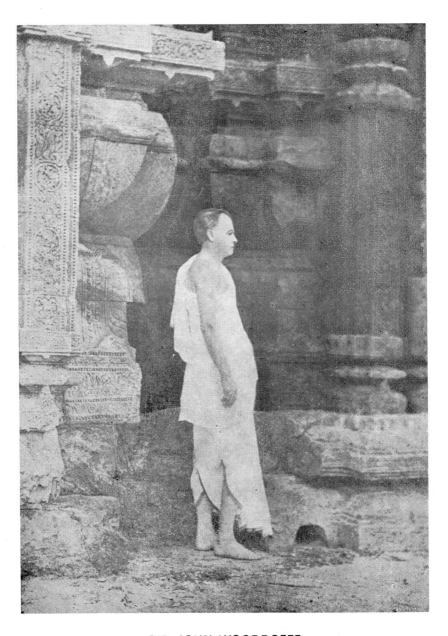

SIR JOHN WOODROFFE

(At the Konarak Temple of Sun-god in Orissa)

THE GARLAND OF LETTERS

STUDIES IN THE MANTRA-S'ĀSTRA

BY

SIR JOHN WOODROFFE

WITH A FOREWORD BY

Prof. T. M. P. Mahadevan, M.A., Ph.D.

University of Madras

GANESH AND COMPANY
MADRAS

Reprint   2011

ISBN   978-81-8598-812-2

Price Rs.350

Published by Ganesh & Co.,
An Imprint of Productivity & Quality Publishing Pvt Ltd.
New No. 38, Thanikachalam Road, T.Nagar
Madras - 600 017, India: E-mail:service@kkbooks.com
Website: http://www.pqp.in
Printed at All IndiaPress, Kennedy Nagar
Ponducherry - 605 001

FOREWORD

Sir John Woodroffe (Arthur Avalon) was instrumental in removing many of the cobwebs of ignorance that had come to cluster round the Sākta philosophy and practice. The decent Indian mind that had developed a deep-seated prejudice against the Tantras became awake to their excellence after the pioneering work of this great foreigner. By editing the original Sanskrit texts, as also by publishing essays on the different aspects of Sāktism, he showed that this cult had a profound philosophy behind it, and that there was nothing irrational or obscurantist about the technique of worship it recommends.

The philosophy of Sāktism is a kind of non-dualism (*advaita*), similar to that of Kashmir Sāivism. In both the systems, the highest Reality is styled Sīva-Sākti. Sīva and Sākti are not different; they are one. Sīva is consciousness as stasis (*cit*); Sākti is consciousness as dynamis (*cidrūpiṇī*). Sīva is pure awareness, which is the ground of all existence. Through his *Parā Sakti*, he effects the manifestation of the universe. He is the sole and whole cause of the world. Only, he becomes the cause, not in his aspect as stasis, but through his dynamic aspect which is spoken of as his feminine part. The main difference between Kashmir Sāivism and Sāktism is that while the former lays relatively greater stress on the Sīva-aspect, the latter emphasizes more the Sākti. Between the Sāiva and Sākta philosophy on the one hand, and Advaita-Vedānta on the other, there is close kinship. Advaita too teaches that the ultimate Reality is non-dual, and that it is of the nature of pure consciousness. But, for it the world-process is not real. The world, according to Advaita, is *māyika*, illusory appearance. The theory of world-appearance is here called *vivarta-vāda*. The corresponding doctrine of the S'aiva and S'ākta schools is known as *ābhāsa-vāda*. According to this view, the universe consists of appearances which are all real in the sense that they are aspects of the ultimate Reality.

Evolution, we are told, is the result of self-movement (*spanda*) on the part of S'iva-S'akti. It is the movement of God that brings about the distinctions of word (*śabda*), object (*artha*), and cognition (*pratyaya*). These three are, in fact, aspects of God's primal energy. It is the causal impetus of the Divine that makes them emerge out of itself. The world of sounds, things, and thoughts, is the self-manifestation of the non-dual Spirit.

The line of evolution is from the subtle to the gross. The Reality in itself — Para S'iva — is transcendent; it is beyond the levels of Matter, Life, and Mind. It is without parts (*niṣkala*), without activity (*niṣkriya*), and beyond the reach of word (*aśabda*), and mind (*amanaska*). The same Reality as the cause of the world-process is called Parameśvara (the Supreme Lord). From Parameśvara arise at first the five categories of pure (*śuddha*) creation ; and then begins the course of finitization consisting in the emergence of the thirty-one categories composing impure (*aśuddha*) creation.

The five categories (*tattvas*) of the pure creation are) : (1) S'iva-tattva, (2) S'akti-tattva, (3) Sadāśiva or S'ādākhya-tattva, (4) Īśvara-tattva, and (5) S'uddha-vidyā-tattva. The first, S'iva-tattva, is the first in the order of

world-evolution.   Here the predominant aspect of
power is Consciousness (*cit*).   The second, *S'akti-tattva*,
is not a subordinate of the first ; it is more properly to
be regarded as its co-ordinate, manifesting mainly the
aspect of bliss (*ānanda*).   The third, *Sadāśivā-tattva*, is
the stage where the experience of being (*sat*) begins.
Here, it is the power of will (*icchā*), that is dominant.
At the next stage which is *Īśvara-tattva*, the power of
knowledge (*jñāna*) figures prominently ; and at the
final stage, *śuddhavidyā-tattva*, it is the power of action
(*kriyā*) that functions as the dominating influence.
Interpreted philosophically, these five stages or categories represent the gradual differentiation in the pure
Experience, which subsequently serves as the basis of
the evolution of the pluralistic universe.   At first there
is only the distinctionless experience.   Into this the
condition of distinction is introduced by *S'akti*.   When
we reach the *Sadāśiva-tattva*, the experience of the form
' *I* am this ' arises with the emphasis on *I*.   At the next
level of *Īśvara-tattva*, the stress is on the *this* : ' *this* am I.'
In order that the universe of minds and objects may
emerge, there should be a balance between *this* and *I*.
This is what is obtained at the stage of *śuddhavidyā*.
Here in the experience ' I am this ' the two get equali-
sed.   It is in such an experience that there is activity
and movement of thought.

Up to *S'uddhavidyā* what we have is only ideal
creation.   It is after this, and with *Māyā*, that there
commences actual creation—the creation that is called
impure.   *Māyā*, which is the first of the thirty-one
categories of impure creation, is the power of obscura-
tion.   It obscures the infinite spirit, and makes possible
the rise of a plurality of souls and things.   The limitless
Experience gets limited as regards both the experiencer

and the experienced, the ' I ' and the ' this '. The next
five categories called *kañcukas* (constrictors) constitute
the ways in which the limitation is brought about.
Kāla is temporal limitation. *Niyati* is restriction in
regard to space. *Rajā* is attachment to particular things.
Vidyā is limited knowledge. *Kalā* is limited agency. As
enveloped in these *kañcukas*, the soul (*puruṣa*) arises.
This is the seventh category. The eighth is *prakṛti*
which is the corresponding limitation on the objective
side. From this, the rest of the evolution appears,
almost as in the Sānkhya scheme. *Buddhi* (intellect),
ahaṁkāra (individuation or egoity), and *manas*, (mind)
come into manifestation in sequence. From *ahaṁkāra*,
there are evolved besides *manas*, the five organs of sense
(*jñānendriyas*) the five organs of action (*karmendriyas*),
and the five essences of elements (*tanmātras*). Out of
the last five emerge the five gross elements which are
ether, air, fire, water, and earth.

So far we have been speaking of the evolution of
the world of things (*artha-prapañca*). It should be noted
that there is a similiar evolution of the world of sounds
(*śabda-prapañca*). In this context Parameśvara is S'abda-
Brahman. The entire world is said to be born of *S'abda*
(*śabda-prabhava*). Here also the line of evolution is
from the subtle to the gross. Corresponding to the five
categories of pure creation there are five stages of the
emanation of sound. The first is *Parā* which is absolutely supreme and subtle. The second is *Paśyantī* which
is less subtle but still undifferentiated. The third is
Madhyamā which is grosser and undifferentiated, though
not articulate. Articulate sound is called *Vaikharī*. This
is of two forms : subtle and gross . It is from *Vaikharī*
that all the letters (*varṇa*), syllables (*Pada*) and sentences
(*vākya*) are manifested.

Parā which resides in the *S'iva-tattva* represents the first movement of *S'abda*. This is also called *Nāda-tattva*. *Paśyanti* stands for *S'akti-tattva* which is known as *Bindu-tattva*. *Nāda* and *Bindu* are the complements of the ultimate potency of creation. From these arise what is known as the *Tribindu* or *Kāmakalā* which is the root of all *mantras*. The three *Bindus* are the white *sita*, red (*śona*) and mixed (*miśra*). These are the effect-Bindus in relation to the original *Mahā-bindu*. They are also referred to as *Bindu*, *Nāda*[1] and *Bīja*, and represent respectively the *Prakāśa* (effulgence), *Vimarśa* (distinction), and *Prakāśa-vimarśa* (combination of both) aspects of the Lord's Power. In *Tāntrika* ritual they are designated *Caraṇatritaya* (the three Feet). A host of correspondences are made with the three *Bindus:* e.g., (1) Moon, Fire and Sun ; (2) *icchā*, *jñāna*, and *kriyā ;* (3) Vāmā, Jyeṣṭhā, and Raudrī ; (4) Brahmā, Viṣṇu, and Rudra. The three *Bindus* constitute symbolically the points of a triangle. It is the *icchā* (desire), *jñāna* (knowledge) and *kriyā* (action) of the universal Being, represented by Moon, Fire and Sun, that are responsible for world-creation. The Sun is technically spoken of as *Kāma*, and the Moon and Fire together as *Kalā*. So, the great triangle is *Kāmakalā*. From *Kāma-kalā* arise the subtle *śabdas* called *Mātṛkās* (the little Mothers) ; and from them the gross *śabdas*, viz., letters (*varṇa*), words (*pada*), and sentences (*vākya*.)

The three lines constituting the *Kāma-kalā* triangle are named after Brahmā, Viṣṇu and Rudra. The letters of the Sanskrit alphabet are distributed thus : 16 letters from *a* to the Brahmā line ; 16 letters from *ka* to the Viṣṇu line; 16 letters from *tha*, to the Rudra line; and the remaining three letters, *la*, *ha*, and *kṣa* to the three corners.

---

1 Here *Nāda* is the effect-*Nāda*.

S'abda is said to be of the nature of *varṇa* (letters) and *dhvani* (sounds). The latter may be regarded as the manifester of the former. Each element or category of the universe has its own natural sound which is called its *bīja* (seed). For example, the sounds of the five elements, ether, air, fire, water, and earth, are *ham, yam, ram, vam,* and *lam,* respectively. The typal sounds are said to be eternal, as also the relation between them and their objects. These sounds may themselves constitute *mantras,* or by mutual combination. A *mantra* is so called because it *saves* one who *meditates* on its significance. Each *mantra* has its *devatā ;* and each *devatā* has its *mantra.* For instance, the *mantra* of Mother Kālī is *krīm,* and of *Māyā* or *S'akti, hrīm.* The significance of *hrīm, e.g.,* is that it is composed of the letters *ha, ra, ī,* and *ma,* representing respectively *ākāśa* (ether), *agni* (fire), *ardhanārīśvara,* and *nādabindu.* Even the word *aham* is a *mantra : a =* S'iva ; *ha =* S'akti ; *a + ha* (with nādabindu, viz., *m) = aham =* I. The breathing process consisting of inspiration and expiration constitutes the *mantra, ham + sa.* The queen of all *mantras,* and their source as well, is *Om* composed of the letters, *a, u, m.* There is a whole literature on the significance of *Om,* and on the technique of meditation thereon. And, there is the grand conception of the World-Mother wearing the garland of letters.

Mantra-sādhana is an essential part of spiritual discipline. The most potent way of realizing a *devatā* is with the help of the *bīja-mantra.* And when an aspirant gets devoted to the highest of all *mantras,* viz., *Om (Praṇava),* and meditates thereon, he reaches eventually the goal of life which is *mokṣa.*

Madras }
March 18, 1955 }   T. M. P. MAHADEVAN

PREFACE

⊤ This book is an attempt, now made for the first time, to explain to an English-knowing reader an undoubtedly difficult subject. I am therefore forcibly reminded of the saying, "Veda fears the man of little knowledge, since injury may be received from him" (*Bibhetyalpaśsutād-Vedo māmayam praharisyate*). It is natural, given this difficulty and the mystery which surrounds the subject, that strangers to India should have failed to understand Mantra. They need not, however, have then (as some have done) jumped to the conclusion that it was "meaningless superstition." This is the familiar argument of the lower mind which says "what I cannot understand can have no sense at all." Mantra *is*, it is true, meaningless to those *who do not know its meaning*. But there are others who do, and to them it is not "superstition." It is because some English-educated Indians are as uninstructed in the matter as that rather common *type* of Western to whose mental outlook and opinions they mould their own, that it was possible to find a distinguished member of this class describing Mantra as "meaningless jabber." Indian doctrines and practice have been so long and so greatly misunderstood and misrepresented by foreigners, that it has always seemed to me a pity that those who are of this *Punyabhūmi* should, through misapprehension, malign without reason anything which is their own. This does not mean that they must accept what is in fact without worth because it is Indian, but they should at least first understand what they condemn as worthless.

When I first entered on a study of this S'āstra I did so in the belief that India did not contain more fools than exist amongst other peoples, but had on the contrary produced intelligences which (to say the least) were the equal of any elsewhere found. Behind the unintelligent practice, which doubtless to some extent exists amongst the multitude of every faith, I felt sure there must be a rational principle, since men on the whole do not continue throughout the ages to do that which is in itself meaningless and is therefore without result. I was not disappointed. The Mantra-S'āstra, so far from being rightly described as " meaningless superstition " or " jabber, " is worthy of a close study which when undertaken, will disclose elements of value to minds free from superstition, of metaphysical bent and subtle-seeing (Sūkṣmadarśin). A profound doctrine, ingeniously though guardedly set forth, is contained in the Tantras of the Mantra-S'āstra or Āgama. This is an auspicious time in which to open out the secrets of this Adhyātmika science. For here in this country there has been a turn in the tide. The class of Indian who was wont to unite with the European critic of his Motherland in misunderstanding and misrepresenting Her thoughts and institutions, is to Her good fortune, gradually disappearing. Those who are recovering from the dazzle produced on its first entrance by an alien civilization are able to judge aright both its merits and defects as also to perceive the truth of the saying of Schiller : " Hold to your dear and precious native land ; there are the strong roots of your strength (Ans Vaterland ans teure schliess dich an. Da sind die starken Wurzeln deiner Kraft.)" Again in the West there is a movement away from the Materialism which regarded that alone as " real " which is gross sensible matter ; and towards

that standpoint whence it is seen that thought itself is a
thing which is every whit as real as any external object.
Each is but an aspect of the one conscious Self whence
both Mind and Matter proceed. This self or *Cit* is the
Soul of the Universe, and the universe is *Cit* which has
become its own object. Every being therein is Consciousness, that is, *Cit* manifesting as the multiple forms of
Mind and Matter which constitute the universe. This
Western movement is called by its adherents " New
Thought," but its basal principles are as old as the
Upaniṣads which proclaimed that all was Feeling-
Consciousness (*Cit*), and therefore what a man thought,
that he became. In fact thought counts for more than
any material means whatever. I am not however
here entering upon a general defence of so immense a
subject, for this cannot be compassed in a work such as
this. In any case—and this is what I am concerned to
show—the Mantra Śāstra is not the mere senseless
rubbish it has been supposed to be.

This book is, as the sub-title states, a Collection of
Studies in, or Essays upon, particular subjects in the
Mantra-Śāstra, a term which is commonly applied to
the Tantra-Śāstra. It is practically composed of two
parts. After Chapter I, which deals with the " Word,"
Chapters II-IX treat of the Principles of the general
doctrine of Śabda. I am much indebted in the preparation of these Chapters to my friend, Professor
Pramathanātha-Mukhopādhyāya. Chapters X-XXI are
elucidations of some subjects in the Tantra-Śāstra which
adopt the Mīmāṃsā doctrine of *Śabda* with some modifications to meet its doctrine of Śakti. Chapters XXII,
XXVIII and XXIX deal with the Mantras " Om " and
the Gāyatrī. An understanding of such terms as Śakti,
Nāda, Bindu, the Causal Śaktis of the Praṇava, Bīja-

mantras and so forth, is essential for those who would understand the S'āstra in which they appear. Hitherto knowledge of these matters has been confined (where it exists at all) to the Gurus and Sādhakas. This does not mean that my information has been gathered from oral sources only. On the contrary, the substance of it may be found in the Tantras. These are however generally unknown. The definitions must be sought for in many S'āstras. When found they must be explained by the aid of general S'āstric knowledge and of *Upāsakas* who possess the tradition. As regards technical terms I refer my readers to other books which I have published, in particular to " S'akti and S'ākta," " The Serpent Power," and the volumes of the series called " The World as Power " describing the chief concepts of Indian Philosophy and Religion.

Chapters X-XXI and XIV are reprinted from the Journal the *Vedānta-Kesarī*. Chapters XXII-XXIII on " *Om* " and the " Necklace of Kālī " appeared in *East and West*, ānd Chapters XXVIII-XXIX on *Mantrasādhana* and the " *Gāyatrī* " in the Introduction to my edition of the Mahānirvāṇa Tantra, which is now superseded, as regards the Introduction, by the fuller account of the Tantras and Tāntrik ritual given in my volume, " S'akti and S'ākta, " and as regards the Text, by another and more correct edition which I have in preparation. Chapter XXX on the " Gāyatrī as an Exercise of Reasoning " is a reprint of a paper read by me before the Indian Rationalistic Society at Calcutta, and has been previously published in its Bulletin. Ten of the papers dealing with general principles were delivered by me in 1919 as Extension Lectures at the instance of the National Council of Education, Bengal.

As I write the concluding lines of this preface hard by the ancient and desolate Temple to the Sun-Lord at Konāraka in Northern Orissa, a continuous rolling sound like that of the Mahāmantra is borne to me from afar. I heard the same sound many years ago at the Pemiongchi monastery when some hundred Buddhist monks rolled out from the depth of their bodies the mantra *Om*. Their chant then suggested the sea, as the sea now suggests the Mantra. Here where the sound is heard are green woods, bushes of jasmine, cactus in bloom and the rose and yellow of the Karavīra and Kalikā flowers. Travelling however whence it comes some two miles seaward, the eye surveys a wide wild waste of land, with here and there sparse clumps of Ketaki, stretching from the world-famous Temple of the " Lord of the Universe " in the south to the Golra jungle on the North. On the Eastern edge the surf of the Bengal Ocean in great waves, marbled with foam with creaming crests, whipped into filmy vapour by the wind, ceaselessly beats upon a lonely shore. The waves as all else are Mantra, for Mantra in its most basal sense is the World viewed as — and in its aspect of — sound. But as I have explained in the Text we must distinguish between Natural Name in its pure sense as the sound of the constituent forces of a thing and the sounds made by the thing when so produced. All sounds and therefore movements form the " Garland of Letters, " which is worn by the Divine Mother, from whose aspects as *Om* or the General Sound (*Sāmānya-spanda*) of the first creative movement all particular sounds and things come. For all things may be rendered in terms of sound. The Universe is movement. The Letters are the sound of particular movements. These are audible as the gross letters which Kālī, the Source of movement, wears as a garland round Her neck. I record this note on a scene which I have known and enjoyed for many years, since I may now be seeing it for the last time. If (as I hope not) this be so, then I bid farewell to my old friend the Sādhu Jagannātha-Dāsa and to this place set in an air of magic of which the Kapila-Samhitā (Ch. VI) says :

Maitreyākhye vane puṇye rathayātrāmahotsave
Ye paśyanti narā bhaktyā te paśyanti tanu raveh.

KONĀRAKA
22nd April, 1922   J. W.

CONTENTS

THE GARLAND OF LETTERS
(VARṆAMĀLĀ)

VĀK OR THE WORD

THE word Vāk (in Latin Vox) comes from the root Vach which means "to speak". The feminine noun Vāk therefore means literally both voice and the word it utters, as also the sound of inanimate objects. It has the same sense therefore as S'abda. Artha is meaning or object. Pratyaya is mental apprehension. All things have a threefold sense, supreme (Parā), subtle (Sūkṣma), gross (Sthūla). Parā-Vāk is the Causal Stress which, in terms of Pratyaya, is the Cosmic Ideation (Sṛṣṭi-kalpanā) of Īśvara. This is the Divine "Word". But Vāk is also an effect, either subtle or gross. Paśyanti Vāk is Vāk actually going forth as lkṣaṇa (Seeing), producing or manifesting, as Sūkṣma Madhyamā-Vāk, or Hiraṇyagarbha S'abda which is the Mātṛkā state of S'abda as it exists in man prior to its gross manifestation as the Varṇas in spoken speech (Vaikharī-vāk). In the Ṛgveda, Sarasvati (V.43-11) is called Pāviravī or daughter of the Lightning, that is, of the great Vajra which sustains the worlds, which according to Sāyaṇa is Madhyamikīvāk. (See Muir O.S.T.—V.337 ff.) Spoken speech (Vaikhari) is manifested to the ear by the gross physical sound or Dhvani produced by the contact of the vocal organs on the surrounding air by the effort (Prayatna) to speak. In the transcendental quiescent Brahman (Paramātmā) or Paramaśiva there is neither S'abda (Aśabda), Artha (Nirviṣaya) nor Pratyaya. There is therefore neither name (Nāma) nor form (Rūpa). In this Infinite Calm there arises a metaphysical Point of Stress or Bindu or Ghanībhūta-S'akti, which stirs forth (Prasarati) as the multiple forces of the universe. This energising is the cause of, and as Jīvātmā is, the World-experience with its duality of subject and object. This play of S'akti takes place in the Ether of Consciousness (Cidākāśa) in such a way that the latter is neither effaced nor affected when the second condition appears, which last is that of both Transcendence and Immanence. This is creation (sṛṣṭi) or, more properly, seeming development (Pariṇāma), since the English word " creation " does not truly express the process. Creation, in the Christian sense, excludes the notion that God is a material cause, creation being neither out of pre-existing matter nor out of God's own substance. Creation also involves an absolutely first appearance. With this reservation the term " creation " is used. More accurately the Brahman Itself, in the form of its Power (S'akti), goes forth (Prasarati). This Sṛṣṭi endures a while (Sthiti) that is for a day of Brahmā, upon which there is according to some, a complete dissolution (Mahāpralaya). Others say that there is no such Mahāpralaya, but that there is always existing some universe, though one or another may disappear. In Mahāpralaya the second state is potentially contained in the undifferentiated unmanifest Māyā-S'akti. S'abdabrahman as an Ullāsa of S'iva sinks as it were into the eternally existing Calm, just as the rising wave

breaks itself and sinks upon the ocean, or as the spray
of a fountain falls again into the waters which feed it.
This notion of the "Word" is very ancient. God
"speaks" the word and the Thing appears. Thus the
Hebrew word for Light is "Aur". Genesis says, "God
said : let there be Light (Aur) and there *was* Light
(Aur)". The Divine word is conceived of in the Hebrew
Scriptures as having creative power. A further stage
of thought presents to us the concept of an aspect of the
Supreme or Person who creates. Thus we have the
Supreme and the Logos, Brahman and S'abdabrahman.
In Greek, Logos means (as does Aparaśabda) thought,
and the word which denotes the object of thought. To
Heraclitus, Logos was the principle underlying the
universe. (see J. N. Heinze, Die Lehre vom Logos in
der Griech, Philosophie). To the Stoics it was the
"Worldsoul" the uniting principle of all rational forces
working in the world. According to Plato, the Logoi
were supersensual primal images or patterns (Jāti) of
visible things. The Alexandrian Philo, influenced by
Platonism and other philosophies of Hellenism,
combined the two conceptions and read into the Old
Testament and Jewish Theology a Being intermediate
between It (that is *ho on*) and the manifold universe.
This intermediate Being was the Logos. According to
Philo, Ideas moulded matter. God first produced the
intelligible world of Ideas which are types (Aparajāti)
of the physical world. Though in Itself nothing but
the Logos, the latter is the author of the ideal world.
Just as an architect projects in his mind a plan of a town
(Polis) and then produces the real town according to
the ideal, so God acted when He created the world, this
Megalopolis (Brahmāṇḍa). The Author of the Fourth
Gospel took up these ideas but gave them expression in

such a way as to serve Christian theological needs. (See J. Réville, *La Doctrine du Logos dans law quatriéme Evangile et dans les Æuvres de Philon*). It has thus been said that John's adoption of the notion was not a mere copy, but a free adaptation of the Philonian *Logos* and a Christianising of it. According to the Evangelist, the Logos is a Person who was before creation and Himself God. It is the Potency of the External Wisdom proceeding from the unmanifest Godhead for the purpose of world-activity, and in the world It is the *Logos Endiathetos* or immanent divine wisdom (See Moeller, Hist. Ch. Church I, 92-222). The Logos through whom the world was created became flesh (Avatāra), that it was manifested in man (*Verbum caro factum est*). He is the Son who is Jesus Christ, He who in the heavenly pre-existence is called the Logos and after His incarnation the man Jesus who is the Christ, who is neither prophet nor superman but Pūrṇāvatāra of God. The Logos is the perfect self-presentation of God in the Son. In Jesus there was identity of being with God. The fourth Gospel opens grandly, " In the beginning was the Word, and the Word was with God, and the Word was God. " These are the very words of Veda. *Prajāpatir vai idam āsīt :* In the beginning was Brahman. *Tasya vāg dvitīyā āsīt ;* with whom was Vāk or the Word ; (She is spoken of as second to Him because She is first potentially in, and then as Sʹakti issues from Him) ; *Vāg vai paramam Brahma ;* and the word is Brahman. Vāk is thus a Sakti or Power of the Brahman which is one with the Possessor of Power (Sʹaktimān). This Sʹakti which was in Him is at the creation with Him, and evolves into the form of the Universe whilst still remaining what It is—the Supreme Sʹakti.

It is always possible that human thought may develop similarly and yet independently. It is not improbable also, seeing the influence of India on the West, that the philonic and Neo-platonic and Johannean conceptions were, in part at least, indebted for their origin to India. Nevertheless there are, with general points of similarity, others of difference, for which accuracy demands attention. Thus the Brahman is the material cause of the World which the Christian Logos is not. For Christianity is dualism. Vāk is no Person in a Trinity. Vāk is Herself the Mother of the Trimūrthi who are Brahmā, Viṣṇu and Rudra. For She is the Supreme S'akti, one with Brahman. The full incarnation is a concept of Hinduism, yet, in the form of Jīva, Vāk is incarnated not in one historic person only but in all men, beings and things. The Word as Vāk became flesh, not on one particular date in one particular place and in one particular historic person. It appeared and now appears in the flesh and other forms of matter of all limited beings or Jīvas, each of whom may through Veda directly realise the Brahman whose S'akti is the word of Vāk. Jesus alone was God in human form. Others were not, are not and never can become God. Vāk manifests Herself in every man and is knowable and known as She is in Hereself—that is Brahman, in that spiritual experience which is Veda.

The universe is the outcome of the Divine Desire (Kāma) or Will (Icchā). Kāma on the physical plane denotes among other things, sexual desire. In the highest sense it is the first creative impulse of the One to be many, whereby It begets Itself as all creatures. Earthly desire and self-reproduction are but limited manifestations of that first impulse. The Divine Will is continually and presently working through the

individual sexual desire for the continued creation of the
universe. This Divine Kāma is eternal and the origin
of all things. And so Parmenides speaking of Eros or
Love, said *Prōtision mén érota theōn nétisato panton.*
(" He devised Eros, the first of all the Gods "). This is
the Divine Eros through whom things are; (See Plato
Symp. 5-6). The Daughter of Kāma is Vāk. The
latter as the Divine Will speaks the Divine Word upon
which the Thing is. In the Atharvaveda (IX-2) Kāma
is celebrated as a great Power superior to all the Devas.
The Daughter of Kāma is named " The Cow which
sages call Vākvirāt," that is Vāk in the form of the
universe.

In the " beginning " there was Brahman and with
It was Vāk. In the Veda (S'atapatha-Brāhmaṇa
VI. 1-1-8) it is said, " this Being (Puruṣa) Prajāpati
willed ' May I be many ', ' May I be propagated. ' He
energised *(So śrāmyat sa tapo' tapyata).* Vāk was His,
She was produced from Him *(Vāg evā sya sā sṛjyata)* and
pervaded all which exists. " Then on the issue of Vāk,
" By his mind he united with Vāk (S'a. P. Br. X. 6-5-4;
Brih. Ar. Up. Roer p. 50) and thus (S'a. P. VI. 1-2ff)
became pregnant *(Garbhi abhavat).* " In the Kāṭhaka it
is said (XII-5 and XXVII-1) " Prajāpati only was then
this *(Prajāpatir vai idam āsit).* Vāk was a second to Him
(Tasya vāg dvitīya āsit). He united with Her *(Tāṁ
maithunaṁ sambhavat)* and She became pregnant *(Sā
garbhaṁ ādhatta).* She went out from Him and produced
these creatures *(Sā asmād apākrāmat sā imāh prajāh asṛjata)*
and again re-entered Him *(Sā prajāpatim eva punah
prāviśat).* "

Again in the Pañcaviṁśa Br. (XX-14-2) it is
similarly said : " Prajāpati alone was this universe.

He had Vāk too as His own, as a Second to Him. He
thought, 'let me now put forth this Vāk. She will
traverse and pervade all this. That is, the Brahman or
S'iva first willed to be many and His S'akti, which was
one with Him, issued as His Word." The Union of
Will and Word was the potency of creation, all things
being held in un-differentiated mass in the Great Womb
(Mahāyoni) of the Mother of all (Ambikā). This
potency became actual as the manifested universe, and
at its dissolution S'akti, as such universe re-entered
Brahman and remained one with It (Cit) as Cidrūpiṇī.
Meanwhile She pervades, as immanent Spirit, both
Mind and Matter which are Its temporal forms. For
as the Bṛhadāraṇyaka-Upaniṣad says (pp. 50-53), Ed.
Roer): " By that Vāk and that Ātmā He created all
things whatsoever, the Vedas, Metres, Sacrifices and all
Creatures " (Sā tayā vācā tena ātmanā idaṁ sarvaṁ asṛjata
ad idaṁ kiṁca ṛco yajūmṣi sāmānśi chandāṁsi yajñān
prajāh paśun). "First was produced the sacred Vaidik
science " (S'. P. Br. VI. 1-1-8). In the Mahābhārata,
Sarasvatī as Vāk is called the "Mother of the Vedas "
(S'āntiparva, V. 12, 920) and the same is said of Vāk
in the Taittirīya-Brāhmaṇa (II. 8-8-5) where (and in the
preceding parva IV) She is also said to contain within
Herself all words and to have been sought with Tapas
by the Ṛṣis who put forth the Vedic Hymns (Ṛṣayo
mantrakṛtah). In the Bhiṣmaparva of the Mahābhārata
(v. 3019) Acyuta (Kṛṣṇa) is said to have produced
Sarasvatī and the Vedas from His mind; and in the
Vanaparva (V. 13,432) the Gāyatrī is called the Mother
of the Vedas, for Gāyatrī Devī is a form of Vāk. Vāk
is the Mother of the Vedas and of all things which their
words denote. Vāk in the form of Veda is Vedātmikā
Vāk (See Sāyaṇa and other citations given in Muir

O.S.T. I-325ff where, as in other volumes, some of the
Texts concerning Vāk are collected). The substance of
the whole world is Vāk (*Jagat Vānmaya*), for as previously
stated the world (Jagat) is Śabdaprabhava.

The Ṛgveda (X. 125-5) says: "I (Vāk) make him
whom I love formidable, him a Brāhmaṇa, him a Ṛṣi,
him a Sage." It is this Vāk which entered the Ṛṣis, and has
thus made Herself known to men. 'By sacrifice they
followed the path of Vāk and found Her entered into the
Ṛṣis" (Ṛgveda, X. 71-3). The Ṛṣis called their Hymns
by various names, amongst others Vāk, for they are
manifestations of Vāk. Vāk is one with Brahman for
Śiva and Śakti are one. In the Bṛhadāraṇyaka-Upaniṣad
it is said (Ed. Roer, 688), "By Vāk, O Monarch, the
Brahman is known. Vāk is the Supreme Brahman"
(*Vāchaiva saṁrād Brahma jñāyate vāg vai saṁrāt paramam
Brahma*). The Mahābhārata (Śāntiparva V. 12,920),
says: "Behold Sarasvatī, Mother of the Vedas abiding in
me (*Vedōnāṁ mātraṁ paśya mātraṁ paśya matsthāṁ devīṁ
Sarasvatīṁ*). She, this great Śakti, is one with Maheśvara.
And so in the Maṅgalācaraṇa prefixed to the Commentaries on the Ṛk Saṁhitā and Taittirīya-Saṁhitā by
both Sāyaṇa and Mādhava it is said: "I reverence
Maheśvara the hallowed abode of sacred knowledge, of
whom the Vedas are the breathings and who from the
Vedas formed the whole universe." (*Yasya niśvasitam
vedāh yo vedebhyo' khilam jagat, Nirmame tam aham vande
vidyātīrtham Maheśvaram*). The Taittirīya-Brāhmaṇa
(III, 39-1) says) that Vāk is imperishable, the first-born
of Ṛta, Mother of the Vedas and centre-point of
immortality (*Vāg akṣarām prathamājā ṛtasya vedānāṁ mātā
amṛtasya nābhih*). The Śatapatha-Brāhmaṇa says (VII.
5-2-21): "Vāk is the unborn." It was from Vāk
that the Maker of the Universe (Viśvakarmā) produced

creatures (*Vāg vai ajo vāco vai prajāh viśvakarmā jajāna*).
Various texts associate the Lord of creatures (Prajāpati),
called Paśupati in the Śaiva Śāstra, with His Śakti Vāk,
as to which see Weber, Indische Studien, IX. 477ff.
and Muir's Original Sanskrit Texts, V. 391.

　　Śaṁkarācārya (Sūtra 1-3, 28) quoting ' By His
mind He united with Vāk,' says that by this and other
Texts the Veda in various places declares that creation
was preceded by the Word from which the whole universe of Devas and organic and inorganic earth-life are
produced.　But it is said that the world was produced
from Brahman.　How then was it produced from the
Word ?　Creation was preceded by the Word.　He says
that when any man is occupied with any end which he
wishes to accomplish, he first calls to mind the word
which expresses it and then proceeds to effect his purpose.
Using this as analogy he says that before creation the
words of Veda were manifested in His mind and afterwards he created the objects which resulted from them :
Thus the Vaidik text which says " Uttering Bhūh
(earth) he created the earth (Bhūmi) " and so forth,
means that the different worlds and the beings therein
were manifested or created from the word " Bhūh " and
so forth manifested in His mind.　These distinctions of
" before " and afterwards and so forth are Vyāvahārika.
Human analogies are necessarily imperfect.　In
Īśvara as causal body what (as manifested) are
called Pratyaya, Sabda, Artha are one and identical
(and therefore, as manifested, co-ordinate) though
for the purposes of exposition we may say that His
Sṛṣṭi-kalpanā is a fraction of the Pratyaya which He
has of his own Ānandamaya causal body, and included
therein the subtle and gross bodies.　His Paraśabda
involves as effects all Aparaśabdas, and His Artha is the

first stressing mass of Prakṛtiśakti in which are experienced all elements (Vikṛti) and things which are compounded of them. For Īśvara has direct and immediate apprehension of the three bodies, Hiraṇyagarbha of the second and third, and Virāt of the third. Parā-Vāk is therefore what has been previously spoken of as Paraśabda, and Vāk (simply) as Śabda in its subtle form as Mātṛkā (Madhyamā-Vāk) and gross form (Vaikharī-Vāk). The latter is that of the spoken letters (Varṇa) of which the Mantras are made. There is but one Cause of speech, as also of all the things in the universe which it denotes and also, of the mental apprehension (Pratyaya) or " going towards " the object of the mind. That cause is the Supreme Devī Sarasvatī, Mother of the Vedas and of the Worlds, manifesting as the name (Nāma) and form (Rūpa) which is the Universe. She is thus the Supreme Śakti to whom a title is given, taken from one of Her productions, the manifested word or speech. The musical instrument (Vīṇā), which Sarasvatī holds, denotes all sounds (Śabda), of which She is the Mother. White are Her garments and transparent whiteness is the colour of both Ākāśa and Buddhi. Her name denotes " flow " or "motion " (Saras). She is such, in the Supreme sense, as being the activity (Śakti) of the unmoving Śiva or Brahman. She is again such as the play in the manifested World of the dynamic Śaktis in and around the rigid Ether, which appeared at creation with the roaring sound " Haṁ " and then stood still as the steady framework on, and in which the whole universe flows or moves. According to Science, Ether has no such imperfections as we associate with matter. It is the property of the latter to grow old, to decay, to wear out. But such as exists in the Ether remains unchanged. It is this rigid,

unwasting enduring Ether which is Vajra, the hard,
stable, lasting unwasting Vajra, the static manifestation
of the static Brahman, in which the Dynamic Brahman
as Sarasvatī flows or moves. The former is S'ūnya, the
void of space, in which all movement takes place. Just
as in Brāhmanism Ākāśa is transferred to the Brahman-
idea as Cidākāśa: so this Ethereal S'ūnya in Northern
Buddhist Monism as sTongap-nyid (S'ūnyatā) stands for
the Ultimate beyond all categories (See the Demchog
Tantra published as the seventh Volume of my "Tantric
Texts as sTongap-nyid)". Sarasvatī, the Dynamic
Brahman with Her "consort" the static Brahman as
Brahmā is borne upon the Haṁsa which is no material
"bird" but the natural name of the vital function
manifesting as the expiring (Haṁ) and inspiring (Sah)
breath or Prāṇabīa in all breathing creatures (Prāṇi).
She again is the Divine in the aspect as Wisdom and
Learning, for she is the Mother of Veda, that is of all
knowledge touching Brahman and the Universe. She is
the Word of which it was born and She exists in that
which is the issue of Her great womb (Mahāyoni). Not
therefore idly have men worshipped Vāk or Sarasvatī
as the Supreme Power.

CHAPTER II

ARTHA, PRATYAYA AND S'ABDA

THE one supreme Consciousness (Cit) which is the Changeless Principle of all experience evolves by, and from out of, its Power (S'akti), which is both Cit-S'akti and Māyāśakti—the duality of subject and object, mind and matter. In Parasamvit or Saccidānanda the experience is unitary and devoid of every species of duality. I have dealt in my book " S'akti and S'ākta " with the various possible English renderings of the untranslatable word Cit which subject to the reservations there made, may be called Feeling-Consciousness or with less liability to misunderstanding the Changeless Principle of all changing experience. Through the operation of S'akti the homogeneous Unity becomes the Many or universe of subject and object, mind and matter. The Perfect Experience, without ceasing to be such, involves Itself in mind and matter and thus becomes the imperfect or limited experience. As all is the one Self, this apparent dichotomy means that the Self which manifests as a limited subject sees (though it is unaware of it) itself as object.

Cit is without motion (Niṣpanda), without action (Niṣkriya), without mind (Amanah) and without S'abda (Aśabda). It is neither subject nor knows any object other than Itself as Cidrūpiṇi-S'akti. Creation commences by an initial movement or vibration

(Spandana) in the Cosmic Stuff, as some Western writers call it, and which in Indian parlance is Saspanda Prakṛti-S'akti. Just as the nature of Cit or the S'iva aspect of Brahman is rest, quiescence, so that of Prakṛti is movement. Prior however to manifestation, that is during dissolution (Pralaya of the universe, Prakṛti exists in a state of equilibrated energy (Sāmyāvasthā) in which there is Sarūpapariṇāma. It then moves (Virūpapariṇāma). This is the first cosmic vibration (Spandana) in which the equilibrated energy is released.

The approximate sound of this movement is the Mantra Oṁ. Dualism with all its varieties is thus produced. There is thus a bifurcation of Consciousness into Mind and Matter which therefore constitute a parallelism of common origin. The mind as subject has apprehension (Pratyaya) of objects (Artha), and names those objects by word (S'abda) or language. In man S'abda, Artha, and Pratyaya are connected but distinct. Like everything else they are three effectual manifestations of the movement (Spanda) which is the common Causal Stress. At the stage of Causal S'akti however the three are one ; so that then S'abda = Artha = Pratyaya = Spanda, the last being not, as in manifestation, a common denominator but the equivalent of S'abda, Artha, Pratyaya. The state is one of logical unity. Īśvara's Spanda is His S'abda, is His Artha, is His Pratyaya. Doubtless in projecting our standpoint as existence into Divine Being we cannot help using the analogy of aspects. And so we speak of Cit and the Causal Stress (S'akti) of S'iva and S'akti as two aspects and so on. Nevertheless we must not understand that there is any distinctness in the midst of relationships or even of unity which expresses our idea of aspects. Ultimately the relation of S'abda, Artha and Pratyaya is an identical equation and not a ratio, that is a fraction with a numerator and a denominator. Whilst on the absolute plane which is the Cosmic Causal body the three are one, there is, on and with the manifestation of the subtle body, a divergent descent of the three, retaining, as they always do, their mutual connection. The causal aspect is S'abdabrahman, the Stress or Creative S'akti giving rise to motion and bodies produced by it which are forms of the subtle and gross S'akti. What was a simple stress in quiescent and unaffected consciousness with unitary experience becomes bifurcated as mind and matter. It is here most important to remember (for it is the key to that which follows) that the nature of a process in which the One becomes Many involves this :—the essential substance (Spirit) of both Mind and Matter remains the same, and the S'akti elements and the motion of both are similar. Hence they are mutually connected with a natural relation. Feeling and object of feeling are correlated. Thus sensation through the eye and Manas, and colour as an object which is perceived, are at base the one Ātmā thus dually manifested. The sensation of sight and the colour are both again products of Tejas-Tanmātra. The Indriya is Sātvikāmśa of the Apañcīkṛta-Tanmātra, and the object seen is the Tāmasikāmśa of the same. In Sāmkhya, and commonly in the S'ākta-Tantras, both are products of the same Ahamkāra. Sensation and its object are two aspects of one and the same thing. The vibration of the object (Artha) and of the Vṛtti or modification of mind by which apprehension (Pratyaya) is had of it are the same, and the natural (S'abda) of an object (Artha) is the sound produced by the forces which constitute it. There exists all this parallelism because our postulate is that mind and matter are but twin aspects of the one undivided Self. So when an object (Viṣaya, Artha) affects the senses (Indriya), being attended to by that function of mind which is called Manas, there arises in the mind a modification (Vṛtti) of its substance which is an exact counterpart of the external object. In passing I may observe that this is a fundamental principle on which all Tāntric-Sādhana by way of Upāsanā rests. By worship and meditation or Japa of Mantras the mind is actually *shaped* into the form of the object of worship and is made pure for the time being through the purity of the object (namely Iṣṭadevatā), which is its content. By continual practice (Abhyāsa) the mind becomes full of the object to the exclusion of all else, steady in its purity, and does not stray into impurity. So long as mind exists it must have an object and the object of Sadhana is to present it with a pure one.

Before proceeding further it is necessary to have clear notions as to the meaning of Mind, Matter, Pratyaya, S'abda and Artha. Everything is " material " according to the Vedānta which is not Pure Transcendent S'pirit (Anupāhita-Cit). Immanent of Upāhita-Cit is that which is associated with mind and matter. This Cit with Upādhi is either Para = S'uddha-sattva-pradhāna = Utkṛṣṭo-pādhī = Samaṣṭi, or Apara = Malina-sattva-pradhāna = Nikṛṣṭopādhi = Vyaṣṭi. In each of these there are the three bodies causal (Kāraṇa), subtle (Sūkṣma) and gross (Sthūla). This Upādhi is S'akti as Māyā or Prakṛti-S'akti as that term is used in Advaitavāda. As Prakṛti-S'akti is " material " not as being scientific " matter " but as the subtle material cause of all things, all its effects (Vikṛti) are necessarily of the same character as their cause and are material. These Vikṛtis may be divided into the two parallel groups of Mind (Antahkaraṇa) and its outer instruments or senses (Indriya), and matter or Pañca-bhūta derived from the more rudimentary forms of infra-sensible " matter " which are the Pañca-Tanmātras. These are beyond the threshold of sensation of the ordinary Jīva.

What then is Mind? It follows from the above that it is a manifestation of S'akti or Power in the form of force, which is Power translated to the material plane, and is as much a material (Bhautika) substance as is matter (Bhūta) itself. Thought (for, except in Samādhi, mind is never free of thought) is from the creative standpoint a passing thought and matter a lasting thought. Matter is a dense and gross form of the more subtle and tenuous form of the common Prakṛti-S'akti. Mind is Bhautika because it is according to Vedānta composed of the Sāttvik part (Sāttvikāṁśa) of the Tanmātra. According to Sāṁkhya it is Ahaṁkārī. According to Vedāntas, Mind is not Vibhu that is all-spreading, unlimited and indivisible into parts : nor is it Aṇu or atomic, that is limited and indivisible into parts. It is Madhyama-Parimāṇa, that is limited and divisible into parts and thus takes the form of its objects. Mind has parts in the sense that it is divisible into parts, that is one part of the mind can attend to one thing and to another at one and the same time. As it also takes the shape of the object perceived, it spreads or shrinks with it. It pervades the whole body whether in the waking (Jāgrat) or dreaming state (Svapna), but in deep sleep (Suṣupti) it is withdrawn as all else into the causal body and according to one account is then absorbed in the Nāḍī.

What then is the nature of knowing by the mind ? According to the Naiyāyikas who hold that the mind is atomic (Aṇu), it does not go forth, or transform itself into the shape of the object. Jñāna is a Guṇa of Ātma which is produced by the association of Mind (Manas) and Ātmā. According to Vedānta, Jñāna is a transformation (Pariṇāma) of the Antahkaraṇa or Mind which is a Tattva of Madhyama-Pariṇāma. Jñāna is of two kinds, *viz.*, Jñāna Svarūpa and Jñāna Vṛtti. The former is Brahmasvarūpa of Perfect Experience or Cit. The latter is knowledge of objects or the ordinary worldly imperfect experience. Opinion varies as to the mode of operation in the case of the Mind and Jñānavṛtti. According to some, light from the eye goes forth. Hence the eye is called Tejas. Mind going forth with the light of the eye impinges upon and takes the shape of the object. Mind is called " transparent " (Svaccha) because it can take the shape of the object presented to it. Ātma is ever illuminating the mind and when there is a particular Vṛtti, Ātmā illuminates it so that it is present to the limited consciousness.

Knowledge is true or false (Mithyā). Right knowledge or Pramā is defined as *Tadvati tat prakārakajñānaṁ* which means apprehension of an object according to its true nature, that is, in its own class or Jāti. The mind not only perceives a particular thing (Vyakti) but also the genus or class (Jāti) to which it belongs ; for this Jāti is not merely a subjective thing but is inherent in the Vyakti as its nature (Prakāra) and both are perceived in right knowing, as when in the case of Ghaṭa (jar) its Jāti or Ghaṭatva (jar-ness) is perceived. Where however a rope is mistaken for a snake there is Mithya-Jñāna. The particular rope excites knowledge, but it is false knowledge, because through a defect (Doṣa) in the percipient subject, the rope is not perceived under its Jāti but under that of a

serpent. In short in right perception there is true
conformity of thought with its object. To perceive on
the other hand a rope where there is Ghaṭatva is false
perception.

What then is Artha or object (Viṣaya)? This is the
object which constitutes the mind's content. Object is
manifold as the various forms (Rūpa) which make the
universe. It is the "other" which the Self as mind
perceives. These forms are constituted of the five
Bhūtas—Ākāśa, Vāyu, Tejas, Ap, Pṛthivī representing
various densities of Prākṛtic substance. Just as the
mind is a form of motion (Spandana) of that substance,
so the five Bhūtas are five forms of motion of the same
Prakṛti which in the Tantras are symbolised by figures
denoting the forms of the vibration namely a circle with
openings (Chidra) shown as points on it denoting the
interstitial character of Ākāśa ; a circle denoting Vāyu ;
and a triangle, crescent and cube-square denoting Tejas,
Ap, and Pṛthivī respectively. The direction of the
vibration also varies as being in all directions, at an
acute angle to the line of the wave (Tiryag-gamanaśila),
upwards, downwards and " in the middle" where the
forces are equilibrated and matter becomes stationary.
These again are space-giving, general movement
(Calanapara), expansion, contraction, cohesion, stimula-
ting the sense of hearing, touch and feel, (not all forms
of contact), sight or colour and form, taste, and smell
respectively, the centres of which in the Piṇḍāṇḍa are
the Cakras from Viśuddha to Mūlādhāra. The Bīja
Mantras of these are Ham, Yam, Ram, Vam, Lam, the
meaning of which is later explained when dealing with
natural name. They seem like gibberish to the uniniti-
ated. Hence even the common Bengali expression
" What Hayaralava is this ? " These Bhūtas derive

from the Tanmātra commencing with S'abda-Tanmātra
or infra-sensible sound, which by addition of mass
becomes Ākāśa, the Guṇa of which is sensible sound
which generates Vāyu-Tanmātra from which comes
Vāyu Bhūta and so on with the rest, though the mode
of derivation is not always given in the same terms.
The substance of it is that Bhūta or gross sensible
matter is derived from a subtle form of the same which
is not sensible by the gross ear but mentally apprehen-
sible by the Yogī. Hence it is said *Tāni vastūni tanmā-
trādini pratyakṣaviṣayāṇi* (that is to Yogīs). Object
(Viṣaya) is thus not limited to the gross objects seen by
the senses of ordinary men. There are also subtle
objects which may be perceived through the senses or
the mind by the possessor of " Powers " (Siddhi) which
are merely extensions of natural faculty. These are
hidden from ordinary men whose powers vary. Some
can perceive more than others. By scientific instruments we can see (microscope) and hear (microphone)
things beyond the capacity of the highest natural power
of the senses. Is that the end? No, because as we
perfect these auxiliaries of natural instruments we see
and hear more. Once the microscope gave only a
magnification of a few diameters. Now it is of thou-
sands. At each stage more is known. A point however
is reached at which " seeing " takes place not through
the gross senses but by the mind. Everything may be
an object which is not the Asaṅgabrahman or Brahma-
svarūpa that is the Supreme Self or Spirit as It is in
Itself. This is not known by either sense or mind or by
any Pramāṇa or instrument of knowledge. Even
Sabda-Pramāṇa or Veda here fails. Because Brahman
as It is in Itself (Svarūpa) is never an object, being the
true nature of the cognising Self. As such it is beyond

mind and speech. The latter can only give an indication (Lakṣaṇa) of it. Higher objects beyond the
reach of the senses (Atīndrīya) are only perceived by
the heightened powers of the mind of Yogīs. Mind, for
instance, is Atīndriya for it cannot be sensed. Yet
Yogīs can " see, " that is, mentally apprehend the mind
of another which becomes an object for their apprehension. In such cases his mind takes the form of that
other, when everything which was in the latter mind
namely its modification (Vṛittis) or thoughts are known
to him. And so the experience of objects becomes
more and more subtle and inclusive until the state of
Supreme Experience Itself is attained when there is
neither subject nor object. This is Brahma-svarūpa.
This apprehension or image which one has of an object
(Artha) evoked by a word (S'abda) is called Pratyaya.
The third form of divergent descent of the S'abda-
brahman, namely S'abda, will be the subject of a
following chapter.

CHAPTER III

AŚABDA AND PARAŚABDA

INDIAN doctrine revolves round the two concepts of Changelessness and Change. As these propositions cannot be logically predicated of the same substance, recourse is had to the doctrine of aspects. According to this, Brahman as It is in Itself (Brahmasvarūpa) or Śiva does not change, but Brahman as the Power (Śakti) from which the world evolves does, as Māyā, change. It is perhaps more simple to say that Brahman produces and exists as the world without derogation to Its own unchanging unity. How this can be is, like other ultimates, inconceivable. But its truth is said to rest on two established facts, namely the daily experience of the world of the many on the one hand, and the ecstatic (Samādhi) experience of the One on the other. Both are facts of experience though *how* they can be so is a mystery.

When we come to deal with the Mantra-Śāstra the same doctrines are expressed in the language of the subject with which it is occupied, namely Śabda, of which Mantras are forms. Śabda or Sound exists only where there is motion or Spanda. If there is no Spanda there is no Śabda. If there is Śabda there is Spanda. But the transcendent Brahman or Cit (Brahmasvarūpa) is quiescent and changeless. Therefore it is said to be without motion (Niṣpanda) and without Śabda

(Aśabda). From out of this Cit (for there is but one) but without affecting its own changelessness, there arises a creative stir or stress which evolves into the universe. This is the work of the active Brahman or Īśvara. Just as the Parabrahman is Aśabda, Īśvara is Śabdabrahman or Paraśabda. As the former is Niśabda, the latter, as Māyā Śakti, is with motion (Saspanda). Paraśabda, Parā Vāk or Śabdabrahman are each names for the Brahman as the cause of the manifested Śabda. Paraśabda is the causal body of sound. Śabdatanmātra is the subtle body of the sound, Ākāśa is the gross body of sound which (though a Guṇa of it) is only apprehended through the medium of air, the sound waves which strike the ear. Through the latter and mind the sensation of sound is experienced. Śabdatanmātra is pure natural sound as apprehended by Hiraṇyagarbha or Yogīs who share his experience. Gross sound is of two kinds namely Vaidik sound (Śrautaśabda) or approximate natural sound either primary or secondary, and Laukika Śabda, the speech of the ordinary average mortals other than Vaidika Śabda. Taking " cognizance " to mean ' direct apprehension, ' Īśvara has cognizance of all kinds of Śabda, (Paraśabda, Śabda Tanmātra, Śrauta Śabda, Laukika Śabda), Hiraṇyagarbha or Sūtrātma of the last three, Ṛṣis of the last two and ordinary men of the last only. From Paraśabda or Parā-Vāk therefore proceed in their order Śabdatanmātra, Śrauta-Śabda and Laukika Śabda.

Dealing nextly with Pratyaya, Artha and Śabda in their cosmic and individual aspects,—in the Īśvara stage (*i.e.* in so far as there is the causal body) Pratyaya is the Īśvara consciousness of His own body of Bliss (Ānandamaya) and the cosmic ideation (Sṛṣṭi-kalpanā whereby He projects the world. This Sṛṣṭi-kalpanā again *is* the stressing mass of Prakṛti or Māyā and Avidyā śakti, and this *is* the Paraśabda or Parā-Vāk, involving (as the cause involves its effects) the various kinds of Apara-S'abda including the Mātṛkas, Varṇas and Mantras. The approximate representation of the causal (Para) S'abda as a whole to the Ṛṣi-ear is "om." It is however to be noted that Īśvara's whole Pratyaya is Sṛṣṭi-kalpanā, His Artha is the stressing mass of Prakṛti. It is further to be noted that, in Īśvara, Pratyaya, S'abda, and Artha are one and not distinct though co-related, as in Hiraṇyagarbha, Virāt and the individual Jīva. What we may call the elements of the universe namely the Apañcīkṛta Bhūtas or Tanmātras, the Indriyas, Prāṇas, Antahkaraṇa and Sthūla Bhūtas are evolved directly by Īśvara as Īśvara. This is Bhūtasṛṣṭi.

He then, as Hiraṇyagarbha, evolves Bhautika-Sṛṣṭi. The elements themselves must be traced directly to the causal body, but as Hiraṇyagarbha he compounds them. Hence Hiraṇyagarbha's Sṛṣṭi-kalpanā refers to Bhautika Sṛṣṭi, that is the compounding of the elements which have been already provided by Īśvara as Īśvara. S'abda in the Hiraṇyagarbha aspect is S'abda-tanmātra involving the lower or derivative forms. His Artha is everything except the Samaṣṭi causal body.

Bhautika-S'ṛṣṭi may relate either to Sūkṣma or Sthūla elements, the former being everything except the latter; so that theoretically the creative operation may be divided between Sūtrātma and Virāt. But the S'āstra does not in fact contemplate such a division. Virāt is Cit associated with the created whole—a *natura naturata* as it were, to borrow Spinoza's term. Causal activity does not appear to be extended to this. However, if we provisionally leave the compounding of the Sthūla elements to Virāt, then its Pratyaya too may be called Sṛṣṭikalpanā. His S'abda is various grades of sound, gross and subtle, extending to, but not including, S'abda-tanmātra. His Artha is everything except the Samaṣṭi causal and subtle body.

Sūkṣma and Sthūla are relative terms and admit of grades, hence between the limits of S'abda-tanmātra and average gross sounds there will be more and more subtle sounds—all apprehended by Hiraṇyagarbha ; all save the Tanmātra being apprehended by Virāt as Virāt. If we define Sūkṣma as what is of the order of the Tanmātra as the superior limit, then Cit associated with this whole series of Sthūla is Virāt. The latter identifies Himself with Samaṣṭi Sthūla-Deha. It is however a long way from the Annamaya Kośa of average perception to the Prāṇamaya Kośa which comes "next" in order of fineness and which is a modification (Rājasika) of the Tanmātras. What the S'āstra calls Annamaya-kośa is therefore really a graded series. The gross body in made up of visible cells : those of microscopic granules ; those of still finer corpuscles ; and so on. The five Kośas are therefore only five broad landmarks in a series consisting of innumerable gradations as are the seven colours of the rainbow. Hiraṇyagarbha and Virāt are also the types correspond-ing cosmically to our experiences of certain distinctive forms, in a really innumerable series of forms. So that instead of three we may say that there are innumerable creative Cit-śaktis. If the numbers are given differently there is no essential discrepancy. Īśvara, Hiraṇyagarbha, and Virāt are three forms of creative manifestation corresponding cosmically to the Suṣupti, Svapna and Jāgrat. But the truth-seers, as compared with the

system-makers, salute Him as the Many-formed
(Namaste bahurūpāya). Īsvara has direct apprehension
of all three collectively, causal, subtle, and gross. The
cause involves the effects. As Hiraṇyagarbha, He
apprehends directly the second and third (Svapna,
Jāgrat), and as Virāt he apprehends the third (Jāgrat).

We pass now to the individual (Vyaṣṭi) aspect.
Corresponding with Īsvara and with Māyā we have
Prājña with Avidyā. The Pratyaya of Prājña is the
Vyaṣṭi counter-part in S'uṣupti of the Ānandamaya
consciousness which Īsvara has of His own causal body.
Some English writers misunderstand the statement in
the Upaniṣad that the Jīva in dreamless sleep is
Brahman to mean that the experience in slumber is that
of Īsvara, or of the Supreme Brahman. Of course this
is not so, for the Prājña's experience then is associated
with Avidyā whereas Īsvara's is free of all Avidyā. The
comparison is made by way of analogy. For just as in
Suṣupti the Jīva loses the sense of duality, since all
objects as separate things disappear in slumber, so in
Īsvara there is no sense of separateness. All things are
conceived as in and as Himself. The S'abda of Prājña
is Paras'abda-Viśeṣa. This is no sound to him but that
"part" of the causal stress which is the causal body of
the particular Jīva. His Artha is the Vyaṣṭi causal body,
that is, the temporary equilibrium in Suṣupti of the
Stress which makes the Jīva. As in the Samaṣṭi
experience, Pratyaya, Artha and S'abda are one.
Samskāras are latent and all Vṛttis are withdrawn into
the Kāraṇa-Deha. The forces of all subsequent Jīva-
processes are there. Hence the experience of this fund
of causal energy corresponds to Īsvara Pratyaya of His
causal body. Sṛṣṭikalpanā of Īsvara is not the whole
Pratyaya of Īsvara. For though in Pralaya the former

is not there, Īśvara has Pratyaya still, namely the Ānandamaya consciousness of His own causal body. The prājña Pratyaya corresponds to this. The Sʼābdic counterpart of this is Para-śabdaviśeṣa while in Īśvara it is the Para-śabda whole involving all Viśeṣas. The Paraśabda in Jīva is no sound. Artha here is, as stated, the Vyaṣṭi causal body which is the temporary equilibrium of the Stress constituting the Jīva.

Passing to Taijasa, corresponding to Hiraṇyagarbha as Prājña does to Īśvara, his Pratyaya is experience of Sūkṣma-Deha or subtle body in sleep (Svapna). His Sʼabda is that which is not expressed by the vocal organ, being the mental image of articulate or inarticulate sound pushing up in Yoga to the Tanmātras. His Artha is the Vyaṣṭi Sūkṣma-Deha. The Pratyaya of the Sūkṣma Deha is either pleasurable or painful. Hiraṇyagarbha's Pratyaya includes two parts, viz., (a) experience of cosmic (Samaṣṭirūpa) Sūkṣma elements as well as Sthūla elements and (b) Sṛṣṭi-kalpanā referring to the compounding of these elements already evolved by Īśvara. In Taijasa there is (aa) experience of the Jāgrat-vāsanārūpa Svapna or Vyaṣṭi Sūkṣma-Deha, but not quite of the Jāgrat or Vyaṣṭi Sthūla-Deha, (bb) Sṛṣṭi-kalpanā manifesting as a compounding activity as regards various dream forms.

On comparison it is found that the parallelism between Hiraṇya and Taijasa is not complete, a fact due to an important distinction between the two. Īśvara, Hiraṇyagarbha and Virāt are Para or Utkṛṣṭopādhi ; the Upādhi (i. e., Māyā-śakti) is preponderatingly Sāttvika. Hence as regards the relative scope of Sʼabda, Artha, Pratyaya, the three aspects may be respresented by three concentric circles of which Īśvara is the outermost

and Virāt the innermost. Hence Īśvara's Pratyaya,
Artha and S'abda include those of Hiraṇyagarbha;
those of Hiraṇyagarbha, include those of Virāt. It
must not be thought that the S'abda, Artha, and
Pratyaya of Īśvara, Hiraṇyagarbha, and Virāt are
exclusive or ejective. The Sāttvika character of their
limitations implies the concentric arrangement of the
three circles. But Prājña, Taijasa and Viśva have
Upādhis which, though Sāttvika, are impure and
coarse (Malina). Hence practically as regards S'abda,
Artha and Pratyaya we have

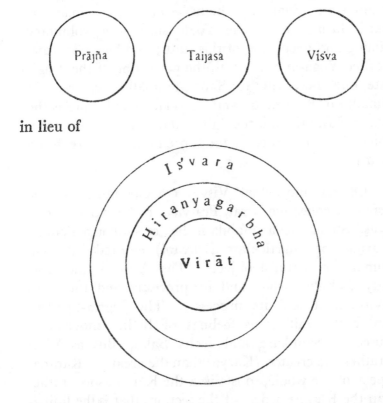

in lieu of

In other words they are practically ejective circles.

Hence the first Pratyaya is practically confined to S'uṣupti, his Artha to the Vyaṣṭi causal body and S'abda to Paraśābda section. Taijasa experiences Svapna and Sūkṣmadeha, but is practically ignorant of Prājña's state and Viśva's state. So with Viśva. But though their experiences apparently exclude one another, the causal unity between them is not in fact wanting.

Taijasa's Artha is Sūkṣma-dcha-vyaṣṭi which contains the seeds of Jāgrat. His S'abda is the subtle form of the gross sound. The mental image of a sound becomes apparent or Prātibhāsika sound during the dream state (Svapna) ; higher sounds even may be heard during this. The Yogic state is a voluntary refining and deepening of this state ; and hence Dhyana is called Yoga-nidrā. With the perfecting of the Yogic state one may rise to S'abda-tanmātra ; or even in Samādhi to Para-śabda and Aśabda. The former is the cosmic Suṣupti and the latter the Turīya state from which, when regarded as the supreme state, there is no return.

Of the individual Viśva, corresponding to the cosmic or collective Virāt, Pratyaya is the experience or Vyaṣṭi Sthūla-Deha ; S'abda is the gross sound articulate (Varṇa) or inarticulate (Dhvani) emitted by men, animals and natural objects. The Artha is the gross body (Sthūla Deha) and its processes and the gross environment and its processes. The Jāgrat-Sṛṣṭikal-panā here manifests as feelings of bodily movements caused by Saṁskāra and Icchā S'akti. But as Virāt is rather the created (Kārya) than the creative (Kāraṇa) aspect of the whole, so is Viśva the Kārya aspect rather than the Kāraṇa aspect of the section, that is the finitiz-ed centre of consciousness or Jīva. The Artha is gross body and its processes together with the environment of that body and its processes. The S'abdas are the sounds emitted by the vocal organs of men and animals or otherwise produced by natural objects. This is Vaikharī sound which is a development from Paraśabda, through Paśyantī and Madhyamā sound. Paraśabda or Parāvāk is Bindu, Paśyantī is Īkṣaṇa or creative thought and action by that Bindu which is the causal body of S'abda. From this arises the subtle body of S'abda which is Tanmātra and Mātṛkā which evolves into the gross body of sound which is the letters (Varṇa) uttered by the vocal organs which are made up into syllables and words (Pada) and then into sentences (Vakya). Mantra, so uttered, is a form of the gross body of S'abda. And this applies both to Bijas and other Mantras.

S'abda-Tanmātra or Apañcī-kṛta Ākāśa is Apañcī-kṛta-Tanmātra. This is sound as such, that is ideal sound or the cognition of sound apart from conditions such as ear, brain and other material conditions such as air, water, earth, whereby sound is transmitted. In the case of S'abda-Tanmātra, sound is known as an object of the higher mind apart from these conditions. Therefore Sabda-Tanmātra is S'abda not conditional to varying perceptive faculties. It is not sound which is heard by this individual or that, on this plane or that; but it is sound as heard by the Absolute Ear and as uttered by the Absolute Tongue. It is invariable and Apauruṣeya. Similarly Rūpa Tanmātra is form unconditional, as seen by the Absolute Eye. By "Absolute Ear" is meant the power (S'akti) of apprehending sound in itself or as such without subjection to the varying conditions of Time, Place, (i. e. Plane) and Person. The Stress by which a thing is generated and sustained is the basis of all the five Tanmātras. It is S'abda-Tanmātra as apprehended by the Absolute Ear, Rūpa Tanmātra as apprehended by the Absolute Eye, and so on. From the gross standpoint S'abda is not the Guṇa of Ākāśa alone. In order to be manifested to the human mind and ear sound requires not only gross Ākāśa but Vāyu and the other Bhūtas. For the transmission of sound to the limited ear there must be a material medium for its transmission whether as air, water or solid body. Virāt sound in short assumes the existence of the whole material universe.

To sum up—There is the unmanifest Lord (Avyakta Īśvara) and the manifest Lord (Īśvara). Both are S'iva-S'akti because there is never S'iva without S'akti nor S'akti without S'iva, whether in creation or dissolution. Only in the latter there is nothing but Consciousness (S'akti being Cidrūpiṇī,) and in the former She assumes the form of the universe. For this reason the supreme state may be called S'iva-S'akti and the manifest state S'akti-S'iva to denote the preponderance of the Cit and Māyā aspects respectively. One state is motionless (Niṣpanda), the other with motion (Saspanda). One is soundless (Aśabda) the other manifests as sound (S'abda). In one is the Unmanī-S'akti, in the other the Samanī S'akti. The manifest Īśvara displays itself in three forms—causal, subtle, gross. The causal form is Paraśabda, Parāvāk, or S'abdabrahman. This is Īśvara. The rest is Aparāvāk. The subtle form is Madhyamā vāk, which is Hiraṇyagarbha sound, which develops into Virāt S'abda or Vaikharī vāk. The sound is accompanied by movement. That of the causal body first projecting the manifold universe from out of itself is general movement or Sāmānya Spanda, the S'abda of which is the Praṇava or " Om. " From Om all other

Mantras are derived.   Hiraṇyagarbha S'abda is accompanied by special motion (Viśeṣa Spanda) and Virāṭ S'abda is clearly defined movement (Spaṣṭatara Spanda) manifesting in man as articulate speech, and therefore as the gross or uttered form of Mantra.

CHAPTER IV

PARAS'ABDA, CAUSAL S'ABDA

S'ABDA which comes from the root *S'abd* "to make sound" ordinarily means sound in general including that of the voice, word, speech and language. It is either lettered sound (Varṇātmaka śabda) and has a meaning (Artha), that is, it either denotes a thing or connotes the attributes and relations of things; or it is unlettered sound and meaningless (at any rate to us) and is mere Dhvani (Dhvanyātmaka-S'abda) such as the sound of a rushing torrent, a clap of thunder and so forth. I say "to us" because every sound may have a meaning for Iśvara. This Dhvani arises from the contact of two things striking one another. So lettered sound is manifested through the contact of the vocal organs with the outer air. As elsewhere more fully explained, S'abda is, and exists as, four S'aktis namely Parā, Paśyantī, Mādhyamā and Vaikharī. These are referred to in connection with Vāk or Devī S'arasvatī, another synonym for S'abda.

S'abda again is either immanent in its manifestation as sound, or transcendent. The first is threefold: (*a*) From an average point of view it means sound of either of these classes as heard by ears and sounds whose capacity (S'akti) is that of the normal or average plane. (*b*) From the Yogic point of view it means subtle sound, that is, subtle sound as apprehended by ears and minds

which are supernormal and therefore whose S'aktis rise
above the average plane. But these capacities can be
greater or less and therefore admit of grades, one person's
capacity being greater than that of another, just as is
the case with individuals in the ordinary plane, some of
whom can hear better than others. (*c*) From the
standpoint of the "Absolute Ear" that is a capacity to
apprehend sound unconditionally such as exists in the
case of the perfect Yogi, it means pure sound or S'abda-
tanmātra. This is apprehended by the perfect Yogi in
its purity.   All these are effects (Kārya). · Transcendent
S'abda means creative movement or Causal Stress itself,
that is, it is not, the effect or manifestation (*i.e.* sound)
to either the relative ear (*a* and *b*) or the "absolute ear"
(*c*) but the cause (Kāraṇa) or Manifesting Fact itself.
This in the S'astra is S'abda-brahman, that is, the source
of all Sabda or name (Nāma) and of all form (Rūpa),
the universe being "Name and Form" (Nāmarū-
pātmaka). Thus we rise step by step starting from
average experience to supreme experience ; from
projections and manifestations to the Thing Itself which
is Causal Stress or S'abda-brahman. The term S'abda is
throughout retained, though the connotations enlarge
and deepen as we proceed upwards. This is in conformity with the concrete way in which Hindu thought
has developed and by which the all-pervading and
all-manifesting power of the Divine S'akti is shown.
In teaching, it is the Arundhatīdarśananyāya, according
to which a husband shows (or rather used to show—for,
is Arundhatī sought now ?) his newly wedded wife the
tiny star Arundhati, emblem of constant chastity, by
drawing her attention first to some neighbouring big
star. "You see this, now look to the left you see this,
well next to it you see Arundhati." So a Guru deals

with his disciple (S'iṣya) in a way suitable to the latter's intelligence. He cannot learn what is the highest all at once. He must make his way upward to it. "Brahman is this; no it is that; no it is this;" and so on until the highest notion of It is capable of being given. Thus the Guru in S'ruti says "Annam Brahma," that is Brahman is the food which the disciple eats as also matter generally. Then as the latter's knowledge deepens, the Guru changes the connotation of the word Brahman but retains the term itself. The disciple then consecutively learns that Life is Brahman (Prāṇāh Brahma). Intelligence is Brahman (Vijñānam Brahma) and finally Bliss is Brahman (Ānandam Brahma) where at last experience rests. Here there are five connotations of "Brahman," each more comprehensive and deeper than the foregoing, gradually evolved as the spiritual life of the S'iṣya unfolds and perfects itself. The connotations of most of the important philosophical terms have been evolved in this way. Thus there are different meanings of Prāṇa, Ākaśa, Vāyu and so forth. S'abda also has the four meanings stated which thought progressively evolves in the manner above stated. Some may think that from the standpoint of pure logic this state of things is unacceptable. We have however to deal with the matter practically. And what life wants is generally not that which pure logic demands. But apart from that the method and the statements are true. For Brahman is all things as S'akti, though the Brahman in itself (Brahmasvarūpa) is beyond them all. If those, before whom all connotations of Brahman are at once placed, complain of ambiguity, this is due to the fact that they have not mastered their subject. And because the subject must be gradually mastered the Guru takes his S'iṣya gradually upwards to the point

where all aspects are seen in relation to the whole
(Pūrṇa) whose aspects they are.

For the present Chapter I will start at the beginning
namely Causal S'abda or S'abdabrahman. S'iva has two
aspects namely Niṣkala (without parts), Nirguṇa
(without attribute), Sakala (with parts) and Saguṇa
(with attribute). The first is the unmanifested transcendent Supreme and the second the manifested and
immanent creative Lord (Īśvara) or Ruling Mother
(Īśvarī). The first is Niṣpanda, without movement, for
it is the eternal changeless Brahman. It is Aśabda
which here means the same thing, for being unmanifest
there is neither S'abda as effect nor S'abda as cause.
The latter means that there is then no Causal Stress.
The other aspect is called S'abdabrahman which appears
at creation from out of Brahman which is the equilibrated condition of S'akti. From the S'abda-brahman all
particular S'abdas as Mantras or otherwise appear.
S'abdabrahman is in Itself Avyakta (unmanifest) S'abda
which is the cause of manifested (Vyakta) S'abda,
Artha and Pratyaya and which uprises from the form
of Bindu on the differentiation of the Supreme Bindu
due to the prevalence of Kriyā-S'akti in Prakṛti.

Kriyāśakti pradhānāyāh śabda śabdārtha kāraṇam
Prakṛterbindurūpinyāh śabdabrahmābhavat param

S'āradā-Tilaka 1-12.

In other words the unmanifest potentiality of power
which subsequently appears as S'abda and therefore as
Artha and Pratyaya becomes manifest through its
activity, manifesting in Prakṛti in the form of Bindu
which is the undifferentiated S'iva-S'akti. With such
activity Bindu becomes threefold as S'abda, Artha,

Pratyaya. Avyakta-Rava is the Principle of sound as such (Nāda Mātra) that is undifferentiated sound not specialised in the form of letters but which is through creative activity the cause of manifested Sabda and Artha which are Its forms.

Tena śabdārtha—rūpa-viśiṣṭasya śabda-brahmatvaṁ avadhāritaṁ—(Prānatoṣinī 13).

It is the Brahman considered as all-pervading Sabda undivided and unmanifested whose substance is Nāda and Bindu, the proximate creative impulse in Paraśiva and proximate cause of manifested Sabda and Artha. *Sṛṣṭyunmukha—paramaśiva—prathamollāsamātram akhaṇḍo-vyakto nādabindumaya eva vyāpako brahmātmaka śabdah* (*See Prānatoṣinī 10. Rāghava Bhatta Com. on v. 12, Ch. I, S'āradā-Tilaka*).

The creative Brahman is called Sabdabrahman. It may be asked why is this so, since the Saguṇa-S'iva (which Sabda-brahman is) is the cause not only of all Sabdas but of all Artha (Rūpa) and Pratyaya. This is so but the S'āstra uses the term Sabdabrahman because it is here considering the origin of Sabda. But Sruti in explaining creation is impartial as between Sabda, Artha or Pratyaya. Now it says "creation is out of Sabda" (Sabda-prabhava) regarding the universe as constituted of Sabda (Vānmaya) in its causal sense. Now it says that creation is out of Pratyaya using that term in the sense of creative ideation (Sṛṣṭikalpanā). Now it says "Creation is out of Artha" that is the supreme Artha, the cosmic "Stuff" or cosmic "Matter" which is Prakṛti-śakti. What is done in such a case is to take an effect (Kārya) known to us, and to refer it to the one cause of all effects, giving that cause however the name of the particular effect which is the subject of consideration. Moreover the S'abda aspect of Brahman is of the highest importance for it is in this aspect that It is Veda.

But what is the sense in which S'abda is used in the term S'abda-Brahman? This has been already indicated in the quotations above cited. S'abda here does not mean either gross or subtle sound. To begin with these are both effects (Kārya) and we are dealing with their cause (Kāraṇa). Manifested sound is a Guṇa of Ākāsa. But in what sense? It is not merely a quality of Ether and thus not anything else; that is the term S'abda is not limited to the Guṇa of Ākāsa. If it were, it would not be possible to explain the well-known scientific experiment (which in early days was supposed to "demolish" all Hindu theories) in which a ringing bell ceases to be heard in a closed vessel from which the Air has been pumped out, but in which Ether still remains. If S'abda were the Guṇa of Ākāsa only and unconnected with anything else it could not be said that sound increases and decreases, appears and disappears with Vayu. Hence the term S'abda is not limited to sound, gross or subtle. It is the Causal Stress or Spanda which inheres in the stressed condition of Cit-S'akti and Māyā-śakti which manifests first as the S'abda Tanmātra to the absolute "Ear," as more or less subtle sound to a Yogic (though not perfect) ear according as the fundamental Ākāsa Spanda is adapted to its relative capacity through other more or less dense media; and which finally appears as average human sound when the fundamental Spanda is adapted to the capacity of the human ear through a

medium of such density as the common air. The
air therefore like the ear is one of the factors of the
manifestation of the fundamental Spanda which is
S'abda as the original creative Causal Stress or agitation in the body of Prakṛti-S'abda. S'abda is the
Cosmic Stress itself which takes place in the Primary
Ether or Saspanda-S'akti which produces the S'abda
Tanmātra which evolves into Ākās'a Bhūta and then
into the Vāyu and other Tanmātras and Bhūtas.
These according to Vedānta are Pancīkṛta; that is,
each Tattva has four parts of its own element and
one of each of the four others. Through the Bhautika-
Sṛṣṭi or indirect causation or Hiraṇyagarba there takes
place the combination of the Tattvas produced by the
Bhūta-Sṛṣṭi in direct causation (Sākṣātkartṛtvam) of
Īśvara producing the gross world of the human senses
which is Virāt. Thus the one initial Stress is communi-
cated as and throughout the chain of its effects. To
distinguish this S'abda it is called Para-S'abda and the
manifested S'abda is Apara-S'abda or commonly S'abda
simply. The latter is subtle and gross sound, the first
being supersensible to the normal mind and senses and
the latter sensible or what we call in its compounds
discrete matter. Paraśabda is thus not sound but a
state of agitation in the Cosmic S'akti when, on the
ripening of the Saṁskāras the hitherto existing
equilibrium (Sāmyāvasthā) of Prakṛti is broken. There
is then a disturbance (Kṣobha) or general movement
(Sāmānyaspanda) in S'akti and this Cosmic Stress which
is Paraśabda or Parāvak reveals itself in manifested
S'abda (Apara). This one stress, which is the potency
of all in which it reveals itself, manifests in man as
Artha, Pratyaya, S'abda, in the objects (Prameya) of
which he as knower (Pramātri) has apprehension

(Pratyaya) and in the names by which he thinks of them as an " after-construction in relation to the intuitive experience of life " as Professor Pramathanātha Mukhopādhyāya has well put it. The primordial S'abda or Parāvāk (corresponding in some ways to the Logos) is the cosmic predisposition to and precondition of creative evolution. The agitation in the primary Substance projecting itself into the sensuous plane becomes audible as Dhvani or sound, but is itself only the possibility and substratum of Sound. Creation is said to be S'abda-prabhava, that is it proceeds from, and is a manifestation of, the Stress or Cosmic S'akti. In this sense every movement or process in the universe is Paras'abda. As'abda Jagat is a contradiction in terms. Whilst the stress or constituting force is one, It manifests Itself differently to the different sense-organs. The Causal Stress when striking the ear and mind produces sound, when striking the eye and mind it produces colour and form, and when striking other sense organs it produces other kinds of sensation. It is to be noted that of the five Bhūtas, Akas'a and Vāyu belong to the formless (Amūrtta) division and the remaining three to the form division (Murtta). The first is sensed by hearing. S'abda as lettered sound is vibration for the ear as name. Tejas the head of the second division is sensed as form (Rūpa). Artha is thus vibration to the eye (mental or physical) as form. It is because the one Power rays itself forth in threefold form that S'abda, Artha and Pratyaya as such have a natural and inseparable relation to one another. It is again because the Vaidika-S'abda is assumed (a matter which I will later discuss) to constitute the natural name of, and therefore to be in complete correspondence with, the Arthas denoted, that it is held to be eternal. S'ruti says that the world is born of S'abda (S'abda-prabhava) and that creation (Sṛṣṭi) is S'abda-pūrvaka, that is S'abda is the antecedent condition of creative process, which cannot be if S'abda be taken to be only that manifestation to the ear and mind (natural or Yogic) which is sound (gross or subtle). This manifestation is a subsequent and consequent fact and is to be distinguished from the antecedent and primordial condition of creation as such. The primordial condition is Causal Stress; that is, in the finite ether of consciousness, homogeneous, quiescent, there is a moving—a stir. Paraśabda is the name for that causal stress as it arises and before it manifests as the universe.

To sum up: In the creative process three stages are to be noted : (1) the transcendental quiescent condition immanent in the others, though veiled, which is Aśabdam, Asparśam, Arūpam and so forth as S'ruti negatively describes it ; (2) the condition of cosmic stress which is S'abdabrahman. The stress is a play of S'akti in the Cidākāśa in such a way that the first condition is not effaced when the second appears. The S'abdabrahman is Veda. After manifestation and at the conclusion of the cycle it is wrapped up as potential Māyā-śakti, when according to some, in Mahāpralaya the transcendental condition alone is. The human parallel is Suṣupti ; (3) S'abda-brahman reproduces itself gradually and partially as countless finite centres of varied finite experiences of Nāma and Rūpa. Hence forms together with sounds, sights and so forth vary as do the S'abdas. The sound which represents the above-mentioned primordial functioning of the Brahmaśakti is the Mahābīja " Om " or Praṇava— *Omityekarang brahma tasya vācakah pranavah.* The nature of this great Bija which is the source of all other mantras will be the subject of a future çhapter after we have discussed what is meant by " natural name " which I have more fully dealt with in the chapter bearing that title.

S'AKTI AS STRESS

THE cosmic states of Sṛṣṭi, Sthiti and Laya, together with the transcendental Parama-S'iva state as also Turīya and the Vyaṣṭi states of Jāgrat, Svapna, Suṣupti, must all be ultimately explained (so far as this can be) by the dynamical theory of S'akti as Stress giving rise to moving forms of Herself. For this purpose it is necessary to investigate conditions of equilibrium and movement.

What is Stress? Let us suppose that two things A and B are attracting each other. The name for the total mutual action is " stress " of which the respective actions of A and B are the elements, partials, or components. Thus there may be Stress for three or four things and so on. Ultimately we reach Universal Stress which is an infinite system of correlated forces. A particular thing may be defined as a partial experience of this infinite system. Professor Pramathanātha Mukhopādhyāya to whom I am indebted in the preparation of this and some of the following papers has given it the appropriate name of " fact-section. " The infinite system is however never really finitized by these partials. When the stress between one such partial and another touches the normal of consciousness in either or both, we may have, under circumstances and within certain limits, sensation of sound in either or both. The stress is S'abda and the sound is Dhvani. There may be several stages from the one to the other. It is stress or S'abda which constitutes a thing. Whether this S'abda is followed or accompanied by a certain Dhvani or not will depend firstly upon the magnitude of its action in relation to a percipient, and secondly upon the conditions of the percipient's perceptive organs. Hence in order that a sound may be heard the rates of vibration of the air must be such and such, the ears and brain must be such and such, and so on. Beyond these limits there are no sounds. Thus most objects of experience though influencing us do not express themselves in sounds to us such as the earth, sun, moon, stars and so forth. In the transcendental Paramas'iva or Turīya state which is Nirvāṇa, all Stress is dissolved and S'akti is then nothing but Cit, Cidrūpiṇi, Cinmātrarūpiṇī. This may be illustrated by the case where causal stress being constituted by a number of forces, all these severally vanish and are each therefore separately zero so that the resultant is zero. This is the Transcendent Niṣkala state in which there is no Sṛṣṭi-Kalpanā, no Artha and no S'abda (Aśabda). In the case of Cosmic Suṣupti we need not take into consideration any external system, for nothing is external to the Cosmos. In this case we have only the static condition where each term is not separately zero, but where each of the forces constituting the Stress balances one another with the result that there is a state of equilibrated energy. There is the state of the Guṇas in Sarūpa-pariṇāma which, with loss of equilibrium in creation, is Virūpa-pariṇāma. Vyaṣṭi Suṣupti may be due two sets of facts. Either the forces constituting this state, without each being separately zero, yet have that resultant, in which case there is equilibrium in the Vyaṣṭi causal body provided the external cosmic system does not disturb this internal equilibrium of the Vyaṣṭi system; or these forces result in something, but this resultant is exactly counterbalanced by the action of the external system. Thus this something which would otherwise be the Vyaṣṭi stress system practically vanishes and equilibrium is established in this last-mentioned system. In the first case the external system has no action on the given internal system but it has action on other Vyaṣṭi systems. Thus the world is not asleep because the individual is so. In the second case the external system has action on the given internal system but this action is just negatived by the reaction of the internal on the external. In both cases the external system is an actual stressing attitude. In Svapna and Jāgrat Avastha the equilibrium of the Samaṣṭi and Vyaṣṭi Suṣupti or causal body is lost, and in Sṛṣṭi there is a system of kinetic stresses which again in Laya lapse into a state of potential stresses. The world process is thus divided into the three stages of Sṛṣṭi (creation), Sthiti (maintenance), and Laya (dissolution) which is a passing from a state of homogeneity (Laya) to one of heterogeneity (Sṛṣṭi and Sthiti) and back to homogeneity again in an unending series of evolution with periods of rest between. The growth of the universe is thus a pulsing forth of the Bindu holding potentially within Itself, as massive (Ghaṇibhūta) S'akti, all into which it subsequently evolves. This great Universe dies down again into that from which it sprang. Though we thus speak of three stages it cannot be properly said that there is Sṛṣṭi, that when it stops there is Sthiti, and then ultimately there is Laya. Evolution (Sṛṣṭi) and involution

(Laya) are going on even during Sthiti. There is always, for instance, molecular birth and death. Each of these terms is employed according as one aspect or the other is emphasised. During Laya the stresses are potential. That is actual movements cease, so that the stresses are due simply to the configuration of relative positions of the units determined by their Karmas up to the time of Laya. There is for instance, stress in a stringed bow though the string may not be in actual movement. The nature of Īśvara experience as the ultimate Fact is as such logical and therefore human categories, if stretched to the fact, will inevitably lead into paralogisms and antinomies. In the same way creation is an unresolved riddle. Why should the spell of cosmic Suṣupti be broken and in what way does the Will of God influence it? Ultimately these questions are unanswerable in all faiths. We may say that Īśvara during Laya has experience of the casual body. The absolute " ear ", " tongue ", " eye " which God possesses are reabsorbed into a massive consciousness of Bliss (Ānanda) as is partially the case with the Jīva in Suṣupti for these are differentiations of His infinite Jñāna-S'akti. These are veiled during Laya, that is the kinetic stresses (S'akti Viśvarūpā) become potential (S'akti Cidrūpiṇī). What is patent becomes latent. The world becomes " Memory " which at the next creation is " remembered " just as in the individual the world is lost to him in dreamless sleep, and when waking he sees and recalls the events of a past day. Yet here the world exists during our sleep for others. But when Īśvara goes to sleep things do not remain as they are. Things return to their causal form or seeds. During Laya, Īśvara has a massive experience of the totality of these " seeds, " for as S'ruti says " I am one, I will now be many. "

To the question whether this creative act is instantaneous or successive it may be replied probably neither the one nor the other. That is the category of time is inapplicable to creation as a whole. Creation considered as an instantaneous flash or a successive flow is Vyāvahārika and not Pāramārthika. On this basis however there is a difference of opinion between Dṛṣṭi-sṛṣṭi-vādā and Karma-sṛṣṭi-vāda. According to the first, and to me preferable, view, as Īśvara thought, so at once the whole world appeared in its stages as subtle and gross. At every moment also creation is taking place. It is not something wholly in the past. According to the second or more commonly accepted doctrine, the Tattvas came out gradually, the one after the other, in a specified order (Krama) though such Krama is not referable to time as we know it and which appeared at a lower stage. This later time is the Janmakāla of the Kālavādins according to whom all is Kāla. The Supreme Time or Mahākāla is Nirguṇa, Nirviśeṣa, Nirvikāra or Brahman.

As regards the cosmic cycle it is claimed to be proved by (a) induction from observed facts of experience which, all giving signs of periodicity, afford a basis for generalization ; and (b) the alleged actual remembrance by Ṛṣis and other super-souls such as Jaigiṣavya of Caturyuga, Manvantara, Kalpa and so forth. Apart therefore from Śruti the proof is inductive and experimental and not deductive.

Creation proceeds from the generic to the specific. When Laya as a state of potential stresses passes into Sṛṣṭi which is a system of kinetic stresses was have first the most generic condition of the latter, namely Sāmānya-spanda, that is general undifferentiated movement. It is the manifestation of the tendency of Laya to pass into Sṛṣṭi. From the standpoint of Consciousness it is the first stage of "seeing" (Īkṣaṇa) that is cosmic ideation on the part of Īśvara. In the individual it is the borderland between Suṣupti and Svapna, the moment that Suṣupti is breaking and Svapna is drawing to pass into Jāgrat. The inertia of the first has passed but the specialised movements of the second and third are not yet in evidence. It is a kind of massive undifferentiated state containing potentially all specialities. The S'abda or acoustic aspect of this tendency of potential stress to pass into kinetic stress is the Praṇava or Mantra " Om."

This tendency realises itself in the first place in Bhūta-sṛṣti by Īśvara. Īśvara has consciousness of his Ānandamaya Body and Causal Body. The latter means the experience, " I am all " (Sarvātmakatva). He experiences Himself as all whether as a whole, as generals or particulars. As Knower of all He is Sarvajña, as Knower of its varieties He is Sarvavit. They are to Him, Himself, for the Māyā with which He is associated does not govern Him and therefore His knowledge does not bind Him. The state of Īśvara though not governed by, is yet associated with, Māyā and is therefore not that of Supreme Mokṣa. Īśvara wills to be many and the Bhūtas issue from him. As Īśvara He does not think Himself to be their creator. The creation of the Bhūtas (Bhūta-sṛṣti) according to the Vedantic order means the evolving of (a) the Apañcīkṛta Bhūtas or Tanmātras and (b) their primary compounds which are again (aa) Sūkṣma that is Antahkaraṇa, Indriya and Prāṇas and (bb) Sthūla that is the Pañcīkṛta Bhūtas. Broadly speaking these are the elements of creation ; the creation of which implies also their natural names or Bījas. Thus from Om are evolved the Bījas of the Bhūtas Ham, Yam, Ram, Vam, Lam and other Bījas such as Hrim the Māyā Bīja or Praṇava of the differentiating Sakti. These elements are special (Viśeṣa) in relation to the tendency and general movement (Sāmānya-spanda) above mentioned, but are general (Sāmānya) in relation to the derivatives which follow.

There then follows Bhautika-Sṛṣṭi by Hiraṇya-garba that is the creation of the secondary compounds ; that is again the mixing up of the " elements " into diverse forms first the typal and then the variational. This is done by Īśvara in His aspect as Hiraṇyagarbha. These too have their natural names (Sabda). Hiraṇya-garbha who is the Lord of Brahmaloka thinks himself to be a creator. This is a state of duality in which He thinks that all things are His. Hence Hiraṇyagrabha as affected by Māyā is a Jīva.

Lastly coming to the completed Sthiti we have actions and reactions of the Bhūtas and Bhautikas such that they continue as a system of the kinetic stresses. These actions and reactions have their natural names which may be called phenomenal Sabdas. Some of these namely those which fall between our limits of sensibility are sensible to us. So much as to Sabdas classified with reference to aspects of creation.

Sabdas may be either directly or indirectly appre-hended. In the latter case they are received. The ordinary individual does not hear the natural name or sound of Agni or " Ram " directly. He is told that it is so having received it from those who have heard that sound. · It is " received " (Āpta) and not directly apprehended (Sākṣātkṛta). For, from the point of

view of apprehension, S'abdas are of two kinds, Sākṣātkṛta
and Āpta. The S'abda range of Īśvara, Hiraṅyagarbha,
and Virāt may be thus represented.

Thus Īśvara has no Āpta or received (indirect)
S'abdas : but all S'abdas are directly apprehended
(S'ākṣātkṛta) by Him. Hiraṇyagarbha, as Hiraṇyagarbha,
that is a particular aspect of Īśvara, has direct apprehension of Bhautika-sṛṣṭi S'abdas and Sthiti S'abdas and
indirect of Bhūta-sṛṣṭi and Laya S'abdas ; Virāt as
Virāt has direct apprehension only of Sthiti S'abda and
indirect apprehension of the rest. This deals with the
Samaṣṭi or collective aspects of Experience.

Coming to the individual or Vyaṣṭi aspects we have
the corresponding state of Prājña, Taijasa and Viśva.
These unlike the collective states are mutually exclusive,
the one of the other, and may thus be figured. Prājña
has direct but veiled or partial apprehension of his own

Vyaṣṭi causal (Laya) S'abda but not of others. This
śabda is however not sound as language for himself.
Taijasa has both direct and indirect experience of
Vyaṣṭi (*i.e.* some) subtle S'abda. And Virāt has the
same of gross S'abdas.

Here in these two cases there is gradation. The
gross ear has capacities of varying degree. A scientist
may by means of a delicately constructed apparatus

hear sounds which are not sensible to the natural ear. A Yogī may hear still more. Thus if either were to hear the rise of sap in a tree that sound would be the direct approximate natural name of that vegetable function. A Yogī in Ṣaṭcakrabheda or piercing of the six centres by Kuṇḍalinī-Śakti may, it is said, directly apprehend the Bījas Om, Ham, Yam and the rest, as the passage of śakti gradually vitalises the six centres. A Yogī by mounting to a higher or the highest plane of existence can have direct experience (Sākṣātkāra) of any or all kinds of Śabdas. The Absolute Ear hears the Śabda Tanmātra in Ākāśa, not through the impact of undulations, but it hears movement as movement.

In Brahmajñāna the Yogī becomes the Brahman Itself when all Stress ceases and there is Peace.

CHAPTER VI

ETERNALITY OF SABDA

THE term "eternal" may mean "always is" (a) without change or (b) with change. The former is existence uncontradicted in the three times. Change again may be either immanent (Svagata) or its reverse (Taditara). Thus if there be only one circle (A) any change going on within it is Svagata change or distinction (Bheda). But if there be two circles A and B of which the latter added a part of itself to the former with the result that A is changed, this is not Svagata. Thus Svagata change is Advaita whilst Non-Svagata change presupposes Dvaita.

Applying then these observations to the Brahman and Jīva, the former has three aspects (a) Brahman as Pure Cit (Brahma svarūpa) (b) Brahman as Cit-Sakti (c) Brahman as Māyā Sakti or Prakṛti. In the first or transcendent sense Brahman is Pure Cit and this always is as such. From the finite point of view we may either ignore (veil) it or accept it, but it is ever given. It is the changeless background of all change ; but Itself has no kind of change. This is the Niṣkala Paramaśiva to whose powers or Saktis we next proceed.

Cit-śakti is Cit as Sakti, that is Cit immanent in the world the forms of which as Mind and Matter are productions of Māyā-śakti. This immanent Brahman

(Cit-śakti) in the sense of the All (which Professor P. N. Mukhopādhyāya aptly calls " Fact " as opposed to " Fact-section ") always is as such. For the All (Pūrṇa) never ceases to be all. All is all. Śruti says that Pūrṇa remains Pūrṇa though Pūrṇa be taken from it. Brahman as Cit-śakti is inseparably associated with Māyā-śakti and has only Svagata change or movement. Brahman as Māyā-śakti—what the author cited calls Stress as distinguished from the background of Cit—is Brahman as Prakṛti. This is eternal in the sense that it always is, though either as latent or as patent, as a kinetic force or as a tendency. Here eternity does not exclude change of condition. Brahman as Prakṛti has Svagata change. We must not then confound the terms Real and Eternal. According to Advaita-Vedānta the transcendent Brahmasvarūpa is both real and eternal, for " real " is here used in the sense of that which does not change (Kūṭastha) whereas Māyā with its changes is neither real nor unreal. " Eternal " therefore includes " change of condition ". Non-eternal or finitized being is, pragmatically con- sidered, marked by three kinds of change and distinction (Bheda), viz., Intrinsic (Svagata) such as the distinction which exists between the leaves and branches of the same tree, and extrinsic which is again of two kinds, viz., Sajātiya such as the distinction which exists between one kind of tree and another kind of tree, and Vijātiya such as the distinction which exists between a tree and the earth and rocks which surround it.

The eternal Śabdabrahman manifests at creation (Sṛṣṭi) and lapses into its quiescent ground in dissolution (Laya). The Śabda of its first creative movement is the Nāda or Dhvani "Om." From this issue all parti- cular Śabdas both Varṇātmaka and Dhvanyāt-maka.

A given particular is obviously not the same for ever. But are particulars as such eternal? The creation of particulars is recurrently eternal in the sense that during each Srṣṭi particulars appear. But are the particulars themselves eternal? The question may mean either of two things. In the first sense the obvious answer is, as stated, in the negative. Then are particulars as such eternal? In other words are there particulars in all times, in Srṣṭi as well as in Laya? This given particular (say the pen with which I am writing) may not be in all times, but will not some particulars (though different from those now given) exist always? There is a genus or type (Jāti) with its particulars (Vyakti). The Jāti never exists without its Vyaktis. Some Vyaktis (though different from those now given) will be associated with the Jātis in all times; though both may be either latent or patent. In Laya for instance the Jātis associated with their Vyaktis become latent. Associated with what Vyaktis? Not the present ones; but the Vyaktis immediately antecedent to the state of Prakṛti equilibrium. A given Vyakti is Vyakti-viśeṣa. Any Vyakti or some Vyakti is Vyakti Sāmānya. The former is not, but the latter is, eternal though it may be either veiled or unveiled. The Jātis are eternal and manifested in every creation and their S'abdas are eternal. The Vyaktis are only eternal in the sense above explained. Each creation is not an exact copy of the previous creation in every particular. Particulars through revolving round certain fixed Jātis (latent or patent) change. Thus a given Jīva may be now a Brāhmaṇa. Through Karma he changes and after death he may change his Jāti and become a S'ūdra or a Devatā. And so he may go on until he reaches the antecedent state of Mahāpralaya. Let it be supposed that at that moment he is a Devatā again. He is a Devatāvyakti associated with Jāti. In Pralaya he will be veiled as such together with his Jāti, and together with all his Saṁskāras active (Prārabdha) as well as nascent (Saṁcita). It is the resultant of these Saṁskāras that will determine his condition of birth after the expiry of Prakṛti's equilibrium. The end of this journey is reached only in Liberation (Mukti).

Then is the Vyakti Śabda eternal? If by this term is meant a Śabda denoting a given Vyakti (Vyakti-viśeṣa) then this is a proper name (non-connotating) and is not eternal. But with the exception of a few proper names (those which are attached as arbitrary signs to this Vyakti or that) all names or words represent Jātis that is groups or classes of things. A Vyakti-viśeṣa is represented by either a proper name or a specific combination of class names, such as, ' this paper I am writing on'; all these being class names the combination of which makes or denotes a Vyakti-viśeṣa.

Only such Śabdas as are approximate natural names (either simple or in combination) are eternal and the rest are not. The Veda claims to give the names of class things and class functions which are approximately natural. Hence (granting this claim) these Śabdas are eternal (Nitya). By Veda is here meant Vaidik language and by natural name Vaidika-Śabda. Thus assuming that the word "Gauh" is an approximate natural name, it has existed in every universe and has there meant the animal cow. If the word "Cow" as a variation of this has originated in some time, in some place and in some persons, then outside this limitation of time, place, and person the word has not existed and has not represented the Artha or animal cow. The ultimate test of a natural name is of course experimental verification. Vaidik language involves different strata. Natural names are of different kinds and degrees. Whether other S'abdas and their combinations are eternal depends on whether those words and their combinations are or are not approximate natural names. Apart from tradition the proof is experimental verification of Yoga. If they are variations of natural names (Vaidika-S'abda) the extent to which they vary, and the conditions of time, place, and person to which they are subject, must determine the nature of their bond with their Arthas. No *a priori* answer is possible. S'abda-brahman thinks creatively, his Pratyaya being cosmic ideation (Sr̥ṣṭi-kalpanā). The S'abda of this is Om and the Artha is the totality of the universe denoted by, and potentially inhering in, the creative impulse of which Om is the sound-expression. From this Om was derived all the letters (Varṇas) and sounds (Dhvanis). These Vaidik-Varṇas are eternal and represent in themselves and their variations all the possibilities of articulate speech in all languages. In Veda the Karma of these Varṇas is eternal and therefore the Vaidik words are also, it is claimed, eternal. The vowels are continuous sounds formed by varying the size of the mouth cavity. The vowel sounds produced by the voice are due (See Catchpool's "Text-book of sound ", p. 290) to the vibrations of two cartilaginous plates, the "vocal chords " placed at the top of the windpipe, edge to edge with a narrow slit between them; air blown through this slit from the lungs keeps the plates vibrating. The apparatus is really a free reed. The vocal chords have muscles attached to them which can vary the frequency of the vibration and the pitch of the sound produced. The different vowel sounds are produced by varying the size and shape of the mouth cavity. The consonants are particular interruptions of those sounds. They cut short the vowel sound but cannot themselves be sounded without vowels. And for this reason the vowels are known as the S'aktis of the consonants.

This subject of the Varṇas occupies an important place in the Tantra-S'astra in which it is sought to give a practical application to the very ancient doctrine concerning S'abda. The letters are classified according to their place of pronunciation (Uccāraṇa) such as gutturals, labials, dentals and so forth. The lips, mouth, and throat form a pipe or musical instrument which being formed in various ways and by the aid of the circumambient air produces the various sounds which are the letters of the Alphabet. Pāṇini (see part I of Siddhānta Kaumudī) and Patañjali's Mahābhāṣya deal with the effort or Prayatna in speech, dividing it into inner (Āntaraprayatna) and outer effort (Bāhya-prayatna). The former is of four kinds Spṛṣṭa, Iṣat Spṛṣṭa, Vivritta, Samvritta according as the effort fully or slightly touches the place of origin of the sound and according as the mouth is open or closed. Bāhyapra-yatna is of eleven kinds namely Vivāra, Samvāra, S'vāsa, Nāda, Ghoṣa, Aghoṣa, Alpaprāṇa, Mahāprāṇa, Udātta, Anudātta, Svarita. Vivāra pronunciation is with the mouth open, Samvāra when it is closed. In S'vāsa there is a predominant use of the breathing, in Nāda there is a humming sound, in Ghoṣa ringing sound, Aghoṣa being the opposite of this. In Alpaprāṇa the sound is quickly pronounced, little demand being made on the Prāṇa, Mahāprāṇa being the opposite of this. In Udātta the sound is given with a loud voice, in Anudātta with a low voice, and Svarita is a mixture of these two. In Pāṇini various letters are assigned to each of these classes of Prayatna. Thus the consonants from Ka to Ma belong to Spṛṣṭa Āntara-Prayatna ; Ya, Ra, La, Va to Iṣat Spṛṣṭa Āntara-Prayatna and so on.

The Tantra-S'āstra in its doctrine and practice of Ṣaṭcakrabheda indicates various parts of the body which are "touched" in the pronunciation of various letters. By this is meant that in the sounding of certain letters various parts of the body take a part. Thus the letter Va is pronounced from that part of the body wherein is the Mulādhāra, and the letter Ha from between the eyebrows in Ājñā-Cakra. The sound produced by the body in motion (for the external cause of sound is something in a state of vibration) is propagated by sound-waves in the circumambient air. The rise and fall of pressure which occur as sound-waves arrive at the ear, produce by their effect on its structures the sensation of sound and the nature of this sensation depends on the nature of the rise and fall of pressure, in other words, on the character of the sound waves.

According to Indian doctrine, God evolved man after having evolved most (if not all) other species of living beings so that language (as also intelligence, moral sense, and many other things which had been less perfectly developed in the lower animals) became more developed in man. The lower animals were "approaches" to man, the difference between man and animal being according to this doctrine a difference of degree and not of kind. It is possible then that there may be an inchoate Varṇātmaka-S'abda in the higher animals, though it is to be noted that the proposition (which is dealt with elsewhere) that " there is no thinking without language " is true only if by thinking is meant some kinds only of cognitive processes. Apart from these man gets on without language and therefore also the animals. It is only the after-construction on perceptive processes which call for language and this we find mainly if not wholly in man alone. Pātañjala-Darśana also discusses the question of transmigration into an animal body. In this case there is a soul which had been in a human body or even in a Devatā body before and has therefore the Saṁskāras (linguistic and others) of those births implicitly given amongst its animal Saṁskāras. Its instinct therefore may be (partly if not wholly) "lapsed intelligence" and its Dhvanyātmaka language a partly veiled Varṇātmaka or human language.

What is eternal then is S'abda in its aspect as Causal Stress or S'abdabrahman, the letter (Vaidika Varṇa) evolved from the primordial Dhvani the Praṇava or " Om ", and the combinations of these letters which constitute approximately natural names. These according to Hinduism are the Vaidika-S'abdas. Whether that claim is well founded is another question which is not here discussed.

CHAPTER VII

S'ABDA AS LANGUAGE

IT has been said that there is no thought without language. This proposition requires examination both from the Brahman and Jiva standpoint. If it be assumed that there is no thinking without language this merely establishes the necessary connection of thought and language and not a law that words or names must come to the mind first and then thoughts. They may be inseparably connected as aspects of one and the same concrete, that is actual, process but between aspects there is no sequence. When a gun is fired the explosion of the cartridge is the causal stress. This manifests to the ear as a report, to the eye as a flash and also it may be by the movement of the object hit. But the last three are co-effects of the first that is the explosion. In the same way when there is a centre of Causal stress in Cit we may have several lines of effectual manifestation. But it cannot be said that one line of effectual manifestation causes another. Now S'ruti as already mentioned calls creation S'abda-prabhava and S'abda-pūrva, both terms implying sequence as between a cause and its consequence. When again S'ruti says " Brahma created Devatās with the S'abda ' Ete '," what is meant is that the causal stress of that special creation manifests to His absolute " Ear " as a sound which is the pure form of what we can *approximately* utter and hear as the sound " *Ete*." We may, as stated, have several lines of effectual manifestation on there arising a centre of causal stress in Cit, one of which is (say) the sound " *Ete* ", and another the appearance of the Devatās. But we cannot say that one line of effectual manifestation causes another. Therefore when S'ruti says that S'abda underlies, precedes and enters Jagat, S'abda is not used in the sense of sound but as the causal stress or initial Spanda which from the subjective aspect is Iccā-śakti. The universe is creative ideation (Sṛṣṭikalpana). To use the terms of human speech this ideation is intuitive and not inferential and therefore does not involve language which is one of Its products. The proposition that there is no thought without language is correct only in a Vyāvahārika sense and is then true if by " thinking " is meant the formation of concepts or general notions, judgments and drawing inferences. For even in us, intuitive processes, such as perception and ideation, are done without language. To use the apt language of Professor Pramathanātha Mukhopādhyāya, words are an " after-thought or after-construction in relation to the intuitive experiences of life." (See as to the principles from which this statement follows " Approaches to Truth " and " The Patent Wonder "). To begin with experience is had without language (Aparaśabda) both in the Turīyā (Aśabda condition) and the Suṣupti (Paraśabda or Causal Stress) states. Coming down to Svapna and Jāgrat it is to be recognised that there are some ways in which language may be associated with thinking processes. On the other hand some processes may go on without language. In Svapna and Jāgrat Avasthā, Arthas and Pratyayas necessarily imply the *possibility* of sound manifestation, that is, vocal language, but do not always *actually* suggest their acoustic counter-parts. In some cases they do go on apparently without language, though there is always the possibility of their being expressed in language. A child sees, hears and so forth almost without language, so does the animal and we ourselves in part. Most of the particular objects of perception have during such perception no specific names for us; still we perceive them and may afterwards recall the class names. Absence of language occurs primarily in two cases, namely in intuitive perception and intuitive ideation. Much seeing and hearing is done intuitively and without language. By intuitive ideation is meant the forming of a mental image of an object. Thus I see a tree: close my eyes and see it again in mental image. Many such sights and sounds pass through our mental range from time to time which do not always call up their names. But though these intuitive processes may actually go on without language, there is the possibility of their being vehicled in language, and in description, analysis, classification, judgment and other mental elaborations such linguistic vehicle is indispensable. For the moment it is required to describe, analyse, classify perceptions, recourse must be had to language. Looking, I see a thing and very well see it. But this seeing is often done without actually remembering the name " tree " or " mangoe tree." To describe, classify and otherwise to elaborate this seeing I must remember the name. In this sense language is called an " after-construction." Language again is a system of signs either natural or arbitrary, either vocal or non-vocal, by which we describe things and consider the attributes and relations of things. In this definition four marks are employed, namely, natural, arbitrary, vocal and non-vocal. Taking two at a time there are six combinations namely natural-vocal, natural non-vocal, arbitrary-vocal, arbitrary non-vocal, natural arbitrary, vocal non-vocal. The last two may be at once rejected as the marks in them are contradictory. The first four give us four kinds of signs which exhaust possible language. Of the first the example is Vaidika-S'abda including Bīja Mantras uttered by the vocal organs and of the second we may instance " expressive " signs made to a man (who does not understand the spoken language) by means of the hand or other bodily organ in order to indicate a particular object. The third and fourth classes refer to arbitrary forms of the first two. Arbitrary-vocal is an arbitrary combination of natural vocal signs, each separately being vocal and natural but their combinations being arbitrary as where two or more natural words are taken and an arbitrary meaning is given to the whole group, *e.g.* code words. In the same way it may be possible to combine two or more non-vocal natural signs and give the whole thing an arbitrary meaning. A particular name attached to a thought or thing may be arbitrary as in the case of some proper names, but names as such are necessary to higher mental processes directly and also to intuitive processes implicitly. All proper names however are not arbitrary. Those that are, are attached as signs to objects to denote them or mark them off from other objects. They do not connote any attributes or relations of the things to which they may be attached. Our perceptions and ideations often go on without language. Many rapid automatic inferences are drawn and habitual actions are performed without language. But sometimes these processes are with their language accompaniment and the moment we want to review, describe, classify, and judge these processes, their language accompaniment appears in consciousness.

Now S'abda according to previously given defi- nitions is either Para or Apara. The former is Movement or Stress considered in itself, that is, apart from conditions of its manifestation to specialised sense organs or sense capacities. One of these sense capacities is the ear which is subject to degrees, since the capacity of one individual is greater than that of another. The gradation points to a highest or absolute capacity which may be called the Absolute Ear. The appea- rance or manifestation of Paraśabda or causal Stress to the highest capacity (wherever that be) is S'abda- Tanmātra. This last is still a manifestation and not the Stress itself. It is the Stress-in-itself appearing to an ideal ear. It is this stress-in-itself regarded from a special standpoint. Just as we conceive an absolute ear, so we may conceive an absolute eye, tongue and so forth. Each means the Ideal limit (a mathematical term) of certain capacities of specialised feeling which are exercised in us in varying degree. S'abda Tanmātra therefore means not sound in general or undifferentiated pure sound *only*, but Sāmānya (general) sounds including the highest, the Praṇava or Mantra " Om, " as well as Viśeṣa (special) sounds. In the Tanmātra form they are both of them sounds as apprehended by the highest capacity and therefore not subject to the conditions of *variability*. " Sound in itself " or " sound as such " therefore does not *necessarily* mean " undifferentiated sound. " Thus a dove is cooing in a grove of mangoe trees hard by. I hear it. You may hear it better. By a Scientific instrument (megaphone, microphone) it may be heard better still and so on. But what is that sound as apprehended by a perfect capacity of hearing? What is this cooing sound in itself or the standard of this cooing sound of which you, I and the Yogī hear so many variations? The answer to this will give us the Tanmātra of a Viśeṣa sound.

Now Paraśabda is not language. Aparaśabda including S'abda-Tanmātra is. In the individual (Vyaṣṭi) consciousness there is intuitive consciousness (which answers to Pratyaya) of veiled Ānanda. The Artha is the temporarily equilibrated causal body. But this Artha does not manifest itself to the sleeper at that time in language. In Suṣupti the individual is without language though he has an Intuitive experience of his Vyaṣṭi Ānandamaya causal body. But the Artha in Suṣupti, though wanting language, must have its Paraśabda.

The individual is a centre correlated to other centres in a cosmic system. For a while he is in equilibrium in Suṣupti. Dynamically this means that the algebraic sum of the forces of the other centres exerted upon the individual and of the forces of his own causal body exerted upon the other centres is zero. It follows therefore that the whole cosmic system need not be in equilibrium whilst the individual (that is, his causal body) is in equilibrium. His slumber does not mean the slumber of the Universe. The question is not here discussed as to the forces constituting the individual causal stress during Suṣupti. This I deal with elsewhere. To explain equilibrium in Suṣupti we require only to assume that the resultant action of the universe on the individual causal body and the resultant reaction of the individual causal body on the universe annul each other during Suṣupti or dreamless sleep. They (at the former) need not be separately nil. Hence the going by the individual into slumber means an actual stressing attitude of the cosmic system which is Paraśabda. But for a certain attitude of the external system there would be no equilibrium in the internal system. Nay more : this Paraśabda may manifest itself as sound (*i. e.*, as language) to other centres such as S'abda-Tanmatra to the Absolute Ear, Sūkṣma-S'abda of varying degree to the Yogic ear, or as the self-produced physical sounds of the sleeper to the gross ear. Just as a Devatā has a Bija mantra or Primary Natural Name so has each other individual Jīva, corresponding to their respective causal bodies, and these may be heard in varying degree by finer ears and fully by the Absolute Ear. But the individual does the sleeping without language just as he may make sounds in his sleep without being conscious of it whilst a person sitting by him hears them. Laya or Cosmic Suṣupti is the dreamless slumber of Bhagavān or Īśvara. If our own analogy can be pushed up to this, then this cosmic Suṣupti is also without language, though it is an intuitive experience by God of His own causal body. Since there are no *other* centres here and no absolute ear other than that of Īśvara (who is *ex hypothesi* in Suṣupti), this intuitive experience is absolutely without language (Mauna). It is silence itself. But Paraśabda is there still, namely equilibrated Samaṣṭi (Causal Stress.) Hence language or no language, the correlation of S'abda and Artha persists. Thus language is not the *whole* of S'abda.

S'abda, Artha and Pratyaya are the three poles of a polar triangle. In all planes of consciousness below the pure or transcendent plane this polar triangle necessarily holds. In Īśvara experience the three poles meet together at a point so that S'abda = Artha = Pratyaya. In the Individual Suṣupti experience also they are not clearly distinguishable. Language can be put for S'abda (causal movement or stress) only when there arises the possibility of its being apprehended as sound by some hearing capacity (either absolute or relative). A name or a word ceases to be such when the apprehension by the appropriate cognitive capacity is not there. A name is a manifestation to such cognitive capacity and when the conditions of manifestations are not there the manifestation disappears. But the causal stress (Paraśabda) of the name remains. Hence in Vyaṣti Suṣupti actual names or words (or vocal language) lapse back into their causal stress. The operation is essentially the same in Samaṣti Suṣupti or Laya. So that S'abda is (that is, equals) language, *actual or possible*, in all cases. In the lower planes (Svapna, Jāgrat), however, language may be put for S'abda but subject to this provision that the language-pole may be regarded as being sometimes above and sometimes below the threshold line of normal or pragmatic consciousness. Thus in the case of the intuitive processes afore-mentioned we may save the polar triangle by assuming that the language pole though not apparent is still there below the threshold line ready to be called up whenever occasion should arise. Thus the development from infancy may be shown by the following diagram in which A = Artha, P = Pratyaya and S = S'abda as language, shown as being above or below the line which is the threshold—

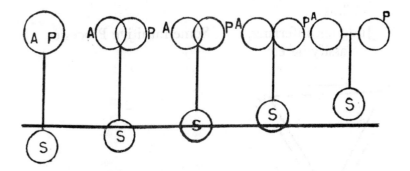

In this diagram, showing the child's development, the five diagrams do not represent definite stages but only the gradual separation of A and P and the rising of S above the line. First no language or more strictly speaking only simple rudimentary sounds—Artha and Pratyaya merge into one, there being no discrimination. Then Artha and Pratyaya are more and more discriminated and their language correlate is more and more developed and brought above the threshold line. Animals probably remain in the first two stages of the child.

In Jāgrat and Svapna, Artha and Pratyaya are all necessarily associated not merely with S'abda but with that condition of S'abda which we call language. But the association may be either manifest or unmanifest. In the latter case whilst Artha and Pratyaya are above the threshold line of normal consciousness, language is below it, so that in the intuitive processes above described Artha and Pratyaya alone *seem* to appear, though their normal associates are waiting for them below the threshold line. The moment it is desired to review, describe and classify Artha and Pratyaya, then the S'abdas as words appear.

Thus :

Judging, inferring,   Some intuitive Processes
classifying etc.

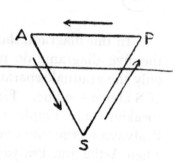

Threshold Line

The above account, whilst saving psychology, would imply that Sabda, Artha, Pratyaya being involved (though as identities) in Iśvara consciousness must be involved in all downward experience also. It is however necessary to clearly understand that Sabda is not necessarily language in all cases, and that language may be either consciously or sub-consciously given. According to the scheme suggested the correlation of Artha, Pratyaya and Sabda as language is essential in the planes of Jāgrat and Svapna, but they may be latent as regards the third partner in some intuitive process, but patent in others as well as in conceiving, judging, inferring and so forth. The conclusion therefore is : (1) The Turiya state is undifferentiated. Hence in it there is no Artha, Sabda, Pratyaya. A, S and P *severally* vanish. (2) The Suṣupti state (Samaṣṭi or Vyaṣṭi) is temporarily equilibrated Consciousness in which there are A, S and P, but their resultant is ineffectual. In the Vyaṣṭi consciousness there are Artha, S'abda, Pratyaya. But these three seem to blend into one and are not clearly distinguishable. Here S'abda is not language to the subject himself. (3) The Svapna and Jāgrat states in which the temporarily equilibrated consciousness ceases are actually stirring Vyaṣṭi or Samaṣṭi consciousness. In them there is S'abda, Artha, and Pratyaya, but in some intuitive processes (perceptional and ideational) S'abda as language is below the threshold line of the normal Consciousness.

Thus the cosmic and individual states must all be ultimately explained (so far as this can be) by the dynamical theory of Stress or S'akti in which an investigation is made as to the conditions of equilibrium and movement.

CHAPTER VIII

NATURAL NAME

WHAT is a natural name ? Everything is composed of moving material forces. Even what seems stable is in movement, though they are sometimes held together as a whole until by design or in the course of nature they are disrupted and dissolved. Matter itself is only a relatively stable form of cosmic energy. Because all is in movement, the world is called Jagat or that which moves. Everything is moving which is not the unmoving (Nispanda) Brahman. This movement, which is the world, is apprehended by man as sound, touch and feel, form and colour, taste and smell. This is its effect on the sense organs (Indriyas) and mind (Manas), which are again themselves in movement, being ultimately composed of the same Tanmātras which are the components of the mind's objects or matter. All movement is accompanied by sound. In other words, movement presented to a subject is apprehended by the ear and mind as sound, just as it is apprehended by the eye as form and colour, or by the tongue as taste. We say ' ear and mind,' for it is to be remembered that according to Indian notions the Indriya or sense is not the physical organ ear, eye and so forth, but the faculty of mind operating through that organ as its instrument. The physical organs are the usual means whereby on the physical plane the functions of hearing and so forth are accomplished. But as they are mere instruments and their power is derived from the mind, a Yogī may accomplish by the mind only all that may be done by these physical organs, and indeed more, without the use of the latter. So also a hypnotised subject can perceive things, even when no use of the special physical organs ordinarily necessary for the purpose is made. The Paramountcy of mind is shown by the fact that an object is not perceived unless the mind gives its attention. So in the Bṛhadāraṇyaka-Upaniṣad it is said, " My mind was elsewhere : I did not hear." Now movement being accompanied by sound, let us suppose we could hear (which we cannot do through the individual natural ear) the sound produced by the generating stress or constituting forces of (say) the household fire, then the sound so heard would be the natural name of that fire. Again the sap rises in the trees. Could we hear the forces constituting this rising sap, then the sound heard would be the natural name of that vegetable function, and so on. Natural name in its purest sense may therefore be defined as the sound produced by the generating stress (Sʼakti) or constituting forces of a thing, not as apprehended by this ear or that (which apprehends within limits and subject to conditions) but by what may be called the supreme and Infinite Ear which apprehends unconditionally a sound, which is sound as it is. By Supreme Ear is meant the power (Sʼakti) of apprehending sound in itself or as such, without subjection to the varying conditions of Time, Place (*i.e.*, Plane) and Person. It is that which hears causal stress of a thing as such or unconditionally. Then the natural name of a thing is that sound which the Supreme Ear hears. Natural language in its highest sense is a language of natural names only. In this sense no language below the absolute plane can be such. In this sense even the Vedic language and its Mahāmantra "Om" is not natural language.

The relative ear does not hear such stress unconditionally. To it therefore a thing has no natural name. In this connection we must distinguish between the sound accompanying causal stress and the sound which a thing gives forth under the action of stimuli. The latter may be heard, but the former not. Fire or heat acting upon various things may produce various sounds which the ordinary relative ear hears, but its causal stress is experienced as a sound which a Yogī alone hears.

Nevertheless there may be according to the S'astra what is called an approximate natural name, that is the sound of the causal stress heard by a Yogī and transmitted imperfectly by him. We say 'imperfectly', because it is transmitted by an imperfect agent as a sound which can be heard by the gross ear. Prajāpati hears the causal sound by His Supreme Ear (not gross or physical) and utters it by His Supreme Tongue to His Sādhaka who, not yet himself possessing the Supreme Ear, hears it a little imperfectly. In him the primordial sound is somewhat veiled. By Sādhana he either attains the Supreme Ear or stops short of it. In the former case he is like Prajāpati himself. In the latter case he communicates by his relative "tongue" the imperfectly heard primæval sound to his disciple (S'isya) who can by Yoga either verify the archetypal sound, or falls short of it. In this way the primordial sounds descend down to our relative planes, where the natural sounds, that

is, causal sounds of many objects, are not represented
at all, and those that are represented are so, suitably to
conditions of relative ears and relative tongues. According to the Mantra-S'āstra the Bīja Mantras represent
approximately natural names. Thus the causal stress
of fire is a sound heard by the Yogī which is said to be
represented for the ordinary relative ear as the sound
or Bīja " Ram " (रं). Vital function under different
stimuli produces various sounds, some of which the
ordinary ear hears, but the causal sound of vital
function as breathing is represented by the Prāna-Bīja
" Hamsa " and so on. If attention is paid to breathing
it will be found that the outward breath is in the form
of the letter Ha and the indrawn breath of Sa. It is not
possible to indraw the breath and say the letter Ha,
but it is pushed forth by the outward breath. And so
with " Om. " The creative energising out of which this
world evolves is S'abda and it is an immense sound
(Nāda) to the Supreme Ear as uttered by the Supreme
Tongue which is also Nāda. But no finite ear can hear
it perfectly and no finite tongue can utter it perfectly.
The sound which has descended to us as " Om " cannot
therefore be a natural name of the creative process in
the full sense; but having descended through the
Mānasaputras and a line of Gurus each of whom more
or less closely approximated to the pure sound in his
personal experience, it is practically taken as an *approximate* natural name of the initial creative action. It is an
open continuous sound, uninterrupted by any consonant
which clips it, vanishing as it were upward in the
Nādabindu which is placed on the vowel. The same
observations apply to Ham (हँ), Yam (यँ), Ram (रं),
Hamsah (हंसः), and other Bījas.

So much for " natural name " in the pure sense and approximate sense of the term.

The term " natural" in this connection can however be interpreted in five different senses :

(1) Sound as produced by causal stress. S'abda is stress which may or may not reach the normal of consciousness. If two things are affecting one another, then the name for the total mutual action is stress, of which the respective actions of each of those things are the elements or partials or components. Thus we have stress for three things, for four things, and so on. Ultimately we reach universal stress which is an infinite system of correlated forces. A particular thing may be defined as a partial experience of this infinite system which has been well called by Professor P. N. Mukho-pādhyāyā (to whom I am indebted in the matter here discussed) "fact section ". This experience is Jīva. The infinite system is however never really finitized by these partials. When the stress between one such partial and another touches the normal of consciousness in either or both, we may have under circumstances and within certain limits sensation of sound in either or both. The stress is S'abda and the sound is Dhvani. It is stress or S'abda which constitutes a thing. Whether this S'abda is followed or accompanied by a certain Dhvani or not will depend upon (a) the magnitude of its action in relation to a percipient subject, and (b) upon the condition of the percipient's perceptive organs. Hence in order that the sound of a thing's constituent stress may be heard, the rates of vibration of the air must be such and such, the ears and brain must be such and such and so forth. Thus most objects of experience, though influencing the individual, do not

express themselves in sound *to him* such as the earth, rocks, sun, moon, and stars. Sound as produced by causal stress and apprehended by the Supreme Ear and uttered by the Supreme Tongue is natural name in its pure sense and in this sense none of our sounds are natural. If by this approximate ' natural name ' of a thing we mean its sound (that is, the sound produced in us by its causal stress) as apprehended by the relative ear to which it is revealed, then most things have no natural names to us, though they may have to other beings with different perceptive conditions. A being who has an experience of the causal stress itself and whose ears (gross or subtle) can respond to it in any form (*i.e.,* whatever be the rates of vibration of air and ether) knows the natural names of all things. Such a Being is Prajāpati Himself and Souls that resemble Him. Hence the natural names of such things are revealed through Vākya which, though the Jīva may not completely verify now, he may progressively verify by personal experience, and ultimately completely verify by personal experience too. In this sense only do Sʹruti and Āgama, that is, the Tantra Sʹāstras, give the natural names of Artha, sensuous or super-sensuous. The test of a natural name is this—If " Supreme or Absolute Ear " be defined as that which hears causal stress of a thing as such unconditionally, then the natural name of a thing is that sound the Supreme Ear hears. The relative ear does not hear this and therefore to it this has no natural name.

(2) Sound as produced by causal stress is projected on to our planes, with necessary limitations, through Mānasaputras and others. This is *approximate* natural language, such as the Mantras Om, Ham,

Ram, and the like; it constitutes one stratum of the Vedic language. In this case the pure sound is represented by a sound capable of being heard by the relative ear. The Yogī who hears the Mantra " Om " does not hear it as the sound " Om," but as a sound which the relative ear can hear as " Om." " Om " is thus only a gross sound which approximates to the real sound only so far as the gross relative ear permits. The pure sound is thus represented by its nearest gross equivalent.

(3) A thing, such as a conch shell or an animal, may under the action of external forces give forth variable sounds of certain kinds. This may be perceived by us and we ordinarily call it its natural sound, and sometimes name it after it as " cuckoo " or " crow." But it is not the sound produced by the " causal stress " (which may be reduced to the motions of electrons and therefore unperceived except by the Yogī). Hence we must distinguish between the sound produced by causal stress, and the sound which a thing gives forth under the action of stimuli such as the crackle (another onomatopoeic name) of fire when wood is thrown on it. The latter may be heard but the former not. These names, " cuckoo " and so forth, are practically regarded as natural names, though according to the definition they are not. Such names enter into all languages, Vaidik and others. Fire or heat acting upon various things may produce various sounds which the relative gross ear hears. But its causal stress produces, it is said, the sound Ram (रं), which Bīja Mantra a Yogī alone hears. Vital function under different stimuli is producing various sounds in the body, some of which may be heard, but the causal stress in the form of vital function is represented by the

Mantra " Hamsa " and so on. Prajāpati (as above
stated) hears the causal sound or Pure Natural Name
by His Supreme Ear (not gross or physical) and utters
it by His Supreme Tongue to His Sādhaka, who, not
yet possessing the absolute ear, hears it only imperfectly.
This, as pointed out before, is the approximate natural
name. The Primordial Sound is thus somewhat veiled
in him. By Sādhana he either attains the Absolute Ear
or stops short of it. In the former case he is like
Prajāpati Himself. In the latter case he communicates
by his relative tongue the imperfectly heard Primæval
sound to his S'iṣya, who can either by Yoga himself
verify the archetypal sound, or fall short of it. In this
way the Primordial Sounds descend down to our
relative planes where (a) the natural or causal sounds
of many objects are not represented at all, and (b)
those that are represented are so represented suitably
to conditions of relative ears and relative tongues. But
these approximate natural names must be distinguished
from what are popularly called natural names (in the
third class), which are not sounds of the causal stress but
are due to the action of external forces on a particular
object which is constituted of the causal stress, the sound
of which is the true natural name, pure or approximate.

(4) There is then a class of secondary natural
names, that is, those which are not, in the primary
sense, purely or approximately natural, as sound of
causal stress, nor natural in the onomatopoeic sense,
but which are secondarily natural in that they are
out of elements of sounds which are primarily (though
approximately) natural.

The Causal Stress when striking the ear produces
sound, when striking the eye produces light and colour ;

and when striking other sense organs produces other kinds of sensation. The stress or constituting force is one and this is S'abda : but it manifests itself differently to the different sense organs. If then, instead of calling a thing in terms of its sound, it is desired to express it in terms of its other manifestations (sensations) to us, we want to state its relations to other perceptive faculties, how in such cases can this be expressed ? The " natural sound " in its primary sense cannot do this ; the thing *as a whole* may be best represented by the natural sound, but not its touch, colour, taste and smell specifically : yet this latter representation is also important and useful. The sound or Bīja Rām (र), for example, may be the approximate natural name of Agni, but unless we can grip the causal stress of Agni itself, it tells nothing about the attributes and relations of the thing with which we are practically concerned. Ordinarily Rām (र), Hrīm (ह्रीं), Aim (ऐं), Om (ओं) are unmeaning. For this reason we hear talk of Mantra being " Jabber " as if any body of men in the world's history deliberately occupied themselves with what was in fact meaningless jabber. That is not necessarily to say that the theory is correct, but that it is not absurd and without sense as supposed. Now-a-days when the S'āstra is nearly lost, it may be so in those cases where the Mantras are said without understanding. These Bījas may be made to *denote* things or processes, but ordinarily (unless it is possible to penetrate into the kernel itself) they do not *connote* qualities or attributes of things ; and hence are what J. S. Mill calls non-connotative terms. They are however according to S'āstra really connotative. Hence in the average plane man requires other terms besides Rām (र) to represent Agni. Suppose we take the quality "burning" (Dāhikā-S'akti). Then in order to express Agni it terms of this quality we may do (or it might have been done for us by linguistic tradition) either of two things : (a) Taking the letters (Varṇas) and remembering that each represents the natural sound of a certain thing or process, it is possible to make such a permutation and combination of them (taken two or more at a time) that "burning" may be represented by the combination thus formed. Here a compound term is formed (either by ourselves or by tradition) by the collocation in due order of elementary approximate natural sounds (viz., the letters). To express the same attribute more than one such combination may be possible. (b) Or there may exist already simple roots (Dhātu) formed in their turn either by the combination of elementary natural sounds or in the onomatopoeic fashion (see 3 ante), which with proper prefixes and suffixes can be made to connote "burning" and thus evolve the term Agni. Here again, to express the same quality or relation, different words may be evolved by ourselves or by tradition. Thus there are synonyms or Paryāya. These secondary names may be arranged in grades in accordance with the degree of their closeness to primary names. Hindu philologists distinguish between S'aktyārtha and Lakṣyārtha, that is, Abhidās'akti and Lakṣaṇās'akti and classify each.

This in itself is a vast subject. It is sufficient to say here that words have two Vṛttis, namely, Abhidā and Lakṣanā. The first is S'akti in the sense that it compels the understanding of the thing denoted by a word. The object "cow" is described by and is the Vākyārtha of the word or S'abda "cow". The second only approximately denotes the object (Artha).

It, so to speak, leads the hearer to the door but does not enter. Lakṣya is that denoted by Lakṣaṇā, which means a sign, that is, object denoted by a sign. Thus the word Brahman is not Vākyārtha of the Supreme Brahman (Nirguṇa-Parabrahman), but it is Vākyārtha of the Saguṇa-Brahman. The word Brahman is only Lakṣyārtha of the Supreme Brahman.

We may say that these secondary names are not indifferent as to their expressiveness of the qualities and relations of things. Some do it better and more closely than others. Agni, Vahni, Hutāśana, and other names of Fire are connected with the Bīja Mantra Ram (र) in this sense, that while the latter approximately represents the natural name of the thing *as a whole*, the former express the attributes and relations of the thing specifically regarded. Hence whilst " Ram " (र) is apparently non-connotative, the former are connotative.

(5) Primary and secondary names may be combined in such order (Krama) and metre or harmony (Chandah) that by vitalizing one another, these in combination may appear as an approximate name of a thing or process. In this manner a Vaidik or Tāntric Mantra (consisting of several words) may, it is said, naturally denote a Devatā or a function.

Beside these five senses of natural sound of which pure and absolute sense is that first given, there is non-natural or artificial sound or name, which means an arbitrary name taken at random to denote a thing such as some proper names.

The test of natural name is, it is said, twofold and capable of experimental verification : (1) Whether the causal stress of a thing makes a sound (say the Bija Yam) may be verified by Yoga. The thing being given, a sound evolves. (2) This sound repeatedly and harmonically uttered, that is in Japa of Mantra, must create or project into perception the corresponding thing. This too is capable of experimental verification. In this case the sound being given, a thing evolves.

VAIDIKA S'ABDA

THE Vedas communicate the natural names of some things, subject to the necessary limitations involved in their representation suitably to conditions of relative ears and tongues. No Vedic word is an absolute natural name. This cannot be. Just as in the Tantra S'āstra we find Bīja mantras, which are said to represent approximately natural names, scattered here and there in a varied mass of ordinary Sanskrit which *remotely* represent natural sounds, so is the case in S'ruti. There are, it is said, closely approximate natural names, combined according to natural laws of harmony (Candah), forming Mantras which are irresistibly connected with their esoteric Arthas (Devatās) ; but these are commented upon, explained, applied and so forth in passages which do not express natural names in this sense. On analyzing these Mantras themselves, both Vaidik and Tāntrik, there are found some sounds which are not and others which are in natural use. Here each word in the Mantra does not necessarily stand for an approximate natural sound (that is produced by causal stress). These tendencies to the archetypal forms may be varying. But in the Mantra it is their order of combination and rhythm that mainly counts. Thus *as a whole* the Mantra may be the approximate natural name of a

Devatā or function. Its creative and projecting power lies in the two things : (a) The mutual aiding and inhibiting of the sounds in the Candah ; the veils of the individual sounds are removed by the order of their collocation. Here the " Curves " of sound are constructive and not destructive. (b) The cumulative effect of the repetition of sounds and strings of sounds also may produce the aforesaid result. By repetition is there summation of stimuli.

So that by analyzing the Vaidik language we get this :

(1) Certain approximate natural names, standing alone or in groups, such as Om, Ham, Hamsah, Svāhā and so on. These are fundamental sounds or primaries.

(2) Certain combinations of sounds which, though not natural distributively, naturalize each other in and by the order and harmony of the combinations. Thus arise Mantras which become approximate natural names of objects and processes. These may gather creative momentum by repetition.

(3) A large mass of sounds or names used to explain the meanings and applications and results of the above which need not be natural names in the above sense.

Hence it follows that the Veda which is heard by the gross ear and spoken by the gross tongue is not a system of natural names. It is however claimed to be a system of approximate natural names in varying degree. The Veda of the Absolute Ear and Tongue is a system of absolute natural names.

Then is the relative and approximate Veda the primordial, universal, unitary language ? The answer

must be in the negative, but in the case of the first class
of names it is amongst all languages most nearly so
upon the basis of the theory here dealt with. In the
second class of names it is less so and in the third it is
least so.

There are four different strata in Vaidik experience.
First there is the nameless Supreme Experience; then
the three above described. S'abda, Artha and Pratyaya
are absolutely connected in the absolute plane but
progressively less so in the lower strata. The natural
connection of S'abda and Artha means that the latter
being given, the former is there whether audible by us
or not; the former being given, the latter is created or
projected. But we must distinguish between what is
here called natural name and what often receives that
term. Thus a conch-shell is blown. What is the
natural name here? Not the sound which we may
make it give forth, for these are produced by our effort
and vary, but the sound of the causal stress which
generates and keeps together the shell. The blowing
sound is only practically natural. What is the basis of
the Vaidik theory? In the final resort experimental
verification is the test as in Āyurveda.

Besides the division of name into natural and
arbitrary, of the former into absolute and relative
and of the latter into primary and secondary, name
may be classified according as it is (a) typal or
(b) variational, as for example of the first the Sanskrit
word "Gauh" and of the second the English word
"Cow". Language according to Indian notions is not
something arbitrary and invented. No man ever
invented a language. Volapuk, Esperanto and the
like are mere combinations of the sounds of pre-existing

language. The Vaidik Language was revealed by Iśvara to the Mānasaputras and others and through them to men. This itself as ordinary worldly (Laukika) speech became corrupted and when rectified was called Sanskrit, that which has been purified. A distinction must therefore be made between the original Vaidik language and current Sanskrit in which however there are words which also occur in the Vedas. Now the ordinary orthodox view is that there is a typal or standard language and that this is the universal language of which all others are variations.

Whenever a typal standard name has a variation, the following questions arise: (*a*) When does that variation appear and for how long does it last? (*b*) In what places or planes does that variation arise? (*c*) In what persons or groups of persons does that variation appear or for whom does it arise?

Briefly stated a variation is always subject to conditions of time, place and person. Then a variation may be (*a*) common (Sāmānya), or (*b*) special (Viśeṣa). The former is what comprises a whole class of objects. Thus " Cow " is a sound variation appearing in a whole class of persons; Gāi or Gābhī with another class of persons namely Bengalis. The special variation is one appearing in an individual object. Thus one individual pronounces the word " Cow " slightly differently from what another does. Every person in fact has his own way of pronunciation.

Again a variation may be (*c*) voluntary, or (*d*) involuntary. The former is due to the free will of a person or a group of persons; the latter is not so.

The typal sounds are eternal. They are latent however during cosmic sleep (Suṣupti). The Sāmānya variations of the typal sounds are not eternal in the sense and to the extent that the types are ; they appear when the conditions of their expressions appear, and disappear when these go.

If we take these four divisions two at a time we get six possible combinations—(1) Common and special variation, (2) Common and voluntary variation, (3) Common and involuntary variation, (4) Special and voluntary variation, (5) Special and involuntary variation, (6) Voluntary and involuntary variation. Of these, the first and last are impossible being self-contradictory. Of the remaining four the second is not eternal. In so far as a common variation is due to the free will of a person or persons it has an absolute beginning ; for if it be simply the repetition of a previous cosmic order, then it is not a free act but predetermined. The third class are eternal but not to the extent the types are. Comparing them with the latter we can say that they are passing, though recurrently. Types too are recurrently passing during creation (Sṛṣṭi) and dissolution (Laya), but their cycles of recurrence are larger. They are eternal in the full sense in so far as they approximate to their type. For the same reasons given as regards the second class, the fourth class is not eternal. The fifth class is not eternal in so far as it is brought about by the part volitions of persons. The whole question is however of so great difficulty, that it is difficult to fully unravel the tangle in which we find it. How and where are we to draw the line between voluntary and non-voluntary, between absolute will and finite will ? Is again the cosmic cycle exactly recurrent or not ? From a practical point of view we may perhaps not greatly err if we say (1) that the general plan and the types are recurrent and

eternal ; (2) that the common variations are recurrent
and eternal subject to more conditions ; and (3) that
the special variations are practically not eternal.
It is claimed for the Veda that it is a system of
standard and typal and therefore natural names. But
natural name has, as already explained, various
meanings. There are therefore different strata of
natural names in Veda. Name may be either (a)
natural or (b) conventional, that is arbitrary. With
the latter we are not here concerned. Natural
name may be (c) Absolute, that is, as apprehended
unconditionally or (d) Relative, that is, as apprehended subjected to varying conditions. Veda as a
manifestation is not the first. Absolute name is only
heard on the unconditioned plane. We are therefore
concerned with the relative natural name. This may
be either (e) primary, or (f) secondary. The first is
the causal stress, thing or functioning as a whole, as
represented approximately to the relative ear and is
again twofold as (g) the elementary sounds or letters
(Varna), and (h) as compound sounds, such as are
found in Bijas and roots (Dhātu). In the Yoga Bhāṣya,
that is Vyāsa's commentary on the Pātañjala-Darśana
(3, 17), it is said : *Tatra vagvarṇeṣvarthavatīti.* According
to this, each letter is intrinsically *Sarvābhidhāna-śakti-
prachita*, that is, possessing the power (S'akti) to denote
and connote all object (Artha). For, as the Viśvasāra-
Tantra says : " What is not here is nowhere " (*Yannehāsti
na tat kvacit*). A letter (Varṇa) is the whole cosmos in
miniature. One Varṇa differs from another in the
relative latency of the universe of Artha involved in it,
the universe being the same in both. They come to
denote special Arthas by virtue of the order (Krama)

of their collocation (*Kramānuro'-vhinorthasaṁketenāvacc-hinnah.*) Their particular meanings or Saṁketa are thus due not to intrinsic difference but to the order (Krama) in grouping.

In the relative secondary natural name, functioning is specifically represented. The specific attributes and relations are given. These again may (*i*) appeal directly to the ear, and be either (*j*) self-produced, or (*k*) induced or excited; or (*l*) they may appeal to other senses and either (*m*) consist of single words which are combinations of Varṇas themselves, or Dhātus, or (*n*) of combination of words which may be either (harmonic, or (*p*) non-harmonic but Kramic.

The first and main division of this scheme is into natural and arbitrary. As to this it is to be observed that all names are made up of elements of sounds or letters (Varṇa). But to naturally connote an Artha, the Varṇas cannot be arbitrarily selected and arranged. To naturally represent a given Artha, certain Varṇas which are in some way connected with that Artha must be chosen and arranged according to a certain order (Krama). A word in which such selection and order are not in evidence is a conventional name, *e.g.*, a telegraphic code (though even in this there is a designed Krama), many proper names, and algebraical symbols. The Krama of the Vaidika S'abdas is said to be eternal. To explain this further; let it be supposed that it is desired to evolve a certain Artha, say an atom of hydrogen. A certain number of moving electrons arranged in a certain order must be chosen. The number and order being different we have a different kind of atom. Suppose again it is desired to evolve water. Two atoms of hydrogen and one atom of

oxygen must be taken and so arranged by electric or
other influence that a molecule H_2O is evolved. So
also is the case of any compound material substance.
The Varnas are in relation to ordinary sounds, what
the atoms are in relation to material substances. The
atoms can be aggregated into molecules and things
only in certain definite proportions and not arbitrarily ;
so with the Varnas and natural words.

Further as radio-activity and other facts prove, an
atom is a system of moving electrons. It is not therefore absolutely simple and elementary. Similarly what
we recognise as the Varnas may not be absolutely
simple or elementary sounds ; they are however so for
all practical purposes, as the atoms are for all chemical
purposes. There are about 75 different atoms but the
electrons which make them up are of the same kind ;
their number and arrangement account for the
differences of Oxygen, Hydrogen, Carbon and other
atoms. In the same way the garland or rosary of letters
(Varnamālā) may be evolved out of the same kind of
elementary sound by differential aggregation. It may
be that the basic elementary sound is the uninterrupted
Anāhata Dhvani finitised into various points
(S'abdabindu) or atoms (S'abdaparamāṇu) of sound.

So again taking any curve, say a circle—its
circumference may be regarded as the sum of an
infinite number of small bits of straight lines : these
are the elements. Any ritualistic diagram, such as,
say, the Sarvatobhadramaṇdala, or a Yajna or Homa
may be similarly regarded. Hence a natural word may
be compared to, and in the case of a Bīja Mantra can
be represented by, a diagram (Yantra) which in that
case, becomes the graph of the Bīja in question, or of

causal stress of which that Bīja is the acoustic manifestation and counterpart. Lastly an electron is an unit
charge of electricity, which after all may be only an
element of ether in stress. This element of ether in
stress is Paraśabda Paramāṇu according to the definition
given ; and as heard by the relative ear it is S'abda
Paramāṇu. So that this last and the electron are
naturally connected. Hence S'abdas (aggregates of
S'abda paramāṇus) and Arthas (aggregates of electrons) are connected. But as electrons aggregated at
random will not make a natural Artha, so S'abda-
Paramāṇus aggregated at random do not make a
natural name.

Physically the vibrations represented by a Varṇa
can be resolved into component vibrations which are
harmonic motions. As Fourier's theorem gives it, a
complex harmonic motion may be analysed into simple
harmonic motions. All the ordinary letters are complex
harmonic motions ; and physically speaking a simple
harmonic motion is S'abdaparamāṇu. Physiologically
each single vibration acting on the ear, nerves and
brain centres, produces a single pulse of cerebral
agitation, a single " nerve-shock, " admits of " more or
less, " so that the primary group gives approximate
natural names *par excellence*, and the secondary group
gives in varying degree approximate natural names.
Within the secondary group the class (*h*), that is
Mantras, represent the closest approximation to natural
names.

The test of a natural name is ultimately experimental, that is the sound (S'abda) being given, the
object (Artha) is evolved : the object being given the
sound is evolved. In absolute natural names these

relations are at once established. In relative names they are established in varying measure through Krama and Japa. Ultimately the question whether Veda is a system of approximate natural names is thus a question of fact.

This leads to a consideration of the claim made by Veda that it is the standard language, an eternal system of natural names of which all others are variations. Hitherto we have dealt with the matter philosophically. We now approach the historical and philological question. The two must be kept apart. Much may be said in favour of the philosophical theory, namely, that the relation between S'abda and Artha is eternal, that there is some S'abda which is the natural name of the Artha, that this natural language is the standard language, that all others are a staying away from and variation of the true norm and so on. But the point now arises as a question of fact, *viz.*, assuming all that is said in theory, is the Vaidika language, that is the language in which the Vedas are as they exist to-day, the eternal standard language? The orthodox affirm that it is, and that the sound " Gauh " is the natural name and standard representation in speech of the object " Cow " for all eternity. That the relation of S'abda and Artha is eternal and that some S'abdas may be natural names of objects are philosophically probable. It is however an entirely different matter when it is affirmed that the Vaidika speech, as existing to-day is that language. Philologists and historians will deny this for they will point out changes in that speech and make claim as regards priority in age for the language of other peoples. Assuming that there was, as the Biblical tradition runs, once, a universal language, it will be denied that the Vaidika language as known to us to-day is that.

It will moreover be shown that even in Veda itself there is evidence to the contrary.   Thus it has been argued that according to the S'atapatha-Brāhmaṇa the original language was monosyllabic.   With this question of philology and history I am not here concerned. But the ultimate philosophical question is, " Who, if any one, first said that *this* sound meant *that* thing?" The Indian answer is that the relation of the word and the object denoted are eternal and not a conventional thing, that there is a system of Natural Names, whatever in fact that may be.   This stands clear of the claim made for the Vedic language, as it exists to-day, that it is that system.

CHAPTER X

THE TATTVAS

A KNOWLEDGE of the Mantra S'āstra involves an understanding of the thirty-six S'aiva-S'ākta-Tattvas. Thus it is said that S'akti is in S'akti-tattva, Nāda in Sadākhya Tattva, Bindu in Īśvara-Tattva. What then are these Tattvas to which reference is made both in the S'aiva and S'ākta-Tantras? Unless these be fully understood, no progress in knowledge of the Mantra Science as here described may be expected.

The S'aiva-S'ākta S'āstras call experience as S'akti by the term Vimarśa. Experience has two elements— the "I" (Aham) and the "This" (Idam), the subjective-knowing aspect (Grāhaka) of the Self and the objective or known (Grāhya) aspect of the Self. For it must be remembered that an object is nothing but the one Self appearing through Māyā as non-Self to Itself as subject. At base the experienced is nothing but the experiencer: though this is not realised until the bonds of Māyā which make subject and object appear to be different are loosened. The "I" side of experience is that in which the Self rests in the light of one's own Self without looking towards another (*Ananyonmukhah aham-pratyayah*) ; just as the experience (Vimarśa) which looks towards another is called—*Idam* (*Yastu anyonmukhah sa idam iti pratyaya*). But this "Other" can only be the Self, for there is in reality nothing but the one Self. It is experienced, however, differently. In the Supreme state it exists with the 'Aham' in a mingled union; in the pure experience between this state and Māyā the "Other" is recognised to be an aspect of the Self; in impure experience governed by Māyā the object appears to be different from the limited self.

Experience again is, at its two poles, Perfect Experience of the Perfect Universe and the Limited experience of the three worlds of reincarnation. Between these two extremes there are intermediate experiences marking the stages whereby the one pure Spirit or Consciousness involves itself in matter.

The Hermetic maxim says: "As above so below". Similarly the Viśvasāra Tantra says: "What is here is there, what is not here is nowhere." (*Yad ihāsti tadanyatra, yan nehāsti na tat kvacit*). S'aiva doctrine says: "That which appears without, only so appears because it exists within." (*Vartamānāvabhāsānām bhāvānām avabhāsanam antahsthitavatām eva ghatate bahirātmanā*). "The manifestation of those things which presently appear, happen in the form of external things because they exist within." Therefore what exists in our experience, evolved from the Supreme also exists in the Supreme experience though in another way." The Supreme experience called Parāsamvit is not a mere abstract objectless knowing (Jñāna). It is the coalescence into one undivided unity of the "I" and the "This," that is, of S'iva and the supreme unmanifested S'akti. The former is the illuminating (Prakāśā) knowing aspect and the latter that Vimarśa aspect which is "the known." But here the two are undistinguishably one. This supreme experience has the immediacy of feeling. It is Bliss (Ānanda) which is defined as "Resting in the Self" (Svarūpaviśrānti). In the Māyika world the Self concerns itself with what it takes to be the non-Self. Here the Universe which is the object of S'iva's experience is the Perfect Universe, that is Supreme S'akti which is but another aspect of Himself as consciousness. She is beautifully called in the Parāprāveśikā : "The Heart of the Supreme Lord" (*Hṛdayam parameśituh*). For the Māyika experiencer (*Māyā pramātṛ*) the universe is the manifested world of objects seen as different from himself. Supreme S'iva and S'akti exist in mutual embrace and love. "Bliss is supreme love" (*Niratiśayapremāspadatvam ānandatvam*) The Supreme state is described by the Bṛhadāraṇyaka-Upaniṣad in the words : "He indeed was just as man and woman in embrace" (*Sā ha etāvān āsa yathā stripumāmsau sampariṣvaktau*) ; when there is neither within nor without, when all thought of lover, loving and loved are forgotten in the joy of blissful unity. The experience is spaceless, timeless, full, all-knowing, almighty. This is the state of S'iva without Kalā (Niṣkalā) or Paramaśiva. This is Parāsamvit which is beyond all Tattvas (Tattvātītā). As the Perfect Universe it is called Parānāda (Supreme "Sound") and Parā-vāk (Supreme "Speech"). Paramaśiva is an experience of the Perfect Universe, that is, of Parānāda (*Amarṣa parānāda-garbhah*). Such universe is pure S'akti (S'akti-svarūpa).

Our worldly experience is as it were an inverted reflection of all this seen in the causal waters of Māyā. Māyā-S'akti is the sense of difference (Bhedabuddhi) which makes the Puruṣa, who is subject to it, see the Universe in the form of an observing self with a multitude of objects conceived of as being outside of and separate from it. In the Māyika world each self excludes the other selves. In the Supreme experience there is one Self experiencing Itself. The Puruṣa is Conscious, subject to Māyā and the five Kañcukas which are limiting forces contracting the natural perfections of the Self. Thus the Perfect state is formless, the world state is with form : the first is spaceless, timeless, all-pervading, the latter is the reverse and so forth. Kāla produces limitations of time. Niyati destroys independence (Svatantratā), regulating the Puruṣa as to what he should or should not do at any given moment of time. The Supreme experience is full and in want of nothing (Pūrṇa). Rāga Kañcuka creates interest in objects as something other than the self and therefore desire for them. The all-knowingness (Sarvajñatā) and all-mightiness (Sarvakartṛtā) of the Supreme S'iva are circumscribed through the action of Vidyā and Kalā, and the puruṣa becomes a "little knower" and a "little doer."

The intermediate Tattvas next described explain the process how from the creative aspect of the Perfect Experience the imperfect World-experience comes into being. S'iva has two aspects in one of which He is Transcendent and in the other creative and Immanent. The creative (Sakala) aspect of the Supreme S'iva (Niṣkala-Paramaśiva) is called S'iva-tattva, wherein is the S'akti called Unmanī. Through operation in His creative aspect S'iva becomes His own object as the Manifested Universe. For in truth there is nothing else than Paramaśiva. S'ivatattva is the first creative movement (Prathama spanda) of the Unmoving Paramaśiva. S'akti-tattva is only the negative aspect of, or in, the S'iva-tattva. The function of S'akti is to negate (*Niṣedhavayāpārupā śaktiḥ*) She who is Consciousness negates Herself, that is, deprives experience of the element of objectivity which is Itself as Parā-S'akti. There is thus left only the other side of experience which is Prakāśamātra, that is, what we should call the "I" (Aham) side of experience when regarded as consisting of an "I" and "This" (Idam). Because in this experience there is no trace of objectivity, whatsoever, either of such objectivity latent or expressed as exists in the Supreme or other lower and derived form of experience, the S'iva Tattva is called "the very void" (S'ūnyātiśūnya). It is the experience in which the self is not looking towards any other (*Ananyonmukhah ahampratyayah*). The objective content, so to speak, of Consciousness is a mere negation. It is S'ūnya because it is empty of objective content. S'akti-tattva is also spoken of as the Will (Icchā) of S'iva as yet Unmanifest and inseparable from him (*Santatasamavāyini*).

This account of S'akti's operation is extraordinarily subtle, explaining as it does how the supreme unitary experience is also the first source of dual experience. Such latter experience and the stages whereby the latter is fully developed can only be produced by positing an aspect in which there is a breaking up of the unitary experience. This is done by first blotting out from the Perfect experience its object or the Perfect Universe (Parā S'akti, Paranāda) thus leaving a mere subjectivity. To the subjectivity thus disengaged there is again gradually unveiled the universe at first as unmanifested and then (through Māyā) as manifested S'akti. In Para Samvit the "I" and the "This" existed as one undistinguishable unity. In S'iva Tattva through the operation of the associated S'akti Tattva, the "This" (*Idam*) is withdrawn from experience so that the "I—experience" (*Aham-vimarśa*) alone remains. To this the 'Idam' or Universe is

again by degrees presented, when there is no longer
an ūndistinguishable unity of " I " and " This, " but an
" I—This " in which both, though distinguishable, are
yet part of the Self which eventually through Māyā-
S'akti becomes an " I " *and* " This " in which the two
are severed the one from the other. How this occurs,
the description of the remaining Tattvas explains. The
S'iva-S'akti Tattva is not an emanation, because it ever
remains the same whether in Creation or Dissolution.
It is the seed and womb of the whole universe.

The first emanation or manifestation (Ābhāsa) of
and by Consciousness is called the Sadākhya or
Sadāśiva Tattva. Here it is to be observed that the
cause ever remains the same and what it was, though
appearing differently in the effect. The Supreme
Experience changelessly endures even though in its
creative aspect it gives birth to the Universe. This
Ābhāsa is like the Vivartta of Māyā-vāda, the difference
between the two lying in the fact that according to the
former the effect is real, and according to S'amkara,
unreal. This difference again depends on the definition
given of " reality ".

Real evolution (Pariṇāma), in which when one thing
is evolved into another it ceases to be what it was, exists
only in the compounded products of the material world.

In Sadāśiva-Tattva there is the commencement of
the first subjective formation of ideas. It is called
Nimeṣa (closing of the eyes) as contrasted with Unmeṣa
(opening of the eyes) of the next stage of experience.
In the former the Universe as S'akti is seen only faintly.
The Self hazily experiences Itself as object. It is the
first step in evolution and the last in involution.
Unmeṣa is the distinct blossoming (Sphutatvam) and

externalization (Bāhyatvam) of the Universe. The
"This" (Idam) is faintly perceived by the "I"
(Aham) as part of the one Self, the emphasis being
therefore on the "I" side of experience. Sadāśiva is
He whom the Vaiṣṇavas call Mahāviṣṇu, and the
Buddhists, Avalokiteśvara who sheds compassion on all.
According to tradition, this is the source whence the
the Avatāras come. It is in this Tattva that there is
what the Mantra-S'āstra calls Nāda-S'akti.

The third stage of the developing consciousness is
Īśvara Tattva, externalization of the last. The Universe
(Idam) is experienced by the "I" (Aham) distinctly
and yet as part of, and not separate from, the one Self.
As in the last experience the emphasis was on the
"Aham," here it is on the "Idam." This Tattva is
called Bindu in Mantra-S'āstra, and is so called because
Consciousness here completely identifies itself with the
Universe as unmanifested Idam, and thus subjectifies it
and becomes with it a Point (Bindu) of Consciousness.
Thus by way of example the mind is completely
subjectified and exists for each of us as a mathematical
point, though the body, to the extent to which it is not
subjectified, appears as an object or extending thing.

The fourth Tattva is known as Vidyā, Sadvidyā,
or S'uddhavidyā. In the experience of this stage,
emphasis is equal on the "I" and the "This"
(*Sāmānādhikaraṇya*). In S'iva-Tattva there is the
I-experience (Aham Vimarśa) ; in Sadāśiva the I-This
experience (Aham-idam Vimarśa) ; in Īśvara-Tattva
the This-I experience (Idamaham Vimarśa). In each
case the stress is laid on the first term. In Vidyā-
Tattva there is an equality of either term in an
experience which is that of the true relation of the

Aham and the Idam, consisting of a synthesis (Saṁga-mana) of the two on a single "basis" (Adhikaraṇa) and not on two different 'bases' according to the experience of those under the influence of Māyā (Māyāpramātṛ), thus eliminating the duality which exists in the latter experience.

By equality of the " I " and the " This ", experience is in the state of readiness for the next stage in which the two are to be severed. Sadvidyā as being the intermediate stage between the pure (S'uddha) and impure (Aśuddha) Creation is called Parāparadasā. It is also spoken of as experience of difference in the form of Mantra (Bhedābhedavimarśanātmaka-mantrarūpa). It is experience of difference because the Idam is separated from the Aham. It is the experience of non-difference because they are still regarded as part of one Self. The experience is compared to that of the Iśvara of the Dvaitavādins, who sees the Universe as different from Himself and yet as part of and in connection therewith. "All this is my manifestation" (Sarvo mamāyam vibhavah). The experience is said to be in the nature of Mantra, because here we are in the region of pure spiritual ideation. As yet there is no objective mani-festation such as exists in our world. Below this Tattva it is said that there were created eight Pudgalas, that is, Jīvas in the from of knowledge (Vijñāna-rūpa) and then seven crores of Mantras and their Maṇḍalas.

At this point Māyā-S'akti intervenes and divides the Aham and Idam, and the Kañcukas or limitations of the natural perfections of Consciousness make It subject to time and space, birth and death, limitation, and desire for object, which It now conceives of as persons and things other than Itself. This is the Puruṣa-

Prakṛti-Tattva. Puruṣa in S'aiva-S'ākta philosophy is the Ātma or Jīva subject to Māyā and the Kañcukas which are limiting forces whereby the Self as Pure Consciousness loses Its natural perfections.

Prakṛti is the S'āntā S'akti of S'iva in contracted form existing as the equilibrium of the Guṇas which are themselves a gross form of the S'aktis of Will (Icchā), Action (Kriyā) and Knowledge (Jñāna). All things exist in Her who is of the nature of feeling in a homogeneous mass. Puruṣa is enjoyer (Bhoktā) and Prakṛti the enjoyed (Bhogyā). The latter is at first the barest objectivity seen as different from the experiencing Self as Puruṣa. Prakṛti then differentiates into the Tattvas of Mind (Antahkaraṇa), Senses (Indriya), and Matter (Bhūta) which constitute our universe.

Puruṣa does not merely mean man nor indeed any animal. Every single thing in the Universe is Puruṣa. Thus an atom of sand is a Puruṣa or consciousness, identifying itself with solidity (Pṛthivī), manifesting its limited Consciousness as atomic memory and other ways. What Consciousness thinks, that is, identifies itself with, that it becomes.

To sum up, the Supreme Experience (Parā-samvit) has a creative aspect (S'iva-S'akti-Tattva), which is a Consciousness of "I" (Aham-vimarśa) which gradually experiences the Universe (Idam) as part of Itself, at first faintly with predominant "I", then clearly with predominant "This", and then as equal " I and This", ready for severance by Māyā. The latter then cleaves consciousness in twain, thus setting up a dichotomy of Subject and Object, though in truth the object is nothing but the Self as its own object. Lastly S'akti, as

Prakṛti differentiates into the multitudinous beings which make the universe. But throughout it is the one and only Śiva whether as the Supreme Experience or as the Consciousness embodied in solid matter. Śakti, Nāda, Bindu mentioned in previous articles are Śakti-Tattva, Sadākhya-Tattva and Īśvara-Tattva (here described), considered from the standpoint of the Mantra Śastra which treats of the origin of Śabda or Sound.

With the Tattvas, the Kalās are associated. These are the forms of activity (Kriyā) of the Tattvas as Śakti. Thus Sṛṣṭi (Creation) is a Kalā of Brahmā. Pālana (Protection) is a Kalā of Viṣṇu and Mṛtyu (Death) is a Kalā of Rudra. It is, however, not always as easy to see the appropriateness of the Kalā as in the simple examples given. The Śākta Tantras speak of 94 Kalās, namely, 19 Kalās of Sadāśiva, 6 of Īśvara, 11 of Rudra, 10 of Viṣṇu, 10 of Brahmā, 10 of Fire, 12 of Sun, and 16 of Moon.

According to Saubhāgya-ratnākara the 19 Kalās of Sadāśiva are Nivṛtti, Pratiṣṭhā, Vidyā, Śānti, Indhikā, Dīpikā, Recikā, Mocikā, Parā, Sūkṣmāmṛtā, Jñānāmṛta, Amṛtā, Āpyāyanī, Vyāpīnī, Vyomarūpā, Mūlavidyā, Mantrakalā, Mahāmantrakala, Jyotiṣkalā.

The 6 of Īśvara are Pītā, Svetā, Nityā, Aruṇā, Asitā, Anantā.

The 11 Rudra Kalās are Tīkṣṇā, Raudrī, Bhayā, Nidrā, Tandrā, Kṣudhā, Krodhinī, Kriyā, Utkārī, Amāyā, Mṛtyu.

The 10 of Viṣṇu are Jadā, Pālini, Śānti, Īśvarī, Rati, Kāmikā, Varadā, Hlādinī, Prīti, Dīkṣā.

The 10 of Brahmā are Sṛṣṭi, Ṛddhi, Smṛti, Medhā, Kānti, Lakṣmī, Dyuti, Sthirā, Sthiti, Siddhi.

The 10 of Fire are Dhūmrārci, Ūṣmā, Jvalini, Jvālinī, Visphuliṅginī, Suṣrī, Surūpā, Kapilā, Havyavahā, Kavyavahā.

The 12 of Sun are Tapini, Tāpini, Dhūmrā, Marīci, Jvālinī, Rucī, Suṣumnā, Bhogadā, Viśvā, Bodhinī, Dhāriṇī, Kṣamā.

The 16 of Moon are Amṛtā, Mānadā, Pūṣā, Tuṣṭi, Puṣṭi, Rati, Dhṛti, Śaśini, Candrikā, Kānti, Jyotsnā, Śrih, Prīti, Aṅgadā, Pūrṇā, Pūrṇāmṛtā.

Out of these 50 are Mātṛkā-Kalās which manifest through the Paśyanti, Madhyamā, and Vaikharī stages (Bhāva) as the gross letters (Varṇa). The 50 Mātṛkā-Kalās are given in the same account as follows : Nivṛtti, Pratiṣṭha, Vidyā, Śāntī, Indhikā, Dīpikā, Mocikā, Parā, Sūksmā, Sūkṣmāmṛtā, Jñānāmṛtā, Āpyāyanī, Vyāpini, Vyomarūpā, Anantā, Sṛṣṭi, Ṛddhi, Smṛti, Medhā, Kānti, Lakṣmi, Dyuti, Sthirā, Sthiti, Siddhi, Jadā, Pālini, Śānti, Aiśvaryā, Rati, Kāmikā, Varadā, Āhlādini, Prītih, Dirghā, Tikṣnā, Raudri, Bhayā, Nidrā, Tandrā, Kṣudhā, Krodhini, Kriyā, Utkāri, Mṛtyurūpā, Pītā, Śveta, Asitā, Anantā. These 94 Kalās are worshipped in the Wine Jar which holds Tārā dravamayī, or the Saviour-Mother in liquid form. She Herself, is called Samvit-Kalā and so the Yoginīhṛdaya-Tantra says—

Deśakālapadārthātma yad yad vastu yathā yathā.
Tat-tadrūpeṇa yā bhāti tam śraye Samvidam Kalām.

CHAPTER XI

S'AKTI—POTENCY TO CREATE

In the previous chapter I have referred to S'akti, Nāda, Bindu. In this and the two next I will deal in greater detail with each of these three concepts of S'akti. One of the clearest accounts known to me of the evolution of S'akti is that given in the authoritative Tāntrika-Prakaraṇa called S'āradā (also spelt Sāradā) Tilaka by Lakṣmaṇācārya. This work was formerly of great authority in Bengal. Its value is much increased by the commentary of Rāghava-Bhatta. As this work with its commentary is of prime importance, and is cited throughout the following chapters, I may here note the following account which Lakṣmaṇācārya gives of himself at its close. Mahābala a great sage was succeeded by his son Ācāryapaṇḍita, a Deśika (Tāntrik-Guru). His son S'rīkṛṣṇa-Deśika had a son Lakṣmaṇa-Deśika who wrote the S'āradā-Tilaka. Rāghava, in his commentary called Padārthādarśa, says that Lakshmaṇa was the disciple of Utpalācārya, who was the disciple of Somānanda, who was the disciple of Vasugupta, who was the disciple of S'rīkaṇṭha. This is the Gurupaṇgkti of Lakṣmaṇa. His disciple was the great *Kāśmirian* Abhinava-Gupta, the author of Paramārthasāra. The latter's disciple was Kṣemarāja, the author of the S'ivasūtra Vimarśini. The date generally assigned to Abhinava-Gupta is the eleventh century. Therefore

Sj. Akṣaya Kumāra Maitra, Director of the Varendra Anusaṁdhāna-Samiti, who has supplied me with these details of the Gurus and Siṣyas of the author, concludes that the Sāradā was written at the end of the tenth or beginning of the eleventh century. Rāghava mentions 1510 as the age of his commentary. Taking this to be the Vikrama Samvat we get 1454 A. D. as its date. These details serve another purpose. There are persons who insist on a total disconnection between ths Saiva and Sakta-Tantras. Lakṣmaṇācārya was a member of the Kāśmirian Saiva School, and his work was, as I have stated, of great authority among the Bengal Saktas.

The Sāradā (Chaper, I, verse 7) says: "From Sakala-Parameśvara vested with the wealth of Sat, Cit, Ānanda issued Sakti; from Sakti came Nāda; and from Nāda issued Bindu."

Saccidānanda-vibhavāt sakalāt parameśvarāt
Asic-chaktis tato nādo nādād bindu-samudbhavāh.

Parameśvara is here Siva-Tattva. He is Sakala, because He is with the creative Kalā or Sakti. As already explained Sakti, when Vyaṣṭirūpā, that is individualised, is called Kalā. Siva is always with Sakti. But in the supreme state, Sakti is unmanifest and exists in Her own (Svarūpa) form as Being-Consciousness-Bliss (Saccidā-nandamayī, Cidrūiṇī), undistinguishable from Siva. Sakala-Siva is thus Saguṇa-Brahman. He is said to be vested with the wealth of Sat, Cit, Ānanda or Being, Consciousness and Bliss to show that His association with Avidyā does not deprive Him of, or affect, His own true nature (Svarūpa). Siva has two aspects. In one of these He is the Supreme Changeless One who is Saccidā-nanda and Saccidānandamayā. This is Parāsamvit. In the other He changes as the Universe ; change being the experience of the Jīva so created. The cause of such change is S'iva-Tattva inseparably associated with S'akti-Tattva.

"There issued S'akti." This is S'akti Tattva of the Thirty-six Tattvas. S'akti evolves Nāda, and Nāda, Bindu. These are aspects of S'akti preparing to create the Universe and are dealt with in future chapters. Here I am concerned with S'akti-Tattva only : that is, with that form of S'akti which is specifically so called ; since Nāda, Bindu and the rest are all but names for different aspects of S'akti.

It may be asked how S'akti can be said to issue from that which was already with S'akti. Rāghava-Bhatta explains that the author here follows the Sāṁkhya principle of the appearance of realities from realities (Sadutpattivāda) and speaks of the condition of readiness (Ucchūnāvasthā) of Her who being without beginning or end existed in a subtle state identified with Caitanya in Dissolution (*Yā anādirūpā caitanyā-dhyāsena Mahāpralaye sūkṣmā sthitā*). Adhyāsa is the attribution of the nature of one thing to another according to which something is considered to be what it is not. In other words during Dissolution there is some potential principle in the Brahman which, as manifest, appears not to be Consciousness (Cit), but which owing to the absence of operation during the dissolved (Laya) state is identified with Cit. The distinction is very subtly marked by the Sanskrit word Cit for S'iva and Cidrūpiṇi for S'akti. Cit is there in either case, for ultimately there is nothing but Consciousness. But that principle which in creation manifests as seeming Acit is in itself Cidrūpiṇi. One is Consciousness and the other is a principle in the form of Consciousness. I prefer to look at S'akti from the Consciousness aspect which is Her own form (Svarūpa) and to say that S'akti in Dissolution is what She really is, namely, Cit. In creation Consciousness, as S'akti, has power to veil Its own true nature, and when we are ourselves subject to this power we attribute unconsciousness to It. The substance in either case is this : in Dissolution, Consciousness and Bliss alone is. Then without derogation to the changelessness of Consciousness there is an apparent dichotomy into subject and object, that is, Consciousness and Unconsciousness. S'akti is conceived as ready to create the Universe composed of Guṇas as its effect (Kārya). In other words, pure Consciousness becomes the world-experience. The Prayogasāra says : " She, who is eternal and all-pervading, the Genetrix of the Universe, issues from Him." Vāyavīya-Samhitā says : " By the will of S'iva, Parā-S'akti is united with S'iva-tattva and at the beginning of Creation appears from It just as oil from sesamum seed when pressed." The Pancarātra is also cited by Rāghava-Bhatta as saying, "The Parama Puruṣa at the begining of Creation, seeing that She who is Saccidānandarūpiṇī is the source (Adhiṣṭhāna) of the manifestation of all Tattvas makes manifest eternal Prakṛti. " These statements, like all our accounts in such matters, are pictorial thinking, being necessarily imperfect attempts to explain the manifestation of activity of Consciousness.

Cause and effect are really one, but appear different. The first aspect of S'akti is its causal (Kāraṇa) aspect. But this again may be analysed into the various stages of its capacity and preparedness to create. These stages are marked by certain names which again are mere labels denoting states of S'akti. Thus Nāda and

Bindu are names for those aspects of S'akti which are more and more prone to Creation (Ucchūnāvasthā). Nāda and Bindu are but two states of Her Creation (*Sṛṣṭyūpayogyāvasthārūpau*). S'akti-Tattva is the first kinetic aspect of Brahman. S'akti then becomes more and more kinetic until, as Bindu, S'akti is Īśvara-Tattva. This Bindu differentiates into the Triangle of Divine Desire called the Kāmakalā upon which there is that Brahman Sound (S'abda-brahman), which bifurcating into S'abda and Artha, is S'akti in its aspect as effect (Kārya) or the manifested Universe of Mind and Matter. This " Tāntrik " account gives firstly an apparent " development " in the causal body of S'akti being in the nature of a resolution of like to like ; and then a real development (Pariṇāma) of the effects (Kārya) produced from the causal body. The whole is necessarily described after the manner of a gradual process stated in terms of our own psychological experience. But such a process exists only in time which first appears with the Sun and Moon. Bhāskararāya in his commentary on the Lalitā Sahasranāma (Verse 117) cites Gorakṣanātha as saying in his Mahārthamañjari, " In a moment the world is created and in a moment it is destroyed."

S'akti-Tattva and S'iva-Tattva are inseparable (Santata-Samavāyinī), the former being only the negative aspect of the latter. Both exist even in Dissolution, the first emanation proper being Sadākhya which corresponds with Nāda in the above-mentioned verse. S'iva-Tattva is defined in the Tattva-Sandoha 1, as follows : " That, beyond which there is none other, moved of His own will in order to create the whole world. The first movement (Spanda prathama) is called the S'iva-Tattva by those who know."

Yad ayam anuttaramūrtir
ṇijecchyākhilam idam jagat sraṣṭum
Paspande sah spandah
prathamah S'iva-tattvam ucyate tajjñaih.

As the Vimarśini on the Pratyabhijñā says—It is
the "I-experience not looking towards another"
(*Ananyonmukhau ahaṁpratyayah*). It is the self-side of
experience, Prakāśa or Jñānamātra, which is such
because of the negation of all objectivity or not-self by
S'akti-Tattva. For this Jñānamātra, She, as Vimarśa-
S'akti, provides through gradual stages the objects of its
experience. Her function is negation (*Niṣedha-vyāpāra-
rūpā S'aktih*) of all objectivity so as to produce the mere
subjective knowing (Prakāśamātra) which is the
Śūnyātiśūnya. She then evolves from Herself the objective
world in order that it may be the content of the S'iva
consciousness. She is pure Will ever associated with
S'iva. She is the seed of the whole Universe of moving
and unmoving things then absorbed in Herself.

Iccha Saiva svacchā
santatasamavāyini sati śaktih.
Sacarācarasya jagato
bījaṁ nikhilasya nijanilinasya.

(Tattva-Sandoha, 2.)

She is thus called the Womb (Yoni), or Seed-state
(Bījāvasthā), and by the Parapraveśikā, "Heart of the
Supreme Lord" (Hṛdayam Paramaśituh). The Yoginī-
hṛdaya-Tantra says that men speak of the heart of
Yoginī; She is Yoginī because She is connected with all
things both as Cause and Effect. This Yoginī is knower
of Herself (Yoginī svavid). She is called the Heart:
for from the Heart all issues. She is the Heart of the

Universe : the pulsing movements of which are Herself
as S'akti. What more can be said than the words of
the Yoginihṛdaya, " What man knows the heart of a
woman ; only S'iva knows the heart of Yoginī "?

In the Pratyabhijnā-Hṛdaya (S. 4) it is said "The
auspicious supreme S'iva desiring to make manifest the
Universe which is one with Himself first of all shines
forth as the one Cit, as the Very Void detached from
Māyā (that is, there is no objectivity) and as
undifferentiated Illumination (that is, Prakāṣa or
Jñāna). He next appears in the form of diverse
experiencers consisting of an infinite, endless number
of Tattvas, words and beings which are in the nature of
a blooming forth of Consciousness and Bliss." (Śrī-
paramaśivah svāt-maikyena sthitaṁ viśvaṁ avabibhāsayiṣuh
pūrvam cidaikyākhyāti māyānāṣrita-śiva- paryāyaśūnyāti-
śūnyātmatayā prakāśyālhedena prakāśamānatayā sphurati ;
tatah cid-rasāśyānatarūpaśeṣa-tattva-bhuvana-bhāva-tattat-pra-
mātrādyātmatayā'pi prathate.

The substance of the matter may be stated thus :
whilst from the static transcendental aspect (Para-śiva,
Parāśakti) Consciousness changelessly endures, there is
from the kinetic creative aspect (S'iva-S'akti) a polarisation in consciousness, the poles of which are S'iva and
S'akti representing the Aham and Idam aspects of
experience. Owing to this polarisation there is in lieu
of the unitary experience a division into the knower,
knowing and known, Mātṛ, Māna, Meya, as it is called.
Consciousness then identifies itself with the products of
its own kinetic S'akti, that is, with mind as the subject
of experience and with matter as its object. This
polarisation is explained in the S'ākta-Tantras by the
illustration of the grain of gram (Canaka). Under the

sheath of the grain of gram two seeds are found in such close union that they appear when held together as one. With, however, the tearing of the outer sheath the two halves of the seeds fall apart. These two seeds are said to be S'iva and S'akti and the encircling sheath is Māyā. Like all attempts to explain the unexplainable, the illustration is to some extent defective, for in the gram there are two separate seeds—but S'iva-S'akti are an undistinguishable unity. Commentator on the Ṣat-cak-raniūpaṇa (*The Serpent Power*) cites the following : (v. 49): "In the Satyaloka is the formless and lustrous One. She is like a grain of gram devoid of hands, feet or the like. She has surrounded Herself by Māyā. She is Sun, Moon and Fire. When casting off (Utsṛjya) the covering She divides in two (Dvidhā bhittvā) and becomes intent (Unmukhī) on creation, then by differentiation of S'iva and S'akti arises creative ideation (Sṛṣṭi-kalpanā)." By " differentiation " is meant the polarisation of Consciousness into subjective (Prakāśa) and objective (Vimarśa) aspects. The Self sees another. The same commentator cites the Prapancasāra Tantra as saying that the Parabindu divides into two parts of which the right is Bindu, the male, Puruṣa or Ham, and the left is Visargah, the female Prakṛti or Sah. Hamṣah is the Union of Prakṛti and Puruṣa and the Universe is Hamsa. In however, the MSS. on which my edition of this Tantra is based it is said that Parabindu divided by Kāla becomes threefold—Bindu, Nāda, Bīja. The difference is of no moment for this Bindu (Kārya) is S'iva and Bīja is S'akti, and Nāda is merely the relation (Mithah-samavāyah) of the two. The combined Hamsah indicates the same relation as is expressed by Nāda. In the Kulacūdāmaṇi Nigama (Chap. I, vv. 16-24), the Devī says of the first stage : " I, though in the form of Prakṛti lie hidden in Being-consciousness-bliss (*Aham prakṛtirūpa cet saccidānandaparāyaṇā*). Then in the initial creative stage when Karma ripens the Devī in the words of the Nigama " becomes desirous of creation and covers Herself with Her own Māyā. " This is the appearance of the kinetic Sakti. The same doctrine is stated with greater or less detail in various ways. Unitary experience, without ceasing to be such, is yet, as Jīva polarised into the dual experience of the Māyika world. Consciousness as Cit-Sakti and Māyā-Sakti projects from itself, in a manner conformable with our own psychological experience, the object of its experience. The Māyika experiencer (Māyā-pramātrī) takes what is one to be dual or many. This is the division of Siva and Sakti which are yet eternally one. All action implies duality. Duality is manifestation. Manifestation is nothing but an appearance to consciousness. As there is ultimately but one Self, the Self appears to itself ; that is, consciousness is polarised. These two poles are the continuity of the " I " (Aham) and its ever-changing content which is " This " (Idam).

Just as there is absolute rest and a world movement, so Sakti or Creative Consciousness is itself of twofold aspect, static and dynamic. Cosmic energy in its physical aspect is potential or kinetic, the first being that state in which the equilibrated elements of power hold each other in check. It is not possible to have one without the other. In any sphere of activity, according to these views, there must be a static background. If one Spiritual Reality be assumed it cannot be actually divided into two. It is possible, however, that there should be a *polarisation* in your experience whereby what is indivisibly one and the self, appears as many and the not-self. How ? The answer is Māyā, that Power of Hers whereby what is impossible to us becomes possible. Māyā is S'akti, but S'akti is not to be identified only with this form of It. In the thirtysix Tattvas, Māyā is a particular and comparatively gross form of S'akti which appears after the evolution of the Sadvidyā-Tattva. It is defined as that S'akti which is the sense of difference (Bhedabuddhi) ; that is, the power whereby the individual consciousness, distinguishing itself from others, considers itself separate from them. S'akti is understood differently in the S'ākta Tantra and in S'aṁkara's Māyāvāda ; a matter of primary importance from the point of view of Sādhana and with which I will deal on some future occasion. Whatever be the description given, all accounts must end in the inconceivable S'akti (Acintyā). She the One, the Primordial S'akti (Ādyā-S'akti) appears as many ; and so the S'ākta Sadhaka saying, " *Aham Devī na cānyo-smi* " (I am the Devi and none other), thinks to himself " Sā'ham " (She am I).

NĀDA—THE FIRST PRODUCED MOVEMENT

S'AKTI-TATTVA dealt with in the preceding chapter is really the negative aspect of the S'iva-tattva. Though spoken of separately the two are indissolubly one. S'akti-tattva, as the Tattva-sandoha says, is the Will of S'iva as yet unmanifest :

Icchā saiva svacchā santatasamavāyinī satī s'aktih.
Sacarācarasya jagato bījam nikhilasya nijanilīnasya.

These two principles (S'iva-S'akti-Tattva) are the ultimate potency of creation, and as and when they (considered as one Tattva) commence to act, the first movement towards manifestation takes place. After the previous restful state of S'iva-S'akti there follows the union for the purpose of creation of the two principles which are S'ivatattva and S'aktitattva. So it is said in the S'ākta-Tantra, " *S'iva-S'akti-samāyogāt jayate sṛṣṭi-kalpanā* " (From the union of S'iva and S'akti arises creative ideation). This union and mutual relation is called Nāda. As the relation is not some substantial thing apart from S'iva or S'akti, Nāda is really S'iva-S'akti ; passing from the state of mere potency into that of the first ideating movement, from which at length, when finally perfected, the whole universe is evolved. The S'akta Tantras frequently employ erotic symbolism to explain the creative process. This has led a missionary author to the conclusion that " throughout its symbolism and pseudo-philosophisings there lies at the basis of the whole system.....the conception of the sexual relationship as the ultimate explanation of the universe." An American author reviewing one of my works has called it "a doctrine for suffragette monists" — "religious feminism run mad." Both statements are examples of those depreciative misunderstandings which are so common in Western descriptions of Eastern belief and which seem so absurd to anyone who has understood the subject. How can "sexual relationship" which exists on the gross plane of matter be the ultimate explanation of That which has manifested not only this but all other relations aed subjects. As for "feminism" and the supposed priority of the feminine principle, the doctrine has no more to do with either than with old age pensions or any other social question. We are not dealing with the biological question whether the female antedates the male principle, of the social question of the rights of Woman, but with those ultimate dual principles, aspects of the one active Consciousness, which projects from Itself both man and woman and all other dualities on the universe. S'iva and S'akti are one and neither is higher than the other. But how are European writers to be blamed when we find a distinguished Indian Sanskritist affirming that according to S'ākta doctrine " God *is* a woman" (the italics are mine).

S'akti is spoken of as female, that is, as Mother, because that is the aspect of the Supreme in which It is thought of as the Genetrix and Nourisher of the universe. But God is neither male nor female. As the Yāmala says for the benefit of all such ignorants, " *Neyam yoṣit na ca pumān na ṣaṇḍo na jadah smṛtah.*"

These are all symbolisms borrowed from the only world which we ordinarily know—that around us. As for the charge of pseudo-philosophy, if it be that, then the same criticism must apply to the Advaitavāda Vedānta. For the Śākta-Tantra is the Sādhana-śāstra of Advaitavāda presenting the teaching of Vedānta in its own manner and in terms of its own ritual symbolism. Thus it is said that Nāda is the Maithuna of Śiva and Śakti and that when Mahākāla was in Viparīta Maithuna with Mahākāli (a form of Maithuna again which is symbolical of the fact that Śiva is Niṣkṛyā and Śakti Sakṛyā) there issued Bindu. For Maithuna, others substitute the logical term Mithasamavāyah as a description of Nāda, which is Kriyāśakti. Before the appearance of Śabda there must be two. Unity is necessarily actionless. Two involves a third— which is the relation of both ; a Trinity of Power which is reflected in the Trimūrti of the Māyika world as Brahmā, Viṣṇu, Rudra.

From Nāda came Mahābindu and this latter differentiated into the Tribindu which is Kāmakalā, the Mūla of all Mantras. In Pralaya, Śiva and Śakti exist as the "two in one"; Śiva as Cit, Śakti as Cidrūpiṇī : the Parā Śakti—not being different or separated from Śiva (*Avinābhāvasambandha*) and being undivided supreme Cit-Śakti (*Akhaṇḍa-paracicchakti*)

The Śāradā-Tilaka (1—7) then says : From the Sakala-Parameśvara vested with the wealth of Saccidānanda (*Saccidānandavibhavāt*) appeared Śakti (Śakti-Tattva); from Śakti, Nāda and from Nāda, Bindu (Mahābindu). Sakala means with Kalā ; that is, the Brahman with what the Sāṁkhya calls Mulaprakṛti, that which the Vedānta calls Avidyā and the Śākta-

Tantras or Āgamas call S'akti. On the other hand Niṣkala S'iva is Nirguna S'iva or that aspect of the Brahman which is unconnected with the creative S'akti; just as Sakala-S'iva is the Brahman so associated. S'iva in either aspect is always with S'akti; for S'akti is but Himself; whereas the S'akti associated with Paramaśiva is Cidrūpiṇī and Viśvottīrṇā or beyond the Universe, the S'akti which is associated with the creative S'iva is that which appears as Universe (Viśvatmika). The Parāśakti is one with Caitanya at rest. The other aspect which ripens into Nāda and Bindu denotes the "swollen" condition of readiness (*Ucchūnāvasthā*) of Her who existed in a subtle state in the great dissolution (Mahāpralaya). These two S'aktis (Nāda, Bindu) are stages in the movement towards the manifestation of the Self as object, that is, as the Universe.

In these, the mere readiness or potency of S'akti-tattva to act develops into action. In Nāda-S'akti therefore Kriyā predominates. When we speak of stages, development and so forth, we are using language borrowed from the manifested world which, in the sense there understood, is not appropriate to a state prior to manifestation; for such manifestation does not take place until after the appearance of the Puruṣa-Prakṛti-Tattva and the development from the latter of the impure Tattvas from Buddhi to Pṛthivī. But a Sādhana S'āstra, even if it had the power to do otherwise, could not usefully use terms and symbols other than those borrowed from the world of the Sādhaka. The Prayogasāra says that the S'akti who is "turned towards" the state of Liberation (*Nirāmaya padonmukhī*) awakes as Nāda and is turned to S'iva (*S'ivonmukhī*) at which time She is said to be male (*Pumrūpā*). For then She becomes Ham in Hamsah. She who was one with Paraśiva in Pralaya as

the coalesced " I " (Aham) and " This " (Idam), now in
Her creative aspect as S'akti-tattva transforms Herself
into Nāda. Nāda is action (Kriyāśaktirūpa). In simple
language, potency and readiness to create, (S'aktitattva),
becomes for the first time active as Nāda, and then more
so as Bindu, which is a further development of Kriyā
S'akti dealt with in the next chapter.

According to Rāghava-Bhatta in his Commentry
on the S'āradā some writers do not speak of Nāda,
though the author of the S'āradā does so in order to
indicate the sevenfold character of Tāra. The Nāda
state is however indicated by those Acāryas who speak
of Kāla. So it is said, "in the Kālatattva which is Sound"
(Ravātmanikālatattve). In the Hymn to Bhuvaneśī also it
is said, " Obeisance to Thee who art called Tattva in
the character of sound " Namaste ravatvena tattvābhidhā me).

Nāda occupies the same place in the Mantra scheme
as the Sadākhya-Tattva of the 36 Tattvas, for Bindu is
Īsvara Tattva. They are each transcendent aspects
of Sabda in the respsctive Tattvas. As Consciousness
reaches forth to enjoyment and the " I " is separated
from the " This," what was mere diffusive consciousness
as Sadākhya-Tattva is objectified into the all-embracing
Ākāśa, the Guṇa of which is gross S'abda ; that is something experienced as an object apparently different
from and other than ourselves.

Nāda which etymologically means " Sound " is a
technical term of the Mantraśāstra. The latter S'astra
is concerned with Mantravidyā, and Mantra is
manifested S'abda which also literally means " Sound."
By " Sound " of course is not meant gross sound which
is heard by the ear and which is the property of the

Kāryākāśa developed as a Vikṛti from the Prakṛti-Tattva which, with the Puruṣa-Tattva, occupies the place (though without its dualities) of the Puruṣa and Prakṛti of the Sāṁkhya. Gross sound belongs to the impure creation as Guṇa of Ākāśa or the ether which fills space. To avoid misconception, it is better to use the word Śabda which with Artha is manifested in the "Garland (or Rosary) of Letters" (Varṇamālā) with which I will later deal.

Nāda is the most subtle aspect of Śabda, as the first putting forth of Kriyāśākti Paranāda and Parā Vāk are Parāśakti. Nāda into which it evolves is the unmanifested (Avyaktātmā) seed or essence (Nādamātra) of that which is later manifested as Śabda, devoid of particularities such as letters and the like (*Varṇādiviśeṣa-rahitaḥ*). It develops into Bindu which is of the same character. From the Mantra aspect, as the source of Śabda, this Mahābindu as it differentiates to "create" is called the Śabda-brahman. Bindu when differentiated is also the source of the Vikṛtis or Tattvas and of their Lords (Tattveśa). In its character as Śabda-brahman it is the source of the manifested Śabda and Artha (*Śabdaśabdārthakāraṇaṁ*). Śabda-brahman is thus a name of Brahman as the immediate creative source of the manifold Śabda and Artha.

What Śabda-brahman is, has been the subject of contention, as Rāghava-Bhatta's Commentary shows. It is sufficient to say here (where we are only concerned with Śabda-brahmātmaka Bindu so far as it is necessary to explain Nāda that Rāghava-Bhatta says the Śabda-brahman is the Caitanya in all beings (*Caitanyam sarvabhūtānām*). This cosmic Śakti exists in the individual bodies of all breathing creatures (Prāṇi) in the form of

Kuṇḍalinī (Kuṇḍalirūpa). Nāda therefore which assumes the aspect of Bindu is also Caitanya and S'akti. Nāda is thus the first emanative stage in the production of Mantra. The second is Bindu, or S'abda-brahman ; the third is Tribindu (Bindu, Nāda, and Bīja) or Kāmakalā ; the fourth is the production of S'abda as the Matṛkas which are the subtle state of the subsequently manifested gross letters (Varṇa) and the last is these gross letters (Sthūlaśabda), which compose the manifested S'abda or Mantra composed of letters (Varṇa), syllables (Pada) and sentences (Vākya). Thus mantra ultimately derives from Nāda which is itself the Kriyā-śaktirūpa aspect of S'iva-S'akti who are the Supreme Nāda (Paranāda) and Supreme Speech (Parā-vāk). The Prayogasāra says: "Oh Devī! that Antarātmā in the form of Nādātmā itself makes sound (Nādate svayaṁ)," that is, displays activity. " Urged on by Vāyu (that is, the Prāṇa-vāyu in Jīvas) it assumes the form of letters." Nāda again is itself divided into several stages, namely, Mahānāda, or Nādānta, the first movement forth of S'abda-brahman; Nāda, when S'akti fills up the whole Universe with Nādānta, in other words, the completed movement of which Nādānta is the commencement ; and Nirodhinī, which is that aspect of Nāda in which its universal operation having been completed, it operates in a particular manner and is transformed into Bindu, which is the completion of the first movement of S'akti, in which She assumes the character of the Creative Lord of the Universe (Īśvara-Tattva). Nādānta considered as the end and not the commencement of the series is that in which there is dissolution of Nāda (*Nādasya antaḥ layaḥ*). Above Bindu, the S'aktis which have been already given in previous articles become more and more subtle until Niṣkala Unmanī is reached which, as the Yoginīhṛdaya says, is uncreate motionless speech (*Anutpannanispandā-vāk*), the twin aspect of which are Samvit or the Void (Sūnya-Samvit) and Samvit as tendency to manifestation in a subtle state (*Utpatsuh samvid utpattyavasthā sūkṣmā*). Unmanī is beyond Kāraṇarūpā-Sakti; where there is no experience (Bhānam) or Kāla or Kalā nor of Devatā or Tattva, in the sense of category, as that which distinguishes one thing from another. It is Svanirvāṇam param padam, the Nirvikalpa-nirañjana-śiva śakti which is Guruvaktra.

Nāda and Bindu exist in all Bīja Mantras which are generally written with the Bindu above and the Nāda below, for this is the form of the written Candrabindu. In however some of the old pictorial representations of Oṁkāra the real position of Nāda is shown as being over Bindu as an inverted crescent. Thus the great Bīja, Hrīm is composed of Ha, Ra, Ī and Ma. Of these Ha—Ākāśa, Ra—Agni, Ī—Ardhanārīśvara and M—Nādabindu. The five Bhūtas are divided into two groups Amūrtta (formless) and Mūrtta (with form). Both Ākāśa and Vāyu belong to the first group, because until the appearance of Agni as Rūpa, there is no colour and form. Agni therefore heads the second division. When Ākāśa is with Agni there is form; for Ra is the first manifestation of Rūpa. This form is in Ardhanārīś-vara, the combined Siva-Sakti, who hold all in themselves. The first three letters represent the Ākāra or form aspect. The Mantra receives its complete form by the addition of the Māhātmya which is Nādā-Bindu which are Nirākāra (formless) and the Kāraṇa (cause) of the other three in which they are implicitly and potentially contained; being in technical phrase Antar-gata of, or held within Bindu, which again is Antargata of all the previously evolving Saktis mentioned. The meaning of the Bija-Mantra then is that the Cidākāśa is associated (Yukta) with Rūpa. It is thus the S'abda statement of the birth of General Form ; that is, Form as such of which all particular forms are derivations. Hiim is, as pronounced, the gross-body as sound of the ideation of Form as such in the Cosmic mind.

The degree of subtlety of the S'aktis preceding and following Nāda is in the Mantra-S'astra indicated by what is called "the utterance time" (Uccāraṇakāla). Thus taking Bindu as the unit, Unmanī is Nirākāra and Niruccāra, formless and without utterance, undefined by any adjective : being beyond mind and speech and the universe (Viśvottīrṇā). The Uccāraṇakāla of Samanī (so named Manahsahitatvat, on account of its association with mind ; the preceding S'akti Unmanī being Tadrahitā or devoid of that), is 1/256, of Vyāpikā 1/128 and so on to Nādānta 1/32, Nāda 1/16, to Ardha-candra which is 1/2 of Bindu and to Bindu itself.

Nāda is thus, in the Mantra-S'āstra, that aspect of S'akti which evolves into Bindu, which latter as differentiating into the Tribindu is called the S'abda-brahman, who is the creative source of S'abda and Artha and thus of the revealed S'abda which Mantra is.

I would in conclusion meet an objection, which I have heard urged, namely that the Mantra-S'āstra treats its subject with unnecessary complexity of detail. It is undoubtedly difficult and requires careful study. Simple minds may be satisfied with the statement that God created the world. Veda too gives an explanation of the cosmic problem in two words "He saw" (sa aikṣata). But who saw, and what, and how did He see? How also if there be only One came there to

be anything to see? And what is " to see " (ikṣaṇa)?
For the process is not like looking out of a win-
dow and seeing a man passing. "He" is Consciousness
which is in Itself (Svarūpa) actionless. How then
did "It" see and thus become active? Because It
has two aspects, one (Niṣkala-śiva) in which It is actionless and the other (Sakala-śiva)in which It is Activity
as the embodiment of all the Samskāras. In this
last aspect It is called S'akti. The latter term denotes
Active Consciousness. How can one and the same
thing have two contradictory aspects, we cannot
say, otherwise than by affirming Svabhāva. By way
of analogy we can refer to what psychology calls
dual and multiple personalities. The ultimate Reality
is alogical and unexplainable (Anirvacanīya). That it
is one and not two is, it is said, proved by Veda and
the actual experience (Svānubhava) had in Yoga.
What is " seeing"? It is not the observing of something
outside which was there before it was observed.
"Seeing" is the rising into consciousness (void of objects)
of the memory of past universes existing in the form of
the Samskāras. Before this can occur, Consciousness
must obscure to Itself Its nature and (though in truth
an unity) must experience itself as an "I" observing a
"This" which it has through Māyā S'akti projected outside Itself. There is no answer again to the question
how this is possible except inscrutable S'akti (Acintya
S'akti). But just as a man rising from deep sleep has
first a more or less bare awareness which is gradually
filled out with the thought of self and particular
objects; consciousness coming to itself, so that in the
waking state it again recognises the world which had
vanished utterly in dreamless slumber ; so it is with the
Cosmic Consciousness. Just as man does not pass at

once from dreamless slumber to the fullest waking perception, so neither does the Cosmic Consciousness. It passes gradually from its dreamless slumber (Suṣupti) state which is the general dissolution (Mahāpralaya) to the waking state (Jāgrat) which is consciousness of the gross universe. The degrees in this emanative process are the Tattvas described earlier. Manifestation, which is nothing but presentation of apparently external objects to the inner consciousness, is, as experienced by the limited consciousness, gradual. The seeds of the " I " and " This " are first formed and then grown. The first principal stage is that before and in Īśvara Tattva of Bindu and which therefore includes Nāda. The second is that of the World-consciousness arising through the agency of Māyā-śakti. These two stages are marked by two principal differences. In the first the " This " (Idam) is seen as part of the self, the two not being differentiated in the sense of inner and outer. In the second the object is externalised and seen as different from the self. In the first, when the Self experiences itself as object, the latter is held as a vague undefined generality. There is, as it were an awareness of self-scission in which the self as subject knows itself as object and nothing more. The degrees in this process have been already explained. In the second not only is the object defined as something which appears to be not the self, but there are a multiplicity of objects each marked by its own differences; for Māyā has intervened. The whole world-process is thus a re-awakening of the Cosmic Consciousness from sleep to the world, into which at Dissolution it had fallen ; and the Tattvas mark the gradual stages of re-awakening, that is re-awakening to the world, but a falling into sleep so far as true Consciousness is concerned. So in Kuṇḍaliyoga when Kuṇḍalini sleeps in the Mūladhāra, man is awake to the world ; and when she awakes, the world vanishes from Consciousness which then regains its own state (Svarūpa). There is no reason to suppose that, judged in terms of our present experience, the change is other than gradual. But how, it may be asked, is this known or what the stages are ; for were we there ? As individuals we were not ; for we speak of that which preceded the formation of the Sakala Jiva Consciousness. But Jiva was there as the plant is in the seed. It is the one Siva who displays himself in all the Tattvas. Those who fall back into the seed have experience of it. There are, however, two bases on which these affirmations rest. In the first place there is correspondence between all planes. " What is without, is so manifested because it is within " ; not of course in the exact form in which it exists without but in the corresponding form of its own plane. We may therefore look for instruction to our daily life and its psychological states to discover both the elements and the working of the cosmic process. These also disclose a gradual unfolding of consciousness from something in the nature of mere awareness to the definite perception of a variety of multiple objects. But the normal experience is by its nature limited. That normal experience is, however, transcended in Yoga-states, when consciousness becomes Nirālambapuri, that is, detached from worldly objects : the experience wherein it is (in part at least) available for the instruction of others. Secondly the Sastras are records of truth beyond the senses (Atīndriya-Tattva). The Tattvas are not put forth as mere speculative guesses or imaginings of what might have been. When however, supersensual truth is described in language it is necessarily expressed in terms, and with the use of symbols, of present experience. That experience is had under conditions of time and space and others. We know and speak of mere potency ripening into actuality, of potential energy becoming more and more kinetic, of shifting states of consciousness and so forth. These are matters the knowledge of which is drawn from the world around us. But this does not necessarily make them wholly untrue or unreal as applied to higher planes. One of the commonest errors is to raise false partitions between things. The experience is real for it is S'iva's and His experience is never unreal. It is according to its degree (that is on its plane) real; an expression (limited though it be) of the ultimate Reality Itself. We can think in no other terms. But it is also true that these terms and symbols, having only complete validity on our plane, are no longer wholly true for Consciousness as it rises from it. But other forms of Consciousness must take their place until the Formless is reached. The Tattvas explain (limited though such explanation be by the bounds of our thought and language) the modes through which the returning Consciousness passes until it rests in Itself (Svarūpaviśrānti) and has Peace. And so the Buddhist Mantrayāna aptly defines Yoga (which in Tibetan is called rNal-rByor) in the sense of result, as the " Finding rest or peace." This final state, as also those intermediate ones which lie between it and the normal individual world-consciousness, are only actually realised in Jñāna-Yoga (by whatsover method Jñāna is attained) when the mind has been wholly withdrawn from without and faces the operative power of Consciousness behind it (Nirāmaya-padonmukhī).

But here we are dealing with Mantra-yoga when the mind is thinking the states which Jñāna, in whatever degree, realises as Consciousness. The Mantra-Śāstra looks at the matter, of which we write, from the standpoint of Mantra that is of manifested Śabda its object. Kuṇḍalinī is both Jyotirmayī, Her Sūkṣmarūpa and Mantramayī, Her Sthūlarūpa. We begin with the latter. All things are then defined in terms of Śabdārtha and of the various causal forms which precede it. The first of such produced forms is Nāda which becomes Bindu and then on the differentiation of the Tattvas the " hiddcn sound " (Avyakta-rava), the Logos or Cosmic Word utters " the Garland of Letters " (Varṇamālā) of which all Mantras are formed. It traces the degrees in which the ideating Cosmic Consciousness becomes, as Supreme Speech (Parāvāk), the Genetrix of the subtle and gross Śabda which are the Mātṛkas and Varṇas respectively. That Supreme Speech (Parāvāk) is without idea or language, but is represented as gradually assuming the state in which it utters both and projects from Itself into the sensual world the objects (Artha) which they denote. The actual manifestation of these from Para-śabda through Paśyantī, Madhyamā and Vaikharī, will be described in another Chapter.

The practice of Mantra-Yoga not only gives, from a merely intellectual standpoint, an understanding of Vedānta which cannot ordinarily be had by the mere reading of philosophical texts ; but also produces a pure Bhāva ripening into Mahābhāva through the purification of mind (Cittaśuddhi) which such practice (according to the rules of Sādhana laid down in the Tantras or Mantra-śāstra) gives, as one of its Siddhis. What a Western, and sometimes the English educated Indian, does not understand or recognise, is the fact that the mere reading of Vedāntic texts without Citta-śuddhi will neither bring true understanding nor other fruitful result. The experienced will find that this apparent complexity and wealth of detail is not useless and is, from an extra-ritual standpoint, to a considerable extent, and from that of Sādhana wholly, necessary. A friend of mine was once asked by a man in a somewhat testy manner "to give him a plain exposition of the Vedānta in five minutes." It takes years to understand perfectly any science or profession. How can that, which claims, to explain all, be mastered in a short talk? But more than this; however prolonged the intellectual study may be, it must be, to be fruitful, accompanied by some form of Sādhana. The Tantra-S'astras contain this for the Hindu, though it is open to him or any other to devise a better if he can. Forms ever change with the ages, while the Truth which they express, remains.

BINDU OR S'AKTI—READY TO CREATE

FROM Nāda, previously described, evolved Bindu (*Nādād bindu-samudbhavah*). What then is Bindu? Literally the term means a "Drop" or a "point" such as the Anusvāra breathing. But in the Mantra-S'āstra it has a technical meaning. It is not, as a distinguished Indian Sanskritist called it, merely a " Drop ". It is not that "red drops" mix with "white drops" and so forth, a description of his, which reminds one more of the pharmacy or sweet shop than the Sāstra. This and other statements betray an ignorance of Indian tradition and a mental attitude alien to Indian thinking which distinguishes so many of those whose souls have been captured in the net of an English education. Those who speak another's language and think another's thought must see to it that their own Indian self is not, through the dangers to which it is thus exposed, lost. But even an educated Western, ignorant of the S'āstra, but with a knowledge of the history of religious thought would have perceived the significance of the term Bindu when he had learnt that one of its literal meanings was a "Point."

In an anonymous Mystical Work published in the eighteenth century by one of the "French Protestants of the Desert" called Le Mystere de la Croix, it is said (p. 9), "Ante omina Punctum exstitit; non to atomon, aut mathematicum sed diffusivum. Monas erat explicite: implicite Myrias. Lux erat, erant et Tenebrae; Principium et Finis Principii, Omnia et nihil: Est et non. "

" Before all things were, there was a Point (Punctum: Bindu) not the Atom or mathematical point (which though it is without magnitude has position) but the diffusive (neither with magnitude nor position). In the One (Monas) there was implicitly contained the many (Myrias). There was Light and Darkness: Beginning and End: Everything and Nothing: Being and Non-being (that is the state was neither Sat nor Asat)." The author says that the All is engendered from the central indivisible Point of the double triangle (that is, what is called in the Tantras, Ṣaṭkoṇa-Yantra) regarded as the symbol of creation. " Le Tout est engennre' du point central indivisible du double triangle." This "Point" is one of the world's religious symbols and is set in the centre of a Ṣaṭkoṇa or in a circular Maṇḍala or sphere. On this symbol St. Clement of Alexandria in the second century A. D. says that if abstraction be made from a body of its properties, its depth, breadth, and then length, " the point which remains is a unit, so to speak, having position; from which if we abstract position there is the notion of unity" (Stromata V. 2. Ante Nicene Library, Vol. IV). Again Shelley in his "Prometheus" says: " plunge into eternity where recorded time seems but a point. "

Where does the Extended universe go at the Great Dissolution (Mahāpralaya)? It collapses so to speak into a Point. This point may be regarded as a mathematical point in so far as it is without any magnitude whatever, but as distinguished from it, in that it has in fact no position. For there is then no notion of space. It need hardly be said that this is a symbol, and a symbol borrowed from our present experience cannot adequately represent any state beyond it. We only conceive of it as a point, as something infinitesimally subtle, which is in contrast with the extended manifested universe which is withdrawn into it. This point is Bindu. But this again is to make use of material images borrowed from the world of objective form. Bindu is an aspect of S'akti or Consciousness; therefore it is interpreted also in terms of our present consciousness. As so interpreted and as Īsvara-Tattva, in which it is, S'akti is called Bindu; because here consciousness completely identifies itself with the universe as unmanifested *Idam* and thus subjectifies it and becomes with it a point of consciousness. Thus by way of example the individual mind is completely subjectified and exists for each of us as a mathematical point (and so it is spoken of by some as being of atomic dimension) though the body to the extent to which it is not subjectified appears as an object or extended thing. We do not conceive of our own minds as extended because of this complete subjectification. In the same way the consciousness of Īsvara completely subjectifies the universe. He does not of course see the universe as a multiplicity of objects outside and different from himself; for if He did, He would be Jīva and not Īsvara. He sees it as an object which is a whole and which whole is Himself. In Sadākhya-Tattva "Otherness" (Idam) is presented to Consciousness by S'akti. This *Idam* is then faintly perceived (to use the language of the Vimarśinī on Īsvara-Pratyabhijñā III. 1, 2) "in a hazy fashion (*Dhyāmalaprāyam*) like a picture just forming itself (*Unmīlita-mātra-citra-kalpam*); seen by the mind only and not as something seen outside by the

senses (*Antahkaranaikavedyam*)." The object thus vaguely
surges up into the field of consciousness in which the
emphasis is on the cognitive aspect or " I " (Aham).
This however is not the " I " or " This " of our
experience, for it is had in the realms beyond Māyā.
The " This " is then experienced as part of the Self.
In Īśvara Tattva all haziness gives place to clarity of
the "This" which is thus seen completely as part of the
Self ; the emphasis being on the " This ". After equal
emphasis on the " I " and " This ", the two are in
Śuddhavidyā-Tattva wholly separated by Māyā.
When therefore the Yogī passes beyond the Māyik
world his first higher experience is in this Tattva.

Nāda and Bindu are states of Śakti in which the
germ of action (Kriyā-śakti) so to speak increasingly
sprouts with a view to manifestation producing a state
of compactness of. energy and readiness to create.
Rāghava-Bhatta (Comm. Śāradā 1.7) speaks of them
as two states of Śakti which are the proper conditions
(*Upayogyāvasthā*) for creation. They are, like all else,
aspects of Śakti, but are names of those aspects which are
prone to and ready for creation (*Uccūnāvasthā*). Bindu is
said to be the massive or *Ghanāvasthā* state of Śakti. The
PrapañcasāraTantra says that Śakti is seized with the
desire to create and becomes Ghanībhūtā (*Vicikīrṣur
ghanībhūta*). Thus milk becomes *Ghanībhūtā* when it
turns into cream or curd. In other words, Śakti is
conceived as passing gradually from its subtle state
through Śakti-tattva and Nāda (in its three-stages) and
becomes what is relatively gross or massive as Power
which is fully equipped to pass from the stage of potency
into that of active manifestation. That stage is Bindu
which is called Mahābindu or Parabindu to distinguish

it from the other Bindus into which it subsequently differentiates.

The commentary of Kālicaraṇa on the Ṣaṭcakra-nirūpaṇa (see *The Serpent Power*, V. 4) citing Toḍala-Tantra (Ch. VI) says that the Supreme Light is formless ; but Bindu implies both the Void (S'ūnya) and Guṇa also. Bindu is the Void in so far as it is the Supreme Brahman. It implies Guṇa as being the creative or S'akti aspect of the Brahman which subsequently evolves into the Puruṣa and Prakṛti-Tattvas of which the latter is with Guṇa. The commentary to V. 49 states that this Bindu is the Lord (Īśvara) whom some Paurāṇikas call Mahāviṣṇu and others the Brahmapuruṣa : and (V. 37) that Para-bindu is the state of "Ma" before manifestation; being S'iva-S'akti enveloped by Māyā. As to this it may be observed that the letter M is male, and Bindu which is the nasal breathing, sounded as M, is the unmanifested S'akti or Ma which is revealed upon its subsequent differentiation into the three S'aktis from which the universe proceeds. Bindu as the Cause is *Cidghana* or massive Consciousness and Power in which lie potentially in a mass (Ghana), though undistinguishable the one from other, all the worlds and beings about to be created. This is Parama-S'iva and in him are all the Devatās. It is thus this Bindu which is worshipped in secret by all Devas (V. 41) and which is indicated in its different phases in the Candrabindu (Nāda-Bindu), S'akti and S'ānta of the Om and other Bija mantras.

This Bindu is in Satyaloka which, within the human body, exists in the pericarp of the thousand-petalled Lotus (Sahasrāra) in the highest cerebral centre. It is, as I have already said, compared to a grain of gram (Caṇaka) which under its outer sheath (which is Māyā) contains the two seeds (S'iva and S'akti) in close and undivided union.

Kālicaraṇa (V. 49) thus cites the following : In the Satyaloka is the formless and lustrous one. She is like a grain of gram devoid of hands, feet and the like. She has surrounded Herself by Māyā (that is She is about to create by the agency of this Power of Hers). She is Sun, Fire and Moon, She being intent on creation (*Unmukhī*) becomes twofold (*Dvidhā bhitvā*) and then, by differentiation of S'iva and S'akti, arises creative ideation (*Sṛṣṭikalpanā*). S'iva and S'akti are of course not actually divided for they are not like a *chapatti* or some other material thing. It might seem unnecessary to make such obvious remarks, did not experience tell me of the absurd misunderstandings which exist of the Scripture. When we read that God "*is* a woman," that the S'ākta Tantra is "Feminism" with a doctrine similar to that of Prof. Lester Ward's primacy of the female sex, that "the conception of the sexual relation-ship is the ultimate explanation of the universe" and so forth, no caveats, however obvious, are unnecessary. What of course is meant is that, whereas in Praḷaya, S'iva and S'akti existed as one unity of consciousness, They in creation, whilst still remaining in themselves what They always were, project the universe which is S'akti ; and then we have the Paramātmā and Jīvātmā consciousness which seem to the latter to be different.

Although Parabindu and all which evolves from It are nothing but aspects of S'akti and in no wise different from it, yet as representing that state of S'akti which immediately precedes creation, it is this state of S'akti which is said to be the cause of the universe of name

and form (Nāmarūpa) ; concepts and concepts objectified ; or S'abda the word and Artha its meaning. The
states of S'akti preceding Bindu are those in which the
Bindu state is in process of being " evolved " according
to what we may call an Avikṛta-Pariṇāma and when
evolved it is the cause of the universe. Really they are
merely aspects of one and the same pure S'akti. This
is not an evolution in time. As Plotinus says, the
universe " was formed according to intellect (here the
Cosmic Power or Prapañca-S'akti which manifests as
Mahat) and intellect not preceding in time but prior "
(in the sense that cause precedes effect). This again,
as all descriptions, (in so far as they are applicable to
the transcendent S'akti) is imperfect, for sequence of
cause and effect involves to our minds the notion of
time. This Supreme Bindu as containing in Himself
all Devatās is the ultimate object of adoration by all
classes of worshippers (V. 44) under the name of S'iva,
or Mahāvisṇu or the Devī as those call it "who are
filled with a passion for Her Lotus Feet." The sec-
tarianism of the lower mind, still existent in both East
and West, is here shown to be a matter of words (the
fight for which is of such interest to many) and is
reduced to its real common denominator. As the Lord
says in the Gītā, Whomever men may worship, all
such worship comes eventually to Him.

Para-bindu is thus the Head of every line of creation ; of the Tattvas from Buddhi to Pṛthivī and their
Lords (Tattveśa) and of the S'abda or Mantra creations;
all belonging to the Vikāra-Sṛṣṭi or Pariṇāma-Sṛṣṭi.
The development after the manifestation of Prakṛti is a
real evolution (Pariṇāma), for Consciousness has then
been divided into subject and object in time and space.
What is spoken of in terms of a development in the

Īśvara body is not that. There S'akti assumes various aspects with a view to create but without manifestation. S'akti-tattva, whilst remaining such, assumes the aspects of Nāda and Bindu.

The next stage is thus described in the S'āradā-Tilaka (Ch. 1-8, 9) as follows:

Paraśaktimayah sākṣāt tridhā, sau bhidyate punah.
Bindur nādo bījamiti tasya bhedāh samīritāh.
Binduh śivātmako bījam śaktir nādas tayor mithah.
(Samavāyah samākhyāth sarvāgamaviśāradaih

That which is supreme S'akti again divides Itself into three, such divisions being known as Bindu, Nāda, Bīja. Bindu is said to be of the nature of S'iva and Bīja of S'akti, and Nāda as the mutual relation between these two, by those who are learned in the Āgamas).

One Mss. I have seen has 'Bindur nādātmako', but the commentary of the Ṣaṭcakra (V.40) explains this as S'ivātmaka. These form the three Bindus (Tribindu). Nāda here again is Trait d'Union, the Yoga of the other two Bindus as the Prayogasāra calls it, (See Rāghava's Comm. to V. 8 of Ch. I S'āradā). These are S'iva, S'iva-S'akti, S'akti. By this it is not to be understood that S'iva or S'akti are ever altogether dissociated but the aspects may be regarded as S'iva or S'akti-pradhāna respectively. Bhāskararāya in his valuable commentary on the Lalitā-Sahasranāma says "From the causal (Kāraṇa) Bindu proceeds the effect (Kārya) Bindu, Nāda and Bīja. Thus these three which are known as supreme, subtle and gross arose." *(Asmacca-kāraṇabindoh sākṣāt krameṇa kāryabindustato nādastato bījam iti trayam utpannam tadidaṁ parasūkṣmasthūlāpadair apy ucyate.* V. 132).

One text of the Prapañcasāra-Tantra says that the Parabindu divides into two parts, of which the right is Bindu, the Male, Puruṣa or Ham, and the left Visarga the Female, Prakṛti or Sah making the combined Hamsah. Hamsah is the union of Prakṛti and Puruṣa and the universe is Hamsah. In however the Mss. on which my edition of that Tantra is based it is said that the Bindu (Para) divided by Kāla becomes threefold as Bindu, Nāda, Bīja. Substantially the matter seems one of nomenclature, for the two Bindus which make Visarga become three by the addition of the S'iva-Bindu. Moreover as Ham is S'iva and Sah is S'akti, the combined Hamsah implies the relation which in the S'āradā. account is called Nāda. So it is also said from the first vowel issued "Hrīm," from the second Hamsah, and from the third the Mantra "Hrīm, S'rīm, Klīm", the first indicative of general form ; the second being a more Sthūla form of Ākāśa and Agni (Sa = Ākāśa ; Ra = Agni) held as it were within the "skin" (Carma) of the enveloping Ardhanārīśvara ; the third commencing with the first and last letters including all the 24 Tattvas and all the fifty letters into which the general Form particularises itself.

Para-bindu is S'iva-S'akti considered as undivided, undifferentiated principle. On the "bursting" of the seed which is the Parabindu the latter assumes a threefold aspect as S'iva or Bindu, S'akti or Bīja and Nāda the S'iva-S'akti aspect which, considered as the result, is the combination, and from the point of view of cause, the inter-relation of the two (S'āradā I. 9) the one acting as excitant (Kṣobhaka) and the other being the excited (Kṣobhya). The commentary on V. 40 of the Ṣaṭcakranirūpaṇa speaks of Nāda as the union of S'iva and S'akti; as the connection between the two and as being in the

nature of the S'akti of action (Kriyā-śakti-svarūpa). It
is also said to be that, the substance of which is Kuṇḍali
(Kuṇḍalinimaya). All three are but different phases
of S'akti in creation (Comm. I. 39) being different
aspects of Parabindu which is itself the Ghanāvasthā
aspect of S'akti.

Thus in the first division of S'akti, Nāda, Bindu,
Nāda is the Maithuna or Yoga of S'iva and S'akti to
produce the Parabindu which again differentiates into
the threefold aspects as the S'aktis, though in grosser
form, which produced it. Though the Guṇas are factors
of the gross S'akti Prakṛti, they are in subtle form contained within the higher S'aktis. This S'akti as the
first potentially kinetic aspect about to display itself is
the Cit aspect of S'akti and Cit S'akti is, when seen from
the lower level of the Guṇas, Sāttvic : Nāda is in the
same sense Rājasik, for S'akti becomes more and more
kinetic gathering together Its powers, as it were from
the previous state of barely stirring potency, for the
state of complete readiness to create which is Bindu, and
which in the aforesaid sense as Ghanībhūta foresha-
dows that Tamas Guṇa which at a lower stage is the
chief factor which creates the world, for the latter is
largely the product of Tamas. Each aspect of Tribindu
again is associated with one or other of the Guṇas.
These divisions of aspect from the Guṇa stand-point
are not to be understood as though they were separate
and exclusively concerned with only one of the Guṇas.
The Guṇas themselves never exist separately. Where
there is Sattva there is also Rajas and Tamas. In the
same way in the case of the three S'aktis Icchā, Jñāna,
Kriyā, from which the Guṇas develop, one never stands
by itself, though it may be predominant. Where there
is Icchā there is Jñāna and so forth. And so again

S'akti, Nāda and Bindu are not to be severed like different objects in the Māyik world. In each there is implicitly or explicitly contained the other. Parameś- vara assumes (for the Jīva) successively the triple aspects of S'akti, Nada Bindu, Kārya Bindu, Bīja, Nāda, thus completing by this differentiation of S'akti the sevenfold causal sound-forms of the Praṇava or Oṁkāra; namely, Sakala Parameśvara (which is Saccidānanda, for even when the Brahman is associ- ated with Avidyā, its own true nature (Svarūpa) is not affected), S'akti (S'akti-Tattva), Nāda (Sādākhya- Tattva), Parabindu (Īśvara-Tattva), Bindu (Kārya), Nāda and Bīja. It is not clear to me where (if at all) the Suddha-vidyā-Tattva comes in according to this scheme, unless it be involved in Nāda, the Mithah- samāvāya; but the Puruṣa-Prakṛti-Tattvas appear to take birth on the division of the Para-bindu into S'iva and S'akti or Ham and Sah, Hamsah being the Puruṣa- Prakṛti Mantra.

The first impulse to creation comes from the ripen- ing of the Adṛṣṭa of Jīvas, on which Sakala Parameś- vara puts forth His S'akti (which means Himself as S'akti) to produce the Universe wherein the fruits of Karma may be suffered and enjoyed. All the above seven stages are included in, and constitute, the first stage of *Ikṣaṇa* or "Seeing" and is that stage in which S'abda exists in its supreme or Para form (Para-śabda- sṛṣṭi). She who is eternal (Anādirūpā) existing subtly as Cidrūpiṇī in Mahāpralaya becomes on the ripening of Adṛṣṭa, inclined (Utsuka) towards the life of form and enjoyment, and reveals Herself on the disturbance of the equilibrium of the Guṇas. As the Vāyavīya-Samhitā says "Parā-S'akti through the will of S'iva is revealed with S'iva-Tattva (for the purpose of creation). Then

She manifests as the oil which is latent in, and exudes from, the sesamum seed." Parameśvara is Saguna-S'iva or the Iśvara of Vedānta Philosophy with Māyā as His Upādhi. He is Sat, Cit, Ānanda in Māyā body and endowed with all S'aktis (Sarva-vedānta-siddhānta-sāra-saṁgraha 312, 313, 315). There is, as the Pañcadaśī says, (3-38), a S'akti of S'iva which is in and controls all things which have their origin in Ānanda or Iśvara. When Iśvara is moved to create, this Iśvaraśakti or Māyā which is the aggregate of, and which yet trans-cends, all individual S'aktis issues from Him and from this Māyā issue all the particular S'aktis by which the universe is evolved and is maintained. The same sub-stance is, to a large extent, to be found in all accounts under a variety of presentment of Symbols ; even where there are real differences due to the diversity of doctrine of different Vedāntic schools. This is not the case here : for the account given is a Sādhanā presentment of Advaitavāda. The S'ākta-Tantra teaches the unity of Paramātmā and Jīva, though its presentation of some subjects as S'akti, Māyā, Cidābhāsa is different (owing to its practical view-point) from S'aṁkara's Māyāvāda. On this matter I may refer my readers to the article which I recently wrote on S'akti and Māyā in the second number of the *Indian Philosophical Review* (Baroda) since incorporated in my *S'akti and S'ākta*.

The three Bindus constitute the great Triangle of World-Desire which is the Kāmakalā ; an intricate subject which I must leave for a future chapter. The three Bindus are Sun, Moon and Fire and three S'aktis Icchā, Jñāna, Kriyā associated with the three Gunas Sattva, Rajas, Tamas. I do not deal here with the order or correspondence which requires discussion. From them issued the Devis Raudrī, Jyeṣṭhā, Vāmā and the Trimurtis Rudra, Brahmā, Viṣṇu.

The three Bindus are also known as the white Bindu (Sita-bindu), the red Bindu (S'oṇa-bindu) and the mixed Bindu (Miśra-bindu). These represent the Prakāśa, Vimarśa and Prakāśa-Vimarśa aspects of the Brahman which are called in the ritual Caraṇa-tritaya (The Three Feet). The Gurupādukā-Mantra in which initiation is given in the last or Ṣaḍāmnāya Dīkṣā represents a state beyond the S'ukla, Rakta and Miśra-Caraṇas. So it is said in S'ruti that there are four Brahmapadas, three here and one the Supreme which is beyond.

As is the case in many other systems the One for the purpose of creation is presented in twofold aspect, for Unity is actionless, and their relation involves a third aspect which makes the Trinity. But this apparent differentiation does not derogate from the substantial unity of the Brahman. As the ancient Rudrayāmala (II. 22) says : " The three Devas Brahmā, Viṣṇu, Maheśvara are but one and formed out of My body."

Ekā mūrtis trayo devā brahmaviṣṇumaheśvarāh.
Mama vigrahasaṁklptāh srjati avati hanti ca.

From the differentiating Bindu are evolved the Tattvas from Buddhi to Pṛthivī and the six Lords of the Tattvas (preceding Paraśiva the seventh) who are the presiding Devatās of mind and of the five forms of matter. Here on the diremption or dichotomy of Consciousness, Mind and Matter are produced. That is, Consciousness functions in and through the Self-created limitations of mind and matter. It was on this division also that there arose the Cosmic Sound (S'abda-

brahman) which manifests as S'abda and Artha. This
is the S'abda-brahman : so called by those who know
the Āgamas.

Bhidyamānāt parād bindor avyaktātmā ravo'bhavat.
S'abdabrahmeti tam prāhuh sarvāgamaviśāradāh.

(*S'āradā-Tilaka I-II*)

It will be observed that in this verse the first
Bindu is called Para and to make this clear the
author of the Prāṇatoṣinī adds the following note :
"By Para-bindu is meant the first Bindu which is a state
of S'akti (*Parādbindority anena śaktyavasthārūpo yah pra-
thamabindus tasmāt*). S'abda-brahman is the Brahman
in its aspect as the immediate undifferentiated Cause
of the manifested and differentiated S'abda, or
language in prose or verse ; and of Artha or the
subtle or gross objects which thought and language
denote. It is thus the causal state of the manifested
S'abda or Mantra.

CHAPTER XIV

MĀYĀ TATTVA

WHAT Matter is in itself the senses do not tell us. All that can be predicated of it is its effect upon these senses. The experiencer is affected in five different ways giving rise in him to the sensations of hearing (S'abda); feel by which is experienced the thermal quality of things (S'parśa); colour and form (Rūpa); taste (Rasa); and smell (Gandha). The cause of these are the five Bhūtas which in the general cosmic evolution, are derived from the Tanmātras or general elements of the particulars of sense perception. These again together with the senses (Indriyas) or faculties of mind operating through a particular physical organ as their instrument and Manas the mental faculty of attention, selection and synthesis of the discrete manifold, derive from the still more general aspects of the Cosmic Mind or Antahkaraṇa which are the personal forms of limited experience respectively called Ahaṁkāra and Buddhi. These again are evolutes from that form of S'akti which is Prakṛti-Tattva and which in the 36 Tattvas scheme comes into being through the instrumentality of Māyā-S'akti from the preceding Tattvas of the pure creation extending from S'uddha-vidyā to S'iva-S'akti-Tattva, the Svarūpa of the last being Saccidananda or Pure Spirit. Matter is thus a manifestation or aspect of Spirit. The two are ultimately one. They seem to be two because the fundamental Feeling (Cit) is able, as S'akti, to experience itself as object. As Professor Haeckel says, in conformity with S'ākta Monism, Spirit and Matter are not two distinct entities but two forms or aspects of one single fundamental Substance (which is here the Brahman). The one entity with dual aspect is the sole Reality which presents itself to view as the infinitely varied picture of the universe. The two are inseparably combined in every atom which, itself and its forces, possess the elements not only of vitality but of further development in all degrees of Consciousness and Will. The ultimate substance is S'akti, which is of dual aspect as Cit-S'akti which represents the spiritual, and Māyā-S'akti which represents the material aspect. These are not separable. In the universe the former is the Spirit-matter and the latter Matter-spirit. The two exist in inseparable connection (Avinābhāva-sambandha) as inseparable (to use a simile of the S'aiva-S'astra) as the winds of the heaven from the ether in which they blow. Manifested S'akti or Māyā is the universe. Un-manifest S'akti is feeling-consciousness (Cidrūpā). Māyā-S'akti appears as subtle mind and as gross matter and as the life-force and is in Herself (Svarūpa) consci-ousness. There is and can be nothing absolutely lifeless or unconscious because S'akti is in itself Being—Feeling—Consciousness—Bliss   (Cid-rūpiṇi,   Ānandamayī) beyond all worlds (Viśvottīrṇā) ; and appears as appa-rently unconscious, or partly conscious and partly un-conscious, material forms in the universe (Viśvātmaka). The universe is S'akti. Therefore it is commingled Spirit-Matter. S'akti beyond all worlds is Conscious-ness. The one Consciousness exists throughout ; when changeless it receives the name of S'iva ; when the source of, and as all moving objects, it is called S'akti.

The universe arises through a negation or veiling of true Consciousness. As the Spandakārikā says " By veiling the own true form its S'aktis ever arise " *Svarū-pāvaraṇe cāsya śaktayah satalotthitāh*). This is a common doctrine of the three schools here discussed. The difference lies in this, that in Sāmkhya it is a second independent principle (Prakṛti) which veils ; in Māyā-vāda Vedānta it is the non-Brahman unexplainable mystery (Māyā) which veils, and in S'ākta-Advaita-vāda it is consciousness which, without ceasing to be such, yet veils itself. This statement shortly describes the difference in the three concepts which may however be more fully elaborated.

The Mahānirvāṇa-Tantra says that the vākya " All this verily is Brahman " (*Sarvam khalvidam Brahma*) is the basis of Kulācāra. But Brahman is Conscious-ness ; and it cannot be denied that there is an element of apparent unconsciousness in things. S'āmkhya says that this is due to another Principle independent of the Puruṣa-consciousness, namely, the unconscious Prakṛti, which is real, notwithstanding its changes. But according to Advaitavāda Vedānta there is only one Reality. It therefore denies the existence of any second independent principle. S'amkara attributes unconscious-ness to the unexplainable (Anirvacanīyā) ·wonder (Māyā), which is neither real (Sat) nor unreal (Asat) nor partly real and partly unreal (Sadāsat), and which though not forming part of Brahman, and therefore not Brahman, is yet, though not a second reality inseparately associated and sheltering with Brahman (Māyā Brahmāsritā) in one of its aspects (Īśvara) ; owing what false appearance of reality it has to the Brahman with which it is so associated. It is an eternal falsity (*Mithyābhūtā sanātani*), unthinkable,

alogical, unexplainable (*Anirvacanīyā*). The reflection
of Puruṣa on Prakṛti gives the appearance of consciousness to the latter. So also the reflection
(Cidābhāsa) of Brahman on unconscious Māyā is
Iśvara and on unconscious Avidyā is Jīva. Though
Māyā is thus not a second reality, the fact of positing
it at all gives to S'aṁkara's doctrine a tinge of dualism
from which the S'ākta doctrine (which has yet a
weakness of its own) is free. The S'ākta doctrine has
no need of Cidābhāsa. It says that Māyā is a S'akti
of Brahman and being S'akti, which is not different
from the possessor of S'akti (S'aktimān), it is, in its
Svarūpa, consciousness. It is then consciousness which
veils itself; not unconscious Māyā which veils consciousness. According to S'aṁkara, man is the Spirit
(Ātmā) vestured in the Māyik falsities of mind and
matter. He accordingly can only establish the unity
of Jīva and Iśvara by eliminating from the first Avidyā
and from the second Māyā, both being essentially—
and from the transcendent standpoint—nothing. Brahman is thus left as a common denominator. The S'akta
has need to eliminate nothing. Man's spirit or Ātma is
S'iva. His mind and body are S'akti. S'iva and S'akti
are one. The Jīvātmā is S'aiva-S'akti, the latter being
understood as its world-aspect. So is the Paramātmā ;
though here S'akti, being uncreating, is in the form of
Consciousness (Cidrūpiṇi). The supreme S'iva-S'akti
exists as one. S'iva-S'akti as the world is the Manifold.
Man is thus not the Spirit covered by a non-Brahman
falsity but Spirit covering itself with its own Power
of S'akti. As the Kaulācārya Satyānanda says in
his Commentary (which I have published) on the
4th Mantra of the Iś'opanisad—" The changeless
Brahman which is consciousness appears in creation

as Māyā *which is Brahman* (Brahmamayī), Consciousness (Cidrūpiṇī), holding in Herself unbeginning
(Anādi) Kārmik tendencies (Karma-samskāra) in the
form of the three Guṇas. Hence She is Guṇamayī (Her
substance is Guṇa) despite being Cinmayī (Consciousness). *As there is no second principle,* these Guṇas are Cit-
Sakti." Hence, in the words of the Yoginī-hṛdaya-
Tantra, the Devī is *Prakāśavimarśasāmarasyarūpiṇi.* There
is thus truly no unconscious Māyā and no Cidābhāsā.
All which exists is Consciousness as Sakti. *"Aham strī"*
as the Advaitabhāva Upaniṣad exclaims. And so the
grand doctrine "All is Consciousness" is boldly and
vigorously affirmed. Those who worship the Mother,
worship nothing unconscious but a Supreme Consciousness which is Love, the body of which Love is all forms
of consciousness-unconsciousness produced by and which
is, Her as Siva's Power. In short, Samkara says that
there is unconsciousness which appears to be conscious
through Cidābhāsa. Sākta doctrine says Consciousness
appears to be unconsciousness or more truly to have an
element of unconsciousness in it (for nothing even
empirically is absolutely unconscious) owing to the
veiling play of Consciousness itself as Māyā-Sakti. The
result is in the end the same—" All is Consciousness "—
but the method by which this conclusion is attained and
the presentment of the matter is reversed.

This presentment again is in conformity with scientific research which has shown that even so-called
"brute matter" exhibits the elements of that sentiency
which, when evolved in man, is the full self-consciousness. It has been well said that sentiency is an integrant
constituent of all existence, physical as well as metaphysical, and its manifestation can be traced throughout
the mineral and chemical as well as the vegetable and

animal worlds. It essentially comprises the functions of
relation to environment, response to stimuli and atomic
memory in the lower or inorganic plane, whilst in the
higher in the organic plane it includes all the psychic
functions such as consciousness, perception, thought,
reason, volition and individual memory. Throughout
it is the one Mother who works, now veiling Her Bliss
in inorganic matter, now more fully revealing Herself
by gradual stages as the vitivity (which She is) displays
itself in the evolving forms of worldly life. As Haeckel
says, sentiency, is like movement, found in all matter.
To reach this conclusion we must assume (as the S'aiva-
S'ākta schools do) that Kriyā and Icchā, its preliminary,
are functions of Consciousness. Abhinava-Gupta in
his Commentary on the Pratyabhījñā-Kārikā says,
"The characteristic of action is the manifestation of
all objects. These objects again characterised by
consciousness-unconsciousness are in the nature of a
shining forth (Ābhāsa). The universe is thus described
as a " going forth " (Prasara) of S'iva.

The ultimate reality is Saccidānanda which, as
the source of appearances, is called S'akti. The latter
in its Sat (Being) aspect is omnipresent, indestructible
(eternal) Source and Basis both of the Cosmic Breath
or Prāṇa as also of all vital phenomena displayed as
the individual Prāṇa in separate and concrete bodies.
S'akti is Life which, in its phenomenal sense as manifested in individual bodies, issues from, and rests upon,
and at basis is, Sat. In this aspect manifested S'akti is
vitality which is the one fixed unalterable potential in
the universe of which all other forms of energy are
particular effects. Life is the phenomenal aspect of
spirit in which, as its Cause, it is at the great dissolution
merged. There is no absolute end of life but only to

certain structures of life. As it had no end it has no
absolute beginning. It appears only in creation from
the depths of Being which is its unmanifested ground.
The search for the "origin of life" is futile; for it
issues from Brahman who, in a supreme sense, is
Infinite Life. Life is throughout the Universe. Every
atom of dust is quivering with it, as are the most
sensitive organic structures. In the latter case it is
obvious, in the former it is not so, but is yet traced.
The existence and functions of life cannot be explained
on exclusively mechanical principles. What is called
mechanical energy is the effect and not the cause of
vitality or vitivity or S'akti as the Mother of all. The
purpose of evolution is to take up the living potential
from some lower grade, develop it and hand it over to
a higher grade of forms.

S'akti as Cidānanda is, as Iccha-S'akti, the source
of all forms of will-power and, in matter, of mechanical energy; and as Jñāna-Sakti, of all forms of
mentality and feeling, and as Kriyā, of all forms of
activity (Kartṛtva), being in itself all-mighty.

The ultimate changeless Reality, in its aspect as
S'akti, veils and contracts in various degrees its power
of will, knowledge and action. This veiling, negation,
limitation or contraction is seen at its fullest in so-called
"dead inert brute" matter. This allegation of lifeless
inertia is however the result of superficial observation.
It is true that in gross matter (Bhūta) the light of
consciousness is turned down to its utmost. It is nowhere however even empirically extinguished. Cit is
faintly manifested by scientific experiment in gross
matter; more clearly in the micro-organisms between
such matter and the vegetable world, in which, as in

the animal world evolved from it, vitality is so obvious
that we have been wont to call these alone "alive."
Śākta doctrine starts with the Full (Pūrṇa) and deals
with the creation of things as a cutting down thereof.
From a scientific point of view we may commence with
the world as it is, taking inorganic matter as the starting point. From such a stand-point we may speak
(See "Veda's vital molecule" and "Notes on the
radical Vitality of all concrete matter" by G. Dubern)
of a Radical Vital Potential in all matter, universal,
omnipresent, indestructible, all-powerful; the source as
will-power of mechanical energy, and as rudimentary
sentiency of all mentality. From the Śāstric standpoint
the process is one of veiling and unveiling. Śakti veils
itself down to and in Pṛthivī-Tattvā of gross matter
(Bhūta) ; and thereafter gradually unveils Herself up to
and in man who in Samādhi realises his *Svarūpa* as pure,
unveiled, Consciousness.

This veiling by Śakti takes place first in Śiva-Śakti-
Tattva by the complete negation of the " *Idam* " of
experience ; and then through action of the *Idam* " on
the subjective aspect of the consciousness of the pure
creation, in which subject and object exist as part of the
One Self ; and then through that form of Śakti which is
Māyā which effects a severance of subject and object
which are then experienced no longer as part of the one
Self but as separate. The point of junction between
Pure and Impure experience is the Tattva variously
called Vidyā, Sadvidyā or Śuddha-vidya, the first truly
realistic stage of the Yogī. Because it is in the intermediate state, it is called Parāpara-daśā (Iś. Prat. III, 1-5) and,
as the Svacchanda-Tantra (IV, 95) says, the" Experience
in the form of Mantra of both difference and non-
difference." After this Tattva, Māyā intervenes.

In the Tattva-Saṁdoha (v. 5) it is said, " *Māyā* is the sense of difference (Bheda-buddhi) in all Jivas which are parts of Her. Just as the shore holds in the sea, so She ever obstructs the manifestation (Vibhava) of Ātmā which but for Her is otherwise unobstructed".

Māyā vibheda-buddhir
nijāṁśa-jāteṣu nikhilajīveṣu
Nityam tasya niraṅkuśa—
vibhavam veleve vāridhe rundhe

So also in the Īśvara-Pratyabhijñā it is said, "That which is nothing but the notion of difference (Bheda-dhi) in things entertained by the Doer (Kartā) though in Himself of the nature of consciousness, is Māyā-S'akti, whom others, as in the case of Vidyeśvaras, call Vidyā".

Bhedadhir eva bhāveṣu kartur bodhātmano' pi yā.
Māya śaktyeva sā vidyetyanye vidyeśvarā yathā.

(III, ii, 6)

" She is Vidyā-S'akti when She reveals in the Paśu state of the Ātmā whose true nature is Lordship (Aiśvarya), but when She veils (Tirodhānakarī) then She is called Māyā."

Tasyaiṣvaryasvabhāvasya paśu-bhāve prakāśikā.
Vidyā-śaktis tirodhānakarī māyābhidhā punaḥ.

(ib. 7)

S'iva has two functions namely Tirodhāna, that by which He veils Himself to His worshipper, and Anugraha whereby He, through His grace, reveals Himself by the " descent of S'akti " or grace (S'akti-pāta). She is both Madhumatī "Honey" and Māyā

(Lalitā-sahasranāma, v. 139). She is that saving (Tāraka) knowledge by which the ocean of the Samsāra is crossed. The Citkalā or Amśā of the great Consciousness enveloped by mind and matter is the S'akti which, as the Padma-Purāṇa says resides as the core of the " inner working " of all Jīvas and the Ānandakalikā or Germ of Bliss therein; She again as the Lalitāsahasranāma says (v. 142) is basis of the false (in the sense of impermanent) universe (Mithyā jagadadhiṣṭhānā) created by, and which is Her Māyā, the power of the Lord (S'āndilya-Sūtra, 86) which obscures and which, as the S'ākta Devī-Purāṇa says, is called Māyā, because it is the marvellous instrument whereby unheard of results are produced like those of dreams or Magic. She is in all systems, whether as Prakṛti, Māyā or Māyāśakti, the finitising principle whereby forms are created in the formless Consciousness. This She effects by causing that duality of feeling of the self and not-self in the grand experience which is Mahāsattā. Under Her influence the Self experiences Itself as object in all the forms of the universe, which when completed is objectively seen as an evolution from Prakṛti-Tattva, that state of S'akti which is evolved by the action of Māyā and the five Kañcukas developed from Her. These are specific aspects of the great general limiting Power (S'akti) which Māyā is. With this Prakṛti is associated Puruṣa-Tattva, the two combined being Hamsa. Puruṣa-Tattva is Ātmā enveloped by the Kañcukas, derived from Māyā and specific of its operation. S'akti as Prakṛti, subject to the influence of the Kañcukas, develops on the dis-equilibrium of Her Guṇas from Herself, as Vikṛtis, the impure Tattvas (Aśuddha-Tattva) extending to Pṛthivī. At this point conscious vital energy materialises, forming, what has been called by the author cited "the crust of the vital molecule" of all forms of solid matter. Subjectively therefore the Māyā process is the establishment of a dichotomy of subject and object in what would otherwise be an unitary experience; and objectively it is the creation of the various psychical and physical forms into which the Universal Substance projects becoming in the course of such emanation more and more gross. Bindu as the Mantra designation of Īśvara-Tattva is Ghanībhūta; that is, the first Ghanāvasthā aspect of Śakti becoming (through Māyā) Prakṛti-Tattva and its evolutes which are more and more gross (Sthūla); until passing the first four states of decreasing subtlety of matter, Substance emerges as the solid atoms of matter of which the physical universe is composed. These compounds being the subject of the senses are the materials of physical science which seeks to work the process backwards. At a point, search on the path of objectivity is closed. If it would know more, the mind must turn in on itself and release itself from all objectivity which Māyā is and fall back into that group of Consciousness (Māyātīta) whence it has emerged. From the Mantra aspect dealing with the origin of language, the undifferentiated Śabda which arises on the differentiation of the Bindu into Puruṣa-Prakṛti or Hamsa develops, with the creation of mind and matter, into the manifested Śabda and Artha which are the Varṇas or letters (springing from the subtle Matṛkas) expressed in Vaikharī speech made up of letters (Varṇa), syllables (Pada), and sentences (Vākya or the uttered Mantra). Mantra again is the thought (*Man*) which saves (*Trā, Trāyate*) : Saves from what? From firstly the evil which man, subject to Māyā, commits; and then, by the thorough purification of the mind (Citta-śuddhi), from

Māyā Herself who is transformed in the Sādhaka into Vidyā-S'akti. Mantra is thus here a pure thought-form ; a pure Vṛtti or modification of the Antahkaraṇa which is Devatā. The senses and mind are also Devatās being operations of the one Divine S'akti. Through Mantra the mind is divinely transformed. Contemplating, filled by, and identified with, Divinity in Mantra form, which is a Sthūla (gross) aspect of Devī, it passes into Her subtle (Sūkṣma) Light form (Jyotirmayī Devī) which is the Consciousness beyond the world of Māyik forms ; the Īśvara and Īśvarī who as S'abdabrahman are the source of, and appear as, that Māyā which is the Creatrix both of the objective world of Mind and Matter and of the manifested S'abda and Artha ; the Word and its Meaning derived from the Mother in Her aspect as Supreme Nāda (Para-nāda) and Supreme Speech (Parā-vāk).

THE KAÑCUKAS

THE six Kañcukas including Māyā which may be regarded as the root of the other five are Kāla, Niyati, Rāga, Vidya, Kalā. The term Kañcuka means sheath or envelope. The same Tattvas are also called contractions (Saṁkoca), for creation is the contracted (Saṁkucadrūpā) form of infinite S'akti. It is to be observed that Māyā, Niyati and Kāla, occupy in the philosophy of Pāñcarātra-Āgama the very place which is held in the S'aiva-S'akta system by the Kañcukas (See as to this Dr. Otto Schrader's Ahirbudhnya-Samhitā 63, 64, 90). The author cited opines that the six Kañcukas are only an elaboration of the older doctrine of the three powers of limitation (Saṁkoca) of the Pāñcarātra which are Māyā, Kāla, Niyati. The same idea is expressed by these two terms, namely limitations by which the Ātmā, in its form as the finite experiencer, is deprived of the specific attributes which It, as the Perfect Experience, possessed. Consciousness reaching forth to the World of enjoyment becomes subject to the Kañcukas and thus becomes the impure, finite, worldly experience where subject and object are completely different ; which experience is, as it were, the *inversion* by the contraction and negation of S'akti of the perfect Experience from whose S'iva-S'akti-Tattva aspect it proceeds. Infinite Consciousness whilst still transcen-

dentally retaining its Svarūpa is, as S'akti, narrowed to
the degree which constitutes our experience on the
material plane. The process may be represented in
Diagram by an inverted triangle representing the Yoni or
S'akti, in the form of the Pure Tattvas, resting on the
point of an upright triangle. The point of intersection
is Māyā from which proceeds the second triangle
representing the impure Tattvas, which constitute
wordly experience. Seen in the waters of Māyā all is
reversed. Through the operation of Māyā and
Kañcukas, S'akti assumes the gross contracted form of
Prakṛti-Tattva which in association with Purūṣa-Tattva
is Hamsa. S'iva and S'akti are the Bird Hamsa. Hamsa
is both male (Pūm or Puruṣa) and female (Prakṛti).
Ham is S'iva and Sah is S'akti. This Hamsa-dvandva
are in their gross form the universe (*Pum-prakṛtyāt-
maka hamsas tadātmakam idam jagat*). Puruṣa is the
Ātmā enveloped by the Kañcukas which are the contractions of Consciousness and Its Powers. Māyā is the
root and cause of all limitations of the powers (Vibhava)
of consciousness (Ātma) for Māyā is the sense of
difference (Bhedabuddhi) between all persons and things.
Each Puruṣa, (and they are innumerable) being as the
Svacchanda-Tantra says, an universe of his own. Each
Puruṣa creates under Māyā his or its own universe.
The Kañcukas are thus the delimitations of the Supreme
in Its form as S'akti. It was Eternity (Nityatā) but is
now orderly and delimitation (Pariccheda) productive
of appearance and disappearace (that is life and death).
This is the operation of the Time-power or Kāla which
is defined as follows in the Tattva-Saṃdoha (V. 11)
"That S'akti of His which is Eternity (Nityatā)
descending and producing appearance and disappea-
rance (birth and death) ; and which ever in regulated

manner performs the function of division or delimitation (Pariccheda) should be regarded as in the form of
Kāla-Tattva. "

> *Sā nityatāsya śakti nikṛṣya nidhanodaya-pradānena*
> *Nityataparic-chedakarīklptā syāt Kāla-tattva-rūpeṇa.* Kāla
is the power which urges on and matures things. It is
not in itself subjective or empirical time, though it
gives rise to it. It is transcendental Time without
sections (Akhaṇḍa-Kāla) giving birth to time as effect
(Kārya-Kāla). This gross time with parts (Sakala-Kāla)
only comes in with the creation of the gross Tattvas.
So it is said " Time leads me in time " (See Ahirbudhnya 64—67. See also the same Author's Ueber
den stand der Indischen Philosophie zur zeit Mahāvīras
und Buddhas 17—30). Consciousness as S'akti is
contracted into the mode of temporal thinking. It was
freedom and independence (Svatantratā). This is now
contracted and the Puruṣa is forcibly subjected to
guidance and regulation in what he must or must not
do in any moment of time. This is Niyati, which is
defined in the Tattva-Saṁdoha (v. 12) as follows :
" That which constitutes that S'akti of His which is
called Independence or Freedom (Svatantratā) ; this
same S'akti, and none other, becoming contracted and
subjecting Him perforce to guidance and regulation
(Niyamayatī) in a definitely ordered and restricted
manner (Niyatam) as regards what is to be done or
not done (that is, what he must not do at any given
moment of time) is Niyati. "

> *Yāsya svatantratākhyā*
> *S'aktih saṁkocaśālinī saiva.*
> *Kṛtyākṛtyeṣvāsam*
> *niyatam amum niyamayan-tyabhun Niyatih.*

Niyati is spoken of in Pāñcarātra Āgama as the
subtle regulator of everything (Sūksma-sarva-niyā-
makah. Ahirbudhnya VI. 46); and is said by Dr.
Schrader to include in that system the functions of the
three S'aiva-S'akta Kañcukas, Vidyā, Rāga and Kalā
(Ahirbudhnya 64-65). It was completely satisfied with
Itself for there was then no other. It was the Full
(Pūrna) and there was nothing else for it to interest
Itself in and thus want. This S'akti becoming limited,
makes the Purusa interested in objects and thus attaches
them to enjoyment. This is Rāga which is defined in
the Tattva-Samdoha (v. 10) as follows :

"There is another S'akti of his which is eternal
complete satisfaction ; the same becoming limited and
attaching him ever to enjoyment, this S'akti is reduced
to the condition of Rāga-tattva. "

Nitya-paripūrnatṛptih
   saktis-tasyaiva parimitā nu satī.
Bhogesu rañjayanti
   satatam amum Rāga-tattvatām yātā.

The Brahman is as the Īsa-Upanisad says Pūrna
the Full, the All which wants nothing ; for there is
nothing to the All which It can want. But when the
one Experience becomes dual, and, subject and object
are separate, then the self as subject becomes interested
in objects that is in things other than itself. Icchā in
the sense of desire implies a want of the fullness which
is that of the Supreme perfect experience. In the
supreme creative sense Icchā is the direction of Consciousness towards activity. The term Rāga is commonly
translated desire. It is however properly that *interest*
in objects which precedes desire. Rāga is thus that
interest in objects, seen as other than the self, which

ripens into desire (Icchā) for them. Such Icchā is thus a limitation of the all-satisfied fullness of the Supreme. The power of the Supreme was to know or experience all things and so it is Sarvajñata. This is limited and the Puruṣa thereby becomes a "little knower." This Kañcuka is called Vidyā which is defined in the Tattva-Saṁdoha (V. 9) as follows : "His power of all-knowingness becoming limited and capable of knowing only a few things and producing knowledge (of a limited character) is called Vidyā by the wise of old."

> *Sarvajñatasya śaktiḥ*
> *parimitatanur alpa-vedya-mātraparā.*
> *Jñānam utpādayanti*
> *Vidyeti nigadyate hudhair ādyaiḥ.*

The supreme is all powerful, mighty to do all things (Sarvakartṛtā). This power is contracted so that the Puruṣa can accomplish a few things and becomes a "little doer." This is Kalā which is defined in the Tattva-Saṁdoha (v. 8) as follows—

"That which was His power of all-doing-ness the same being contracted and capable of accomplishing but a few things and reducing him to the state of a little doer is called Kalā."

> *Tat-sarvakartṛtā sā*
> *saṁkucitā katipayārtha-mātraparā*
> *Kiṁcit-kartāram amum*
> *kalayanti kīrtyate Kalā nāmā.*

Kalā is thus nothing but Kartṛttva or infinite activity, agency, and mightiness cut down to the limits of the Jīva's power ; that is lowered to the possibilities of finite action.

Thus the Saktis of the supreme which are many become contracted. Consciousness thus limited in six-fold manner by its own Sakti is the Puruṣa associated with Prakṛti. Kalā (in its more generic sense) is said in the Saiva-Tantrasāra (Āhnika 8) to be "the cause of the manifestation of Vidyā and the root when She is operating on that Kartṛtva which is qualified by the qualifying conditions of littleness; this limited power of agency having been itself the work of Māyā. Now the moment that Kalā separates from herself what constitutes this qualifying aspect spoken of above as Kiṁcit (little) at that very moment there is the creation of the Prakṛti Tattva which is in the nature of a generality (Sāmānya-mātra) unmarked by any specific form of object of enjoyment, such as happiness, sorrow and delusion ; and of which another name is the equalisation of the Guṇas. Thus the creation under the influence of the Kalā-tattva of the limited experiencer (Bhoktṛ) that is, of the Puruṣa and of the experienced (Bogya) or Prakṛti, is quite simultaneous, that is without any succession whatever in the process. Thus being simultaneous they are ever associated."

The eighth Āhnika of the Tantrasāra (the Saiva and not the Sakta ritual work of Kṛṣṇānanda-Āgamavāgīśa) says : Thus it has been already shown that Kalā is the cause of manifestation of Vidyā and the rest (*i.e.*, the other four Kañcukas leaving out Māyā) when she (Kalā) is operating on that agency or doer-ness (Kartṛ-tva) which is qualified (Viśeṣya) by the qualifying (Viśeṣaṇa) condition of littleness ; this limited power of agency (Kiṁcitkartṛtva as opposed to Sarva-kartṛtva) having been itself the work of Māyā. Now the moment that Kalā separates from Herself that which constitutes this qualifying aspect (Viśeṣaṇa-bhāga) spoken of above as Kiṁcit and is an object of knowledge and action, that very moment there is the creation (Sarga) of the Prakṛti-Tattva which is of the nature of a generality only (Sāmānya-mātra) unmarked by any specific forms of the enjoyable (Bhogya) such as happiness, sorrow, and delusion (which are therefore as yet undifferentiated) and of which another name is the equalisation of their Guṇas (*i.e.*, of Sukha, Duhkha and Moha or of the Guṇas of Her). Thus the creation under the influence of the Kalā-Tattva of the Enjoyer (Bhoktṛ or limited experiencer) and Enjoyable (Bhogya or experienced) is quite simultaneous, that is without any succession whatever in the process and being simultaneous they are conjoined.

(*Evam kiṁcit-kartṛtvam yan māyākāryam, tatra kiṁcittva-viśiṣṭam yat kartṛtvam, viśeṣyam tatra vyāpriyamāṇā kalā vidyādi-prasavahetur iti nirūpitam. Idānim viśeṣaṇabhāge yah kiṁcit ityukto jñeyah kāryaś ca tam yāvat sā Kalā svātmanah pṛthak kurute tāvad eṣa eva sukha-duhkha-mohātmaka-bhogya-viseṣānusyūtasya sāmānya mātrosya tad-guṇa-sāmyā-paranāmnah prakṛti-tattvasya sargah—iti bhoktṛbhogya-yugalasya samam eva kalā-tattvayattā sṛṣṭih.*)

Again in the Tantrāloka (Ahnika 9) it is said " So far it has been shown how Agency (Kartṛtva) which is always accompanied by the power to enjoy (Bhoktṛtva) is (to be found) in that qualified aspect (that is Kartṛtva) of the Tattva called Kalā which (aspect) is characterised by a limited agency (little-doerness)."

Here may be interposed a note of explanation: Kartṛtva is creative activity, ideation and formation as contrasted with a merely induced and passively accepted experience which is Jñātṛtva. Kartṛtva is the power of modifying the Idam. The Sāṁkhyas say that the

Puruṣa is Bhoktā but not Kartā. But the Śaiva-Śāktas hold that there is no Kartṛtva without Bhoktṛtva. In Parā-samvit there is the potential germ of (1) Jñātṛtva, (2) Bhoktṛtva and (3) Kartṛtva held in undistinguishable unity. In Śiva-Śakti Tattva the first exists and the second and third are, through Śakti, suppressed. In Sadākhya there are the first and the incipiency of the second and the third; and in Īśvara-Tattva all three are developed but as yet undifferentiated. The Īśvara consciousness directed to the "Idam" produces equality of attention on "Aham" and "Idam" which is Sadvidyā-Tattva whence arise Māyā and the Kañcukas evolving Puruṣa-Prakṛti. Para-Samvit is the pure changeless aspect of Cit. Īśvara is the fully risen creative consciousness wherein is the undifferentiated Śakti which functions as Icchā, Jñāna, Kriyā, Jñātṛtva or Jñāna. Śakti in Īśvara does not involve limited modification, for the whole universe as the Self is present to Self. But in Puruṣa there is such a modification; the Jñātṛtva functioning through Buddhi, the Vṛttss of which are expressions of the changing, limited, and partial characteristics of the knowledge had through this instrument and its derivatives.

The citation continues, "But in what constitutes therein the part "Kiṁcit" as a qualifying aspect, Kalā gives birth to the Pradhāna which arises from that (Kiṁcit aspect) as a clear but general objectivity which is separate or distinct from (the Puruṣa)."

Evam kalākhya-tattvasya kiṁcit-kartṛtva-lakṣaṇe.
Viśeṣyabhāge kartṛtvam carcitam bhoktṛ-pūrvakam
Viśeṣanatayā yo'tra kiṁcit bhāgas-tadūbitam
Vedyomātram sphutam bhinnam pradhānam sūyate kalā.

That is Kartṛtva is that aspect of Kalā which is characterised by Kiṁcit-Kartṛtva. From the qualifying (Viśeṣaṇa, that is, Kiṁcit) aspect Kalā produces Prakṛti which is distinct from Kalā as Puruṣa, which Prakṛti exists as a mere general objectivity which becomes particular when owing to disequilibrium in the Guṇas the Vikṛtis are produced.

Again it is said (ibid) : " Kalā produces the Bhogya (Prakṛti) and the Bhoktā (Puruṣa) simultaneously by the notion of, or by seeking to establish a difference between the two aspects in Herself, namely, Kartṛtva and Kiṁcit ; by working on Kartṛtva alone), (yet), the Bhoktā and Bhogya are inseparate from one another. And because what is thus the barest objectivity (Samvedya-mātra) is known (or experienced) later as (or in the form of) happiness (Sukha) sorrow (Duhkha) and delusion (Vimoha) it is therefore called the equalisation of these (three) in the beginning."

Samāmeva hi bhogyam ca bhoktāram ca prasūyate
kalā bhedābhisaṁdhānād aviyuktam parasparam.
Evam samvedyamātram yat sukhaduhkha-vimohatah,
bhotsyate yet tatah proktam tatsāmyātmakam āditoh).

When Māyā-S'akti first severs the " Aham " and " Idam " this latter is still experienced as an unlimited whole. The next step is that in which the whole is limited and broken up into parts, for our experience is not of an all-pervading homogeneous whole but of a heterogeneous universe. Kalā, as a development of Māyā-S'akti, belittles the Puruṣa's hitherto unlimited Agency which thus becomes Kiṁcit-Kartṛtva. Agency which exists both as to the Knowable (Jñeya) and object of action (Kārya) has two aspects, namely the qualified power of action (Viśeṣya-Kartṛtva) on the part of the Puruṣa and the object or " little " in respect of which Kartṛtva operates, namely the " little " or universe (Kiṁcit or Viśeṣaṇa) which is the " Idam " as viewed by Puruṣa after the operation of Kalā Śakti. Kalā operates on agency (Kartṛttva) and not on the " this " which is by such operation necessarily Kiṁcit. For if the power and experience of the Self is limited, the object is experienced as limited ; for the object is nothing but the Self as object. In other words the production of Puruṣa is a positive operation of Kalā whereas the production of Prakṛti is a negative operation due to the limitation of the Puruṣa which as so limited, experiences the universe as Kiṁcit. Prakṛti is thus nothing but the object of Kartṛttva, as it exists when the latter has been whittled down by Kalā. Puruṣa and Prakṛti thus both emerge as the result of the action by Kalā on the Puruṣa. For this reason Puruṣa and Prakṛti are simultaneously produced and are also inseparable.

The following chapters deal with Puruṣa and Prakṛti or Hamsa ; the Kāmakalā or three Bindus arising on the differentiation of the Para-bindu which differentiation witnesses the birth of Hamsa ; and then with the creation of the impure Tattvas (Aśuddha-Tattva) from Prakṛti and the Varṇamālā or the Garland or Rosary of Letters the evolution of which denotes the origin of speech and of Mantra.

CHAPTER XVI

HAMSA

HAMSA is Puruṣa-Prakṛti-Tattva. Ham is "Male" or Śiva ; Sah is "Female" and Śakti. Śiva-Śakti are therefore Hamsa which combined mean the "Bird" Hamsa, the material shape of which is variously said to be that of the goose, flamingo, brāhminī duck and rightly by others to be legendary. The universe is made of, and informed by this Hamsa Pair (Hamsa-dvandva) who are Puruṣa and Prakṛti and in all the latter's varied forms (*Pumprakṛtyātmako hamsas tadātmakam idam jagat*). Of these the Ānandalaharī says (39) "In Thy Anāhata Lotus I salute the Wondrous Pair who are Ham and Sah, swimming in the mind of the Great who ever delight in the honey of the blooming lotus of knowledge." That is, they manifest in the mind of the Great delighting in the honey of Consciousness. This Hamsah reversed is the Vedantic "So'ham" of which the Sammohana-Tantra (Ch. VIII) says "Hakāra is one wing. Sakāra is the other. When stripped of both wings then Tāra is Kāmakalā." Jīva is Hamsa. The same Tantra says that the Sādhaka of Tāra is the Lord of both Kādi and Hādi Mata. The Hamsatārā-Mahā-vidyā is the sovereign mistress of Yoga whom the Kādis call Kalī, the Hādis Śrīsundarī and the Ka-Hādis Hamsah.

The Jñānārṇava-Tantra (xxi-22) speaking of the Citkuṇḍa as the Maṇḍala in the Mūlādhāra where Homa is done, defines as follows the four Ātmās, viz., Paramātmā, Antarātmā, Jñānātmā and Ātmā which form the Cit-kuṇḍa and by the knowledge whereof there is no rebirth. Ātmā is Prāṇarūpī, that is the Ātmā which is in all beings as their Prāṇa. It is Hamsa-Svarūpī or Jīvātmā manifested by outer and inner breathing (Svāsa, Ucchvāsa). It is compared to the ether in a pot, which the potter's wheel separates from the surrounding Ākāśa but from which there is no distinction when the pot is broken. The individual breath is the Cosmic Breath from which it seems to be different by the forms which the latter vitalises. Jñānātmā is Sākṣat-sākṣirūpaka. It is that which witnesses all and by which the unity of all is known. It is reflected in Buddhi and the rest, and is yet in its own form distinguishable therefrom, just as the rays of the moon are reflected on water and seem to be, and are yet not, one with it. It is thus the substratum of Buddhi and of all the subjective or mental Tattvas derivable therefrom. By "Antar" in the term Antarātmā is meant the subtle (Rahasya-sūkṣmarūpaka) Ātmā which pervades all things; the spark of Paramātmā which indwells all bodies (Antargata). It is the Hamsa known only by Yogīs. Its beak is Tāra (Praṇava or "Om" Mantra), Nigama and Āgama are its two wings. Śiva and Śakti its two feet. The three Bindus are its three eyes. This is the Paramahamsa; that is Hamsa in its supreme aspect as the Consciousness ground of the manifested Hamsa or Jīva. When this Paramahamsa is spread (Vyāpta), that is, displayed, then all forms of matter (Bhūta) viz., Ākāśa, Pavana and the rest spring up in their order. Of these five the root is Citta. This Hamsa disports itself in the World-lotus sprung from the Mud of Delusion (Mohapaṇka) in the Lake of Ignorance (Avidyā). When this Hamsa becomes unworldly (Niṣprapañca) and in dissolving form (Samhārarūpī) then it makes visible the Ātmā or Self (*Ātmānam pradarśayet*). Then its "Birdness" (Pakṣitva) disappears and the So'ham Ātmā is established. "Know this" says the Jñānārṇava "to be the Paramātmā."

Puruṣa is Ātmā subject to Māyā-Śakti and the other limiting Śaktis called the Kañcukas. Prakṛti is that state of Śakti which arises as the result of the collective operation of Māyā and the Kañcukas; a transformation of Śakti existing as a homogeneity and general objectivity which develops of its own power, which is the summation of the Śaktis producing it, into the heterogeneous universe. The Puruṣa-Prakṛti-Tattvas arise as a bifurcation in Consciousness on the differentiation of the Para-bindu into the three Bindus which form the Kāmakalā which again may be pictured as the triangular base of the pyramidal (Śṛṁgātaka) figure in the Śrī-Yantra at whose apex is the Baindava-Cakra and Parabindu. The first two Bindus represent the Śiva aspect and the Śakti aspect of the one Consciousness, and the third the mutual relation or Śiva-Śakti aspect of the two. From this differentiation arises in the Mantra line of creation, Paraśabda and manifested Śabda and Artha; in the Tattva line, Buddhi and the rest; and in the line of the Lords of the Tattvas (Tattveśa), Śambhu and the rest. In its most general and philosophical sense Puruṣa-Prakṛti represent that stage in the evolving Consciousness (Śakti) in which, after passing from the mere I-experience (*Aham-pratyaya-vimārśa*), and the "I-this" or "Aham-Idam," experience, in which the object or Idam is still experienced as part of the self (the completed type of such experiencer being Īśvara). Consciousness emerges as the experience of duality in which the object is seen as outside of, and separate from, the self. This however is a state of mere general objectivity. The final state has yet to be described when undifferentiated objectivity and supreme Sound (Paraśabda) evolve, the first into the differentiated objects of the universe (Aśuddha-Tattva) and the second into the differentiated word (S'abda) and its meaning (Artha) which is the birth of Mantra consisting of letters (Varṇa), syllables (Pada) and sentences (Vākya). With the differentiation of Prakṛti appear multitudinous Puruṣas of varying experience, each living in a universe of its own.

Puruṣa is not merely confined to man but is applicable to every Jīva who is the Enjoyer (Bhoktā) or Puruṣa of the enjoyable (Bhogya) or Prakṛti. Puruṣa again is not limited to the organic life of animals and plants or the micro-organisms which hover between organic and inorganic matter. The term includes the latter also. For whatever may be the popular signification of the term Jīva as living organic bodies, in its philosophical sense all is Jīvātmā which is not Paramātmā. And in this, modern science bears out the notions here described. The former arbitrary partitions made between the living and non-living are being broken down. We may for practical purposes call that " living " which obviously displays certain characteristics which we call " life " such as the so-called vital phenomena manifested by plants, animals and men. But the life and consciousness displayed in organic bodies is not something wholly new which had no place in the inorganic material of which they are composed. All such vital phenomena exist in subdued or potential form in every kind of matter which contains the potentiality of all life. Life as we know it is the phenomenal aspect of Being-Itself (Sat). Feeling-Consciousness as we know it is the limited manifestation (manifestation being limitation) of the undifferentiated Feeling-Consciousness which is Cit, Sat and Ānanda. All which is manifested exists potentially in its ground. Each of such manifestations is such ground (Bhūmi) veiled in varying degrees ; now more, now less, fully displaying the nature of Spirit, the source of all life, feeling, will and consciousness. Superficial notions based on appearances have given rise to the notion of " dead " matter. But science has given new instruments for and extended the range of our observation and has shown that life and consciousness, though in a subdued or veiled form, exist throughout the universe. Vedānta in its Sākta version says that all forms are the operation of Consciousness as Māyā-Sakti. As the ancient Upaniṣad says and modern so-called " New Thought " repeats " What one thinks that one becomes." All recognise this principle to a certain point. If man thinks inhuman thoughts he dehumanises himself. Vedānta carries the application of this principle to its logical conclusion and affirms that not only does thought operate modifications in and within the limits of particular types or species, but actually evolves such and all other types through the cosmic or collective Thought of which the universe is a material expression. Thus every unit or atom of matter is a Puruṣa identifying itself with the solid (Pārthiva) " crust " of matter, which is the gross expression on the sensual plane of more subtle forces emanating from that Ground Substance, which is the source both of the

experiencing subject and the object experienced. If
the operation of gross matter gives the appearance of
rigid mechanism, this does not imply that such operation is wholly unconscious and lifeless, but that life and
consciousness are veiled by the Tamas Guṇa of Prakṛti
in which Kalā, Niyati and other Kañcukas are operating
to their fullest extent. But however intense may be their
operation, life and consciousness can never be destroyed, for being S'akti Herself they are indestructible.
Thus every molecule of mineral substance is Puruṣa
or Consciousness identifying itself with matter in its
solid and apparently unconscious inert state. For
Consciousness becomes that with which it identifies
itself. When it completely identifies itself with
mineral matter it becomes that matter. What we think
that we become. Nothing however is absolutely
unconscious or inert. Every single atom in the universe
is in constant movement and hence the world is called
Jagat or that which moves. This scientific doctrine is
in India an ancient inheritance. And so the Mantra
runs " Hrim. The Supreme Hamsa dwells in the
brilliant Heaven." The word Hamsa is here said to be
derived from the word Hanti which means Gati or
motion. Sāyaṇa says that it is called Āditya because
it is in perpetual motion. The Tattva-Saṁdoha
(vv. 13, 14) says :

" She is considered to be Prakṛti who is the
collectivity of all the S'aktis, (Will, Knowledge and
Action) who is the peaceful, that is, quiescent (S'āntā)
S'akti of Him in contracted form (Saṁkucadrūpā) ; who
is in the form of the equilibrium of Sattva, Rajas and
Tamas Guṇas which again are Will, Knowledge and
Action gathered together (Saṁkalita) ; who is in the
nature of general unparticularised feeling (Citta) which

is in the form of the undifferentiated Buddhi (and other Tattvas). "

Icchādi-tri-samaṣṭih
  śaktih śāntā'sya saṁkucadrūpā.
Saṁkalitechādyātmaka
  sattvādika-sāmya-rupiṇī saiva.
Buddhyādi-sāmarasya-
  svarūpacittātmika matā prakṛtih.

" Ham " or the male (Pumān) or Puruṣa is again in the same work (v. 6) described as :

" He who having by Her become of limited form with all His powers contracted is this Male (Pumān or Puruṣa) like the sun which becoming red at eventide and His Power (of shining) contracted can scarce reveal Himself (by shining abroad) "

Sa tayā parimitamūrtih
  saṁkucita-samastaśaktir esa pumān.
Raviriva saṁdhyā-raktah
  samhṛtā-śaktih svabhāsane' pyapatih.

Again in the same work (v. 7) it is said :

" His S'aktis are many consisting of complete Kartṛtva (power of action) and others, but on His becoming contracted (that is, limited) they also become contracted in the forms of Kalā and the rest and make him thus manifest (as Puruṣa) "

Sampūrṇa-kartṛtādya
  bahvyah santyasya śaktayas tasya.
Saṁkocāt saṁkucitāh
  kalādirūpeṇa rūdhayanty evam.

Again in the Īśvara-Pratyabhījñā it is said :

"He who is Experiencer commencing with S'ūnya (S'iva-tattva) and the rest, He being clothed by the five Kañcukas, Kāla and the rest, and becoming object to Himself, is then the Experiencer of objects as separate form Him".

Yas' ca pramātā śunyādih prameye vyatirekiṇi
Māta bhavati meyah san kālādi-pari veṣṭitah.

(III-ii 9)

That is, object is the Self appearing as such. He retains His own Self-hood and becomes at the same time the object of His' own experience. Māyā, is not something apart from Brahman, for it is Brahman who through Māyā, an aspect of Brahman, Himself becomes His own object. In the first act of creation He commences to become His own object, but it is only when the subject as Puruṣa is clothed, that is limited, by the Kañcukas, that the latter sees objects as other than and outside Himself. At this stage duality is established and exfoliates in the Vikṛtis of Prakṛtis as the multiple experience of the World of Mind and Matter.

The Guṇas of Prakṛti are inadequately translated as "qualities", because the latter word involves some substance of which they are the qualities. But Prakṛti S'akti is, as Prakṛti, the Guṇas and nothing else, though Her Svarūpa, as that of all S'aktis, is Sat-Cit-Ānanda. The Guṇas Sattva, Rajas, Tamas are properly factors or constituents of Prakṛti. Of these it is commonly said that Tamas Guṇa is the veiling principle of Prakṛti. This is so. But nevertheless it is to be remembered that all the factors of Prakṛti in one way or another veil ; the difference being that whereas Sattva to some

degree veils (for Sattvaguṇa is not as such the same as
absolute Sat) it is in its highest degree of potency, that
is, predominance, the least degree of veiling, and therefore it represents the tendency to unveil, that is, to
reveal and manifest Being (Sat) and Consciousness
(Cit) ; whereas Tamas is in its highest potency the
greatest degree of veiling and therefore specifically
represents the tendency to veil. Rajas is the operative
power in both cases. In all bodies there are the three
Guṇas (for these cannot separately exist though one or
other may predominate), and it is because of this and
therefore of the presence of Sattva-Guṇa in organic
matter that it exhibits the rudiments of sentiency and
consciousness. But in inorganic matter Tamas Guṇa
prevails. As bodies evolve, the strength of the operation of Tamas gradually diminishes and that of Sattva
increases until in man it becomes predominant. The
whole object of Sādhana is to increase Sattva-Guṇa
until, on man becoming wholly Sāttvika, his body
passes from the state of predominant Sattva-Guṇa into
Sat Itself. These Guṇas represent in the Jīva or Paśu
the Icchā, Kriyā, Jñāna and Māyā-Śaktis of the Lord.
As regards Māyā, the Lord (Māyin), as the Kulārṇava-
Tantra says, wields and controls and is free of it; Jīva
is controlled by it. So the Īśvara-Pratyabijñā (IV. 1, 4)
says, " What are Jñāna and Kriyā (on the part) of the
Lord (Pati) in all beings and things (Bhāveṣu) which
(to Him) are really of the nature of His own body (or
limbs)—it is these two (that is Jñāna and Kriyā) and
nothing else (eva) which together with Māyā as the
third are the Sattva, Rajas, and Tamas. (Guṇas in
respect) of the Paśu ".

Svāṅga-rūpeṣū bhāveṣu patyurjñānaṁ kriyā ca yā.
Māyā tṛtīyā tā eva paśoh sattvam rajas tamah.

Siva-śakti has a threefold aspect as Icchā, Jñāna, Kriyā, which are inseparably associated, just as the Guṇas are, though, as in the latter case, one or other may be predominant. Of these again Icchā and Kriyā may be considered together ; for as resolve is directed to action it is the preliminary of it. Icchā in the Śaiva-Śāstra is described as a state of wonder (*Sa camatkārā Icchāśaktih*) in the Puruṣa. But Kriyā considered (for the purpose of analysis only) as apart from Jñāna is blind. For this reason Kriyā has been associated with Tamas. It is very clearly explained by Kṣemarāja in his Tattva-Sandoha (vv. 13-15), that Icchā or resolve to action becomes at a lower stage Rajas Guṇa, the principle of activity in Prakṛti ; Jñāna becomes Sattva or the principle of manifestation in the same ; and Kriyā becomes Tamas Guṇa or the specific veiling principle of the same form of Śakti. He says, " His Will (Icchā) assumed the form of Rajas and became Ahaṁkāra which produces the notion of ' I ' (Aham). His knowledge (Jñāna) likewise became Sattvarūpa and Buddhi which is the determining form of experience. His Kriyā being in the nature of Tamas and productive of Vikalpa (and Saṁkalpa) *i.e.*, rejection (and selection) is called Manas " (*Icchāsya rajo-rūpāhaṁkṛti-rāsid ahampratītikari jñānāpi śattvarūpā nirṇaya-bhodhasya kāraṇam buddhih, Tasya kriyā tamomaya-mūrtir mana ucyate vikalpakari*).

The evolution of these Tattvas (Aśuddha) is the subject of a future chapter. But before dealing with these it is necessary, in the creative order, to further describe the Kāmakalā in which the Hamsa arises and the Rosary or Garland of letters (Varṇamālā) which is the Mantra aspect of the Tāttvika evolution will come later.

CHAPTER XVII

KĀMAKALĀ

IN the previous chapters it has been shown that the Parabindu or Īśvara Tattva assumes in creation a threefold aspect as the three Bindus,—Bindu (Kārya), Nāda, Bīja. These three points constitute symbolically a Triangle which is known as the Kāmakalā. Kāma is of course not here used in the gross sense of desire, sexual or otherwise, but of Icchā, the Divine creative Will towards the life of form, which·is here explicated from Bindu, the aspect previously assumed by Śakti through Nāda (*Bindutām abhyeti*). The undivided supreme Cit-śakti (*Akhaṇḍa-paracicchakti*) becoming desirous of appearing as all the Tattvas (*Samasta-tattva-bhāvena vivarttecchāsamanvitā*) assumes the Bindu aspect (*Bindubhāvam paryeti*) characterised by a predominance of activity (*Kriyā-prādhānya-lakṣaṇā*). Here it may be observed that Icchā or Will is a form of Kriyā (action), in the sense that it is the preliminary to action and sets the Self in motion. Śakti passes from potency through Will to action, which through Para Bindu manifests. Bindu-bhāva is that state (Īśvara-tattva) in which it is fully equipped to work and does so. Its threefold aspect as it works are Bindu Śivātmaka, Bīja, Śaktyātmaka and Nāda. Nāda is Samavāya that is relationship or connection (Sambandha) as exciter (Kṣobhaka) and that which is excited (Kṣobhya), which relation is the cause of

creation (Sṛṣṭihetu). The Sārada (I. 10) then proceeds
to deal with the appearance of the three Devīs and
three Devas which are in the nature of the three Sáktis
(Icchā, etc.) and Fire, Moon and Sun. Having then
dealt with Sʼabda-sṛṣṭi it proceeds to describe Artha-
sṛṣṭi (I. 15), giving first the line of Devas from Sʼambhu
who are the Lords of the Tattvas (Tattveśa) and then
that part of Artha-sṛṣṭi which is Tattva-sṛṣṭi or the
evolution of the Tattvas of mind and matter from
Buddhi to Pṛthivī.

It is not easy in all cases to discover and set forth
an accurate summary of the Devīs, Devas, Sʼaktis and
so forth in Sʼabda-sṛṣṭi : because the Texts being in verse
are not always to be read as they stand, the order of
words being in some cases regulated by the metre. As
the author of the Prāṇatoṣiṇī says in dealing with a
citation from the Gorakṣa-Saṁhita, the texts must not
be read " Pratiśabdam ", that is, according to the order
of the words, but "Yathāsambhavam", according to the
facts. But this does not relieve us from the difficulty of
ascertaining what is the fact; that is the real order.
Other elements may also enter into the calculation : for
instance, as Rāghava-Bhatta points out, the order of
Sʼaktis varies in Īśvara and Jīva. In the former it is
Icchā, Jñāna and Kriyā and in Jīva, Jñānā, Icchā and
Kriyā. In Īśvara's ideation (Pratyabhijñā) when He
desires to do anything, an act of volition proceeds
from Him (*Svecchayā kriyā*) to know or to do it (*Tat
jñātum karlum vā*); next there is the capacity for
cognising such acts (*Tat kārya-jñāna-darśana-sahtitā*)
which is Jñānaśakti ; thirdly the gross efforts (*Sthūlah
samudyamah*) is the Kriyā-śakti (*Kriyāśaktitā*) from which
the whole world proceeds (*Tatah sarvam jagat param*).
Rāghava also points out that there is a difference of

order in S'abda-sṛṣṭi and Artha-sṛṣṭi. Thus in dealing with the Praṇava it is said, " A (the letter) which is Sun is Brahmā ": but here in the S'āradā verse, " Viṣṇu is Sun." I will first give the order as it is given in the S'āradā Text (v. 10): " From Bindu came Raudrī; from Nāda Jyeṣṭhā, from Bijā, Vāmā. From these came Rudra, Brahmā, Ramādhipa (Viṣṇu)".

Raudrī bindos tato nādaj jyeṣṭhā bijād ajāyata
Vāmā, tābhvah samutpannā rudrabrahmaramādhipāh.

It then continues, " Who are in the nature of Jñāna, Icchā, Kriya and Fire, Moon and Sun (v. 11) (*Samjñanecchākriyātmāno vahnindvarkasvarūpiṇah*), who are in the form (Rūpa) of Nirodhikā, Arddhendu and Bindu." These are all different states of S'akti (*S'akterevāvasthāviśeṣāh*), for it is owing to their arising from S'akti (*S'aktitah utpannatvāt*), that they are identified with the S'aktis Icchā and so forth.

According to the Yoginī-hṛdaya-Tantra (I) the order is (*a*) Icchā, Vāmā, Paśyantī; (*b*) Jñānā, Jyeṣṭhā, Madhyamā; (*c*) Kriyā, Raudrī, Vaikharī. It says that when Icchā-S'akti in the form of a goad (Aṁkuśakāra, that is, the bent line Vakrarekhā) is about to display the universe which is in seed (Bija) form, She is Vāmā and in the form of Paśyantī S'abda. Paśyantī " She who sees," Īkṣaṇa. Vāmā is so called because this S'akti vomits forth the universe (*Vamanāt Vāmā*). Jyeṣṭhā which is in the form of a straight line (Ṛjurekhā) attaining the state of Mātṛkā (*Mātṛkatvam upapannā*) is Madhyamā vāk. Raudrī is Kriyā in triangular or pyramidal (S'ṛṅgātaka), that is, three-dimensional form, and is the manifested Vaikharī-S'abda. According to the Kāmakalāvilāsa (Comm. v. 22), Yoginī-hṛdaya-Tantra (Saṁketa 1), and the Saubhāgyasudhodaya (cited in Saṁketa) (2) of the last S'āstra), the order would appear to be (*a*) Icchā Rajas Vāmā Brahmā Paśyantī-S'abda ; (*b*) Jñāna Sattva Jyeṣṭhā Viṣṇu Madhyamā-S'abda ; (*c*) Kriyā Tamas Raudṛī Rudra Vaikharī-S'abda.

I will not however here attempt a discussion, which would be both lengthy and technical, of the texts on this point. For present practical purposes it is sufficient to know that the three Bindus are S'iva, S'akti, S'ivaśakti; Prakāśa, Vimarśa, Prakāśa-Vimarśa ; White, Red and Mixed ; Bindu, Nāda, Bīja ; Supreme, Subtle, Gross ; the three Devīs, the three Devas, and the three S'aktis of Will, Knowledge and Action. The Supreme at this point thus becomes a Trinity of Energy.

The division of the Mahābindu may de memorised by writing in Sanskrit the "Fire" Bīja or "Raṁ", that is Ra with Candra-bindu. Then invert the Nāda sign which will thus represent the Moon (Indu), the Bindu, the Sun (Ravi), and the Ra, Fire (Agni). The Triangle may be formed by drawing two sides or a bent line and then completing it with a straight line. At the apex place the Ravi-bindu (Sun) and at the left and right hand corners Vahni-bindu (Fire) and Moon (Candrabindu). Between Sun and Moon place Vāmā Vakrarekha and Brahmā ; between Fire and Moon, Jyeṣṭha, and Viṣṇu, and between Moon and Sun, Raudrī, Ṛjurekhā and Rudra. Between each of the points are lines formed by all the letters (Mātṛkāvarṇa) of the alphabet called the A-Ka-Tha triangle. The Pādukāpañcaka, a Hymn attributed to S'iva, (See *The Serpent Power*) speaks of A-Ka-Tha in the second verse on which Kālīcaraṇa comments as follows : Here S'akti is Kāmakalā in form and the three S'aktis (Vāmā,

Jyeṣṭhā, Raudrī) emanating from the three Bindus are
the three lines. The sixteen vowels beginning with A
form the line Vāmā, the sixteen letters beginning with
Ka form the line Jyeṣṭhā and sixteen letters beginning
with Tha form the line Raudrī. The abode of S'akti
(Abalālaya) is formed by these three lines. The other
three letters Ha, La, Kṣa are in the corners of the
Triangle. Kāluyrādhvamnāya says, " The Tribindu
is the Supreme Tattva and embodies in Itself Brahmā,
Viṣṇu, Siva (*Brahma-viṣṇu-śivātmakam*). The Triangle
composed of the Letters has emanated from the Bindu;"
also "The letters A to Visarga make the line Brahmā,
the letters Ka to Tha the line Viṣṇu, and the letters
Tha to Sa the Rudra. The three lines emanate from
three Bindus. The Guṇas, as aspects of S'akti, are also
represented by this threefold division. The Tantrojīvana
says : "The lines Rajas, Sattva, Tamas surround the
Yonimaṇḍala." Also "above is the line of Sattva, the
line of Rajas is on its left and the line of Tamas on its
right."

The S'abda-brahman in its threefold aspect and
Energies is represented in the Tantras by this triangular
Kāmakalā which is the abode of S'akti (Abalālaya).
The Triangle is in every way an apposite symbol, for
on the material plane if there are three forms there is
no other way in which they can be brought to interact
except in the form of a triangle in which whilst they
are each, as aspects, separate and distinct from one
another, they are yet related to each other and form
part of one whole. In the Āgamakalpadruma it is said
that the Bindu is Ham (one point) and Visargah (two
points) is Sah or S'akti. The Yāmala thus speaks of
this abode. ' I now speak of Kāmakalā," and proceeding says, " She is the Eternal One who is the

three Bindus, the three S'aktis and the three forms (Trimūrti) ". The Māheśvarī-Samhitā says : "Sun, Moon and Fire are the three Bindus and Brahmā, Viṣṇu, Rudra the three lines." The Lalitasahasranāma calls the Devi Kāmakalārūpā. Bhāskararāya in his commentary thereon (v. 73) says that Kāma or creative will (Icchā) is both S'iva and Devī and Kalā is their manifestation. Hence it is called Kāmakalā. This is explained in the Tripurasiddhānta : " Oh Pārvati, Kalā is the manifestation of Kāmeśvara and Kāmeśvari. Hence She is known as Kāmakalā. Or, She is the manifestation (Kalā) of Desire (Kāma), that is, of Icchā-Sakti. The Devī is the great Tripurasundari. Bhāskararāya's Guru Nṛsimhānandanātha wrote the following verse on which the disciple comments :

" I hymn Tripuré, the treasure of Kula, who is red of beauty ; Her limbs like unto those of Kāmarāja who is adored by the three Devatās of the three Guṇas; who is the desire or Will of S'iva (according to the Anekārthadhvani-manjari lexicon, I = Manmatha = Kāma = Icchā) who dwells in the Bindu and who manifests the Universe." She is red because She is the Vimarśa-śakti. She is called (says the Commentator cited) Tripuré as She has three (Tri) Purās (literally cities or abodes), here meaning three Bindus, lines, angles, syllables and so forth. She has three angles (in the triangular Yoni, the source of the universe) as well as three circles (the three Bindus) and Bhūpura of Her Yantra has three lines. Yoni does not here mean generative organ, but Kārāṇa—the Cause of the universe. She has three aspects and creates the three Devatās through the three S'aktis, Vāmā and others, and manifests as Will, Knowledge and Action. Thus since She the Supreme Energy is everywhere triple, She is

called Tripurasundari. The three syllables of Her
Mantra are the three divisions of the Pañcadaśī, namely
Vāgbhava, Kāmarāja and Śakti Kūtas, which according
to the Vāmakeśvara-Tantra are the Jñāna and other
Śaktis. The Kāma bīja is Klīm and Klīm-kāra is
Śivakāma. Here "Ī" is said to denote the Kāmakalā
in the Turīya state through which Mokṣa is gained,
and hence the meaning of the saying that "he who
hears the Bīja without Kā and Ī does not reach the
place of good actions"—that is he does not go to the
region attainable by good actions but to that (Mokṣa)
attainable by Jñāna alone. The Bhāva-cūḍāmaṇi says :
" Meditate on the face in the form of Bindu, and
below on the twin breasts (the two other Bindus) and
below them the beauteous form of the Hakārarddha.
The commentator on the Ānandalahari says: In the
fifth sacrifice (Yajña) let the Sādhaka think of his
Ātmā as in no wise different from, but as the one and
only Śiva ; and of the subtle thread-like Kuṇḍalinī
who is all Śaktis extending from the Ādhāra Lotus to
Paramaśiva. Let him think of the three Bindus as
being in Her body indicating Icchā, Jñāna, Kriyā ;
Moon, Sun, Fire ; Rajas, Sattva, Tamas; Brahmā,
Viṣṇu, Rudra ; and then let him meditate upon the
Cit-kalā who is Śakti below it." The Bindu which is
the "Face" indicates Viriñci (Brahmā) associated
with the Rajas Guṇa. The two Bindus which are the
" Breasts " and upon which meditation should be done
in the heart indicate Hari (Viṣṇu) and Hara (Rudra)
associated with the Sattva and Tamas Guṇas. Below
these meditate upon the subtle Cit-kalā which indicates
all three Guṇas and which is all these three Devatās.
Similar meditation is given in Yoginī (and other)
Tantras winding up with the direction, "and then let
the Sādhaka think of his own body as such Kāmakalā.

As regards this it is to be observed that in the
Mūlādhāra there is a Traipura-Trikoṇa, so-called
because of the presence of the Devī Tripuré within the
Kā inside the triangle. This Kā is the chief letter of
the Kāma-Bija and Kam is the Bija of Kāminī, the
aspect of Tripurasundari in the Mūlādhāra. Here also
are the three lines, Vāmā, Icchā and so forth. Thus
the Traipura Trikona is the Sthūla aspect of the
Sūkṣma-Śakti in the region of the upper Sahasrāra
called Kāmakalā. It is to this Kāminī that in worship
the essence of Japa (Tejo-rūpa-japa) is offered, the
external Japa being given to the Devatā worshipped in
order that the Sādhaka may retain the fruits of his
Japa. (*Nityapūjāpaddhati 8*). Man physically and
practically is a limited manifestation of this threefold
Śakti which resides within himself and is the object of
worship. Such worship leads to identification and so
the Śritattvārṇava says: "Those glorious men who
worship that Body in Sāmarasya are freed from the
waves of poison in the untraversable sea of the universe
(Samsāra)." Sāmarasya, I may here observe, is a term
which is ordinarily applied to the bliss of sexual union
(*Strīpumyogāt yat saukhyam tat sāmarasyam*). For the
benefit however of those who are always reading gross
meanings into parts of the Śastra alien to them it is
necessary to explain that Sāmarasya is both gross
(Sthūla) and subtle (Sūkṣma). Here the latter is meant.
An erotic symbol is employed to denote the merger of
the Jīva and Supreme Consciousness in Ecstasy
(Samādhi). The Tantras largely employ such imagery
which is to be found in the Upaniṣads and in non-
Indian scriptures. Thus the highly sensual imagery of
the Biblical " Song of Songs " is said (whether rightly
or not, I will not here inquire) to symbolise Christ's

love for His Bride, the Church. Spiritual union is symbolised by terms borrowed from the world of man. By Mantra-yoga is sought that perfection and unity of Bhāva which leads to Jñānayoga Samādhi.

" On the division of the Supreme Bindu (into the threefold Kāmakalā) there was the Unmanifested Sound " (*Bhidyamānāt parād bindor avyaktātmā ravo'bhavat,* Sārada-I-11). This is the Sabda-brahman or the Brahman as the cause of manifested Sabda and Artha and therefore of Mantra. This causal " Sound " is the unmanifested (Avyaktātmā), undifferentiated (Akhaṇḍa) principle of Sabda (Nādamātra), composed of Nāda and Bindu (Nādabindumaya) devoid of all particularity such as letters and the like (Varṇādiviśeṣa-rahita). Some, as the Sārada says (V. 12), have thought that the Sabda-brahman was Sabda and others Sab-dārtha, but this cannot be, for both are unconscious (Jadatvāt). " In my opinion," its author says (v. 13), " Sabda-brahman is the Consciousness in all beings " (*Caitanyaṁ sarvabhūtānāṁ śabda-brahmeti me matih*). For if Sabdārtha or Sabda be called Sabda-brahman then the meaning of the term Brahman is lost (*Brahmapada-vācyatvaṁ nopapadyate*); for the meaning of the term Brahman (Brahmapadartha) is Sat-Cit-Ānanda (Sacci-dānandarūpa), whilst these are unconscious (Jada). Rāghava-Bhatta says that Sabda-brahman is Nāda-bindumaya Brahman (Brahmātmaka) Sound (Sabda) unmanifested (Avyakta), undifferentiated (Akhaṇḍa), all prevading (Vyāpaka), which is the first mani-festation of Paramaśiva in creative mood (*Sṛṣṭyunmukha-paramaśiva-prathamollāsamātram*). He also cites a passage from some work unnamed which says that out of Prakṛti in Bindu form in whom Kriyā-Sakti prevails (*Kriyāśaktipradhānāyo prakṛter bindu-rūpinyāh*) arose the

Supreme S'abda-brahman, the cause of S'abda and Sabdārtha (Sabdaśabdārthakāraṇam). The Sound (Rava) here spoken of is in the form of Bindu-rūpa), which later appears in all bodies as the Mātṛkās and Varṇas in their respective places. The S'āradā (1.14) having thus dealt with Paraśabdāsṛṣṭi concludes in a general way, " Consciousness which is the Svarūpa of, and appears as, Kuṇḍali-S'akti in the bodies of all living beings manifests as Letters in prose and verse, having obtained the instruments for utterance which are the throat and so forth."

Tat prāpya kuṇḍalīrūpaṁ prāṇināṁ dehamadhyagam.
Varṇātmanāvirbhavati gadyapādyādibhedataḥ.

The subsequent Sabdasṛṣṭi is derived from Kuṇḍalinī. The Kāmakalā is thus called the root (Mūla) of all Mantras, for it is the threefold aspect of the S'abda-brahman, the cause of all manifested S'abda and Artha and therefore Mantra. In a future article I will continue the account of the creative process, namely, the Artha-sṛṣṭi in which are included the Tattvas from Buddhi to Pṛthivī and the Lords (Tattveśa) or forms of Consciousness which preside over them. These are necessarily dealt with in connection with Tattvas over which they preside. In the same way Paśyantī, Madhyamā, and Vaikharī states of sound are also dealt with, because Paśyantī and the others only exist in the created body. Paraśabda is unmanifested Caitanya, but the other Three Feet of the One Brahman are set in the manifested world of Mind and Matter.

CHAPTER XVIII

THE GROSS TATTVAS AND THEIR LORDS

THE S'aradā-Tilaka (Chapter I) having first
dealt with S'abdasṛṣṭi on account of its priority
(*Prādhānyadyotanāya prathamoddiṣṭam*) commences with
the fifteenth verse to speak of the creation of objects
(Artha-sṛṣṭi), for Paśyantī and the other Bhāvas assume
the existence of the manifested body. It says that from
S'ambhu who is in the nature of Kalā (*Kalātmanah*) and
Bindu (*Bindvātmanah*) and friend of Kāla (Kālabandhu),
issued (Ajāyata) the "Witness of the World"
(Jagatsākṣi), the all-pervading (Sarvavyāpī) Sadāśiva.
Rāghava says Kalā is here either used generally, or
as refering to the Nivṛtti and other Kalās which
S'ambhu produces. By "friend of Kāla" is meant
that S'ambhu is in the nature of Nāda (Nādātmā),
because in unbeginning and unending Time He is
the helper of Kāla which is Sṛṣṭi (*Anādyanante kāle
sṛṣṭirūpakālasahāyāt*). The connection again is one
between cause and its possessor. Again "friend"
indicates the causality (Nimittatvam) of Kāla. For it
has been said : "It has its beginning in Lava and ends
in Pralaya and is full of Tamas S'akti." Lava is the
time taken to pierce with a needle a lotus-petal. Thirty
Lavas = one Truṭi. This Kāla is Apara, for there is
also Para Kāla. Kāla or Māyā is the cause of the
occurrence of birth and destruction. Rāghava

concludes that Prakṛti and Kāla exist in even Mahāpralaya. But their permonence (Nityatā) is a dependent one (Apekṣakanityatā). For the permanence of the Puruṣa in which all things have their goal is alone independent (Svatabnityatvaṁ).

From Sambhu emanated the Sadāśiva who is the Doer of the five forms of work, namely Creation, Preservation and Destruction, Favour (Anugraha) and Disfavour (Nigraha). From Sadāśiva comes Īśa, from Him Rudra, from Rudra Viṣṇu, from Viṣṇu Brahmā (v. 16). On this verse Rāghava says : " It has been said before how they arise in Sabda-sṛṣṭi. Here they arise in Artha-sṛṭi. "

The five Sivas are known in the Tantras as the " Five great corpses " (Pañca-mahāpreta). Siva is constantly represented in corpse-like (Savarūpa) form. This symbolises that Consciousness in Itself (Svarūpa) is actionless and inert. All action is by Sakti Hence the Devi is in pictures imaged as standing on the inert corpse-like body of Siva. The same notion is represented by *Viparita-maithuna*, a prominent example of the use of erotic symbolism in the Sākta-Sastra. These Pañcamahāpreta form the couch on which the Devi, Wave of Consciousness and Bliss, rests in the house of Cintāmaṇi adorned with a garden of Nīpa trees, which is in the Island of Gems, surrounded with a grove of celestial trees, in the midst of the ocean of nectar (Ānandalahari). This is the well-known Tāntrika meditation on the Heart-lotus of worship below the Anāhata-cakra. The Bahurūpāṣṭaka and Bhairava-yāmala say : " There is the supreme abode (Mandira) of Devi full of Cintāmaṇi stones (which grant all desires) The great couch is Siva, the cushion or

mattress (Kaśipu) is Sadāśiva, the pillow the great
Īśāna. The four supports (Pada) are Īśāna, Rudra,
Hari, and Brahmā. On that bed reclines the supreme
Tripurasundarī." Hence the Devi in the Lalitāsahasranāma (v. 73) is called Pañca-brahmāsanasthitā. The
"Jewelled Island" is a high state of Consciousness in
that ocean of nectar which is the infinite all-pervading
Consciousness Itself. The Devi is united with Paramaśiva in the Praṇava ; the Nāda over the Oṁkāra being
the couch on which is resting Para-śiva in His Bindu
form. A, U, M, Nāda, Bindu the five component parts
of Om and the Srī-cakra Yantra are here referred to.

The supreme Paramaśiva abides in Satyaloka
beyond mind and matter. Saṁbhu presides over mind
and His abode is Maharloka. Ether, air, fire, water,
earth are presided over by Sadāśiva, Īśa, Rudra, Viṣṇu,
Brahmā whose abodes are Tapoloka, Janaloka, Svarloka,
Bhuvarloka, Bhūrloka ; and their centres in the human
body are in the Ājñā, Viśuddha, Anāhata, Maṇipūra,
Svādhiṣṭhāna and Mūlādhāra-Cakras, respectively.
Kuṇḍali-Sakti manifests as the six. But notwithstanding all Her subtle and gross manifestations She remains
ever the same Cit and Ānanda ; for the Ātmā in its own
nature (Svarūpa) as distinguished from its Powers and
their products is the same in all times and places.

Turning then to the Tattvas the Sārada says (v. 17)
that from the unmanifest Mūlabhūta (Prakṛti or root of
all creation) of the Supreme (Paravastu-Bindu) when
subject to change (Vikṛti) issued, through inequality of
the Guṇas, the Sāttvika-Tattva Mahat in the form of
the Antahkaraṇa and Guṇas.

Mahat is the cosmic Buddhi which is said to be in the
form of the Antahkaraṇa (Buddhi, Ahaṁkāra, Manas)

for all three are implicitly contained in the first (Upacārādubhayātmakah), as also the Guṇas which here mean the Tanmātras of sound, touch, sight, taste and smell. According to Nyāya the Guṇas appertain each to each (Tattadviśeṣaguṇāh) ; or according to Sāṁkhya Ether has one Guṇa, Air has two, Fire three and so forth. From Mahat was derived Ahaṁkāra which is threefold as Vaikārika, Taijasa, and Bhūtādi or the Sāttvika, Rājasa, and Tāmasa-Ahaṁkāras (v. 18) ; Rāghava says that it is called Vaikārika because it issues from Parameśvara when His Sāmarasya with S'akti becomes Vikṛta or disturbed. The Devas also are Vaikārika because produced from it. According to Sāṁkhya the Vaikārika nature is due to its generation from Pradhāna when Vikṛta. The Vaikārika Devas are Dik, Vāta, Arka, Pracetā (Varuṇa), Aśvins (two Aśvinīkumāras), Vahni, Indra, Upendra (Viṣṇorekā-mūrtih), Mitra (the third sun) and Ka (Candra). These are the Presiding Devatās of the senses (Indriyas). From the Taijasa-Ahaṁkāra were evolved the Indriyas. The five Tanmātras and the derived Bhūtas came from Bhūtādi-Ahaṁkāra.

The Text and Commentary speak of the derivation of Ākāśa from S'abda-tanmātra, Vāyu from Sparśa-tanmātra and so forth. But as the word Pūrva occurs, others read this as meaning that each becomes cause of what follows in association with what had gone before. Thus S'abda-tanmātra produces Ākāśa. From S'abda-tanmātra together with Sparśa-tanmātra come Agni and so forth.

The Sāradā then gives the colours of the Bhūtas namely transparent (Svaccha) ether, black air, red fire, white water, and yellow earth, the Ādhāras of which are the Tanmātras and the Guṇas of which are sound, touch, sight, taste and smell. Rāghava-Bhatta says that it is for the purpose of worship (Upāsanā-sthānam) in pursuance of Śāstra (Svaśāstrānurodhena) that certain invisible things are here said to have colours *Atra keṣāṁcit arūpidravyānām varṇakathanam*). This might perhaps seem to suggest to some that the colours are not real. But if this be so, is it correct? Ether is transparent which is no colour, black is the absence of colour. With Rūpa there must be colour. For what is colourless is formless. Form is only perceived by means of colour : and the last three Bhūtas are with form. Their colours are widely adopted. Thus in China also yellow is the colour of earth, and red and white are generally assigned to fire and water, respectively. Possibly what is meant is that the colours are here mentioned for the purpose of worship : that is, the mentioning is for such purpose. Else how could the Yogi perceive them? For it is said : " Tāni vastūni tānmātrādini pratyakṣa-viṣayāni " (that is to Yogis). Elsewhere it is said that ether is hollow or pitted (Suśiracinam), air is moving (Calanaparah), fire is digesting (Paripākavān), water is tasteful (Rasavat) and earth is solid (Ghana). All the universe is composed of the four Bhūtas entering into one another (*Parasparānupraviṣṭaih māhābhūtaiś catur-vidhaih*) pervaded by ether (Vyāptākāśaih).

Thus Consciousness as Śakti evolves mind and matter. The principles (Tattvas) of these are not always clearly understood. They may, and indeed must be, considered from the point of view of evolution —that is according to the sequence in which the limited experience of the Jīva is evolved—or from that in which they are regarded after creation when the experience of concrete sense objects has been had.

According to the former aspect, Buddhi is the state of
mere presentation; consciousness of being only, without
thought of " I " (Ahaṁkāra) and unaffected by
sensations (Manas, Indriya) of particular objects which
ex hypothesi do not yet exist. It is thus a state of
impersonal Jīva consciousness. Ahaṁkāra of which
Buddhi is the basis is the personal Consciousness which
realises itself as a particular " I ", the experiencer.
The Jīva wakes to world experience under the influence
of Māyā-Śakti. In the order of awakening he first
experiences in a vague general way without consciousness of the limited self, like the experience which is had
immediately on waking after sleep. It then refers this
experience to the limited self and has the consciousness
" I am so and so." Manas is the desire which follows
on such experience, and the senses and their objects are
the means, whereby that enjoyment is had which is the
end of all will to life. The cosmic mind projects its
content as ideas and desires on to the gross sensual plane
and there the individual mind enjoys them as such.

I may here observe that the same scheme exists in
Buddhism where the root is given as Avidyā, from which
arises Samskāra. This gives birth to Vijñāna (which is
Buddhi) and then to Nāmarūpa that is an external world
at first vaguely perceived. The desire to take cognisance
of this gives rise to the six sense organs (Ṣaḍāyatana)
namely Manas and the Indriyas. From this follows
contact (Sparśa) of the sense organs with the external
world giving rise to feeling (Vedanta) called forth by
such contact in the form of pleasure and pain. This
experience produces Desire (Tṛṣṇa) which a recent work
on the Unconscious calls Libido, for pleasant sensations
resulting in attachment and enjoyment (Upādāna), and
then the individual Jiva consciousness (Bhāva) is born

(Jāta), ages and dies and is again reborn until Nirvāṇa is attained. Throughout it is the will to life, the root of which is in Avidyā which produces the instruments namely the mind and senses whereby enjoyment is to be had and which creatively imagines the content of its experience from out of the store of past lives in past universes. True experience therefore can only be had by destroying the root which is Avidyā. One of the tasks which yet remains to be done is to show the essential similarities of Buddhism and Hinduism instead of dwelling, as is usually done, on their differences, alleged or real. When it is fully realised that Buddhism took its birth in India and the implications necessary therein truer notions will be entertained of it than generally prevails.

An example from science has been given which illustrates the process stated. In some animals there are no specialised sense organs but when stimulus is often given to a particular part of a body that part gets specially sensitive to it and a particular organ is developed. The illustration of course assumes that objects have been already created. But in the evolution of the world similar principles come into play as those which exist after it has been evolved. The effect exists in its cause. Consciousness awakening to world-experiences reaches forth and as it seeks to come by recollection to its limited self, its desire evolves the instruments of enjoyment into the sensual world. This is the action of the Samskāra operating in and upon consciousness.

Whilst however in the order of evolution Buddhi is the first principle, in the actual working of the Antahkaraṇa, after creation has taken place it comes last. It is more convenient therefore for ordinary exposition to commence with the sense objects and the sensations they evoke. Matter as the objective cause of perception is not, in its character, as such, under the cognisance of the senses. All that can be predicated of it is its effect upon these senses which is realised by the instrumentality of mind in its character as Manas. In science the notion of indestructible matter in atomic form is no longer held, for all matter it is now shown can be dissociated and the atom is dematerialised. The old duality of Force and Matter disappears, these two being held to be differing forms of the same thing. The ultimate basis is now recognised as Māyā or Prakṛti-S'akti. Matter is a stable form of force into which on disturbance of its equilibrium it disappears. Sensible matter (Bhūta) affects the experiencer in five different ways giving rise to the sensations of hearing (Ākāśa), touch and feel (Vāyu : not in the sense of all forms of contact, for form and solidity are not yet developed), colour and form and sight (Rūpa), taste (Rasa) and smell (Gandha). Sensible perception however exists only in respect of particular objects. But there exist also general elements of the particulars of sense-perception. There is an abstract quality by which sensible matter (Mahābhūta) is perceived. This abstract quality is Tanmātra the "mere thatness" or abstract quality of an object. These are the general elements of sense perception which necessarily come into existence when the senses (Indriyas) are produced. This is supersensible (Atīndriya) matter, the existence of which is ordinarily only mediately perceived through the gross particular objects of which they are the generals and which proceed from them. Sensations aroused by sense objects are experienced by the outer instruments

(Bāhya-karaṇa) or senses (Indriyas), whether of cognition (Jñānendriya) or action (Karmendriya) which are
the afferent and efferent impulses respectively. The
Indriyas are not however sufficient in themselves. In
the first place unless attention co-operates there is no
sensation (Ālocana) at all. Nextly as the experiencer
is at every moment besieged by countless sensations
from all sides, if any of these is to be brought into the
field of consciousness it must be selected to the exclusion
of others. Lastly, the manifold of sense or " points
of sensation " must be gathered together and made
into a whole. These three functions are those of
Manas the function of which is said to be Saṁ-
kalpa-vikalpa, that is selection and rejection of material
provided by the Jñānendriya. These sensations,
to affect the experiencer, must be made his own and
this is done by Ahaṁkāra or "Self-arrogation." It is
then passed on to Buddhi which determines either by
way of forming percepts and concepts of resolutions
(*Kartavyam etat mayā*). Thus all the Tattvas work for
the enjoyment of the Self or Puruṣa. They are not to
be regarded as things existing independently by themselves but as endowments of the Spirit (Ātmā). They
do not work arbitrarily as they will but represent an
organised co-operative effort in the service of the
enjoyer, the Experiencer or Puruṣa.

   The Tantras speak of three Tattvas namely of
Ātmā, Vidyā, S'iva. The first includes those Tattvas of
the Thirtysix which are called impure (Aśuddha)
namely Pṛthivī to Prakṛti; the second the pure-impure
(S'uddha-Aśuddha) or Māyā, the Kañcukas and Puruṣa;
and the third, the pure Tattvas (S'uddha) from S'uddha-
vidyā to S'iva-Tattva. I have dealt with the last two
in previous Chapters and deal with the first in the present

one.   It is also said (see Jñānārṇava-Tantra XXI-1-22)
that there are four Ātmās constituting the Citkuṇḍa or
Maṇḍala in the Mūlādhāra where the inner Homa is
made. By knowledge thereof there is no rebirth. These
are Ātmā, Jñānātmā, Antarātmā and Paramātmā.

The Ātmā (Prāṇarūpī) which is in all creatures
(Jantu) as the basis of their Prāṇa or vital principle is
their Ātmā. It is Hamsāsvarūpī and is manifested in
individual   bodies   by   inspiration   and   expiration
(Svāsa, Ucchvāsa).   This is Jīvātmā.   It is like the
Ākāśa separated in a pot which when broken becomes
mingled with the total Ākāśa.   Jñānātmā is said to be
Sākṣāt-sākṣirūpaka.   That is, it is that aspect of Ātmā
which witnesses all and by which the unity of all is
known.   It is thus the basis of Buddhi and all mental
Tattvas derived therefrom. By " Antar " in Antarātmā
is meant the subtle Ātmā of atomic dimension (Rahasya-
sūkṣma-rūpaka-paramāṇu) which pervades every object. It
is the "inner bodiness" (Antarangatā), the spark of
Paramātma.   It is Hamsa known only by Yogis.   Its
beak is Tāra (Mantra Om).   Its two wings are Āgama
and Nigama.   Its two feet are Siva and Sakti.   The
three Bindus are Its three eyes.   When this Paramahamsa is spread (Vyāpta) throughout Creation then all
Bhūtas spring up in their order (Ākāśa, Pavana etc).
Of these five the root is citta. This Hamsa Bird disports
Itself in the Lake of Ignorance (Avidyā) in the mud of
illusion and infatuation (Mohapaṅgka) which is the
world.   When this Hamsa becomes other-worldly
(Niṣprapañca) and dissolving (Samhārarūpī), then it
reveals the Self (Ātmānam pradarśayet).   Then its
" Birdness " (Pakṣitva) ceases.   Then the Sohamātma
is established which is the Supreme Experience or
Paramātmā.

To complete the creative process it is now necessary to resume the creation of S'abda (S'abdasṛṣṭi) from its supreme state (Para-śabda or Parabrahman) through its three Bhāvas, Paśyantī, Madhyamā and Vaikharī manifesting in bodies composed of the Tattvas above described; for in this way the birth of the letters composing Mantras is shown. I will deal with this in Chapter XXI under the title "Garland of Letters" (Varṇamālā), a subject of primary importance in the Tantras, after a description of the Causal S'aktis of the Praṇava or Mantra Om and an explanation of the Kalās.

CHAPTER XIX

CAUSAL S'AKTIS OF THE PRANAVA

THE present Chapter is but a short summary of the result of some enquiries recently pursued in Kashmir with a view to ascertain the notions of the Northern S'aiva school on several matters which I have been studying in connection with my work on the awakening of the spiraline energy or Serpent Power. I was already aware, as the Kulārnava-Tantra (one of the foremost Tantras of the "Bengal" school) indicates, that the S'aiva-S'ākta-Darśana and not S'amkara's exposition of Vedānta is the original philosophical basis of the S'ākta faith, though some who call themselves S'āktas seem now-a-days to have forgotten, if they were ever aware of, that fact. In Kashmir, Kula-S'āstra is, I believe another name for the Trika. But amongst several other objects in view I wished to link up the connection of certain S'aktis mentioned in the Kriya portion of the S'āstras with the thirtysix Tatıvas of the S'ākta school, their position in the scheme not being in all cases clear to me according to the information previously at my disposal. I have worked the matter out in more detail and the present Chapter will summarise conclusions on certain points.

Being (Sattā) is of two kinds, formless (Arūpa) and with form (Rūpa). In the first the "I" (Aham) and the " This " (Idam) or universe representing the Prakāśa

and Vimarśa aspects of experience are one. S'iva
and Sakti exist in all the planes. But they are here
undistinguishably one in the embrace of the Lord (S'iva)
and the Heart of the Lord " (S'akti). S'iva is *Cit*.
S'akti is *Cidrūpiṇī*. He is Para and She, Parā. This is
the Perfect Experience which is Ānanda or " Resting
in the Self " (Svarūpa-viśrānti). S'iva then experiences
the universe as Parāśakti, that is, Paranāda and Parā-
vak. This is the Love of the Self for the Self. The
Supreme experience is the bliss of unalloyed Love. The
Idam then exists as Parā-śakti. The two aspects are as
it were one (*Ekam tattvam iva*), to use a phrase in the
Ahirbudhnya-Sambitā of the Pāñcarātra-Āgama. The
" Supreme Sound " and " Supreme Speech " are thus
the perfect Universe which is the supreme Kailāsa.
This is the supreme unitary experience in which, though
the " I " and the " This " do not cease to exist they
are both in their *Svarūpa* and thus mysteriously coalesce
in one unity of Being which is the " Two in one." The
whole process then of creation, that is the rise of imperfect or dual experience, is the establishment through
the negation of S'akti (*Niṣedha-vyāpārā-rūpā-S'akti*) of a
diremption in the one unitary consciousness whereby
the Aham and the Idam, which had then existed,
coalesced in one, diverge, in consciousness, until in our
own experience the " I " is separated from the " This "
seen as objects outside ourselves.

The process of manifestation of Mantra is that of
cosmic ideation (*Sṛṣṭi-kalpanā*) in which Jñāna-S'akti
first merely formulates as thought the outlines of the
limited universe which is about to emerge from, and
for, consciousness, and which is called the " thinkable "
(*Mantavya*), which through Nāda which is *Kriyāśaktirūpa* moves towards the " speakable " (*Vācya*), with

which again consciousness identifies itself as Bindu which is characterised by a predominance of activity (*Kriyāprādhānyalakṣaṇā*). Diversity (*Pṛthagbhāva*) is then produced by Bindu as Ma-kāra in the Māyā-Tattva. S'akti as U-kāra creates objects (*Prameya*) as separate existences and by the completion of the Tattvas objectivity is completely revealed as A-kāra. To describe however adequately this grand system of Ābhāsa, as it is called, would require a full exposition of the Northern and monistic S'aiva and the allied S'ākta-Darśana on which the S'ākta doctrine and practice of the Āgamas is based. I can here only indicate shortly the S'aktis of the Mūla-Mantra or Praṇava, which are the correspondences from the S'akti aspect of S'aiva-Sākta-Tattvas. The account of the S'aktis vary, but such variance is rather due to the fact that some accounts are fuller than others than to any substantial difference in principle.

The gist of the matter may be shortly stated as follows : In creation, the three S'aktis, Jñāna, Icchā, Kriyā, manifest. These are manifested powers of the supreme Bindu. " What is here is there," and these S'aktis of the Lord (Pati) appear as the Guṇas of Prakṛti in the Paśu ; or as it has also been said, Jñāna and Kriyā with Māyā as the third appear as Sattva, Rajas, and Tamas of the Puruṣa-Prakṛti stage which is the immediate source of the consciousness of the Paśu.

Svānga-rūpeṣu bhaveṣu patyur jñānaṁ kriyā cha yā
Māyā tritīyā tā eva paśoh sattvam rajas tamah.

(*Īsvara-Pratyabhijñā, IV 1, 4*)

The creative consciousness (S'akti) projects the universe as all-diffusive Consciousness (*Sadākya-Tattva*), which considered from the Mantra aspect is all-diffusive

"Sound" that is movement or Nāda. Here the emphasis is on the Aham, which is yet coloured by the Idam as the universe faintly rises into the field of the changeless consciousness. Consciousness then identifies itself with the clearly perceived Idam and becomes Bindu. Here the emphasis is on the Idam with which consciousness becomes a point (Bindu). Then the evolving consciousness holds the " I " and the " This " in equal balance (Samānādhikaraṇa), at which point Māyā S'akti, which is the sense of difference (Bhedabuddhi) intervenes to separate the Aham (as Puruṣa) and Idam (as Prakṛti) hitherto held as parts of the one Consciousness, and the divisive power of Kalā-S'akti breaks up the universe so separated from the Self into that plurality of objects which is our ordinary worldly experience. The universe which in the Puruṣa Prakṛti stage was seen as a whole, though different from the Self, is now also seen as separate but as a multitude of mutually exclusive beings.

There is first a fivefold division of the " five rays " of Om, namely, A, U, M, Nāda Bindu, S'ānta. The Prapañcasāra-Tantra says that Jāgrat is Bija, Svapna is Bindu, Suṣupti is Nāda, Turīya is Sakti and the Laya beyond is S'ānta. This is the simplest form of statement setting forth one S'akti for each of the Varṇas, and the Candra-Bindu. In other words from S'iva-S'akti (which includes all the Tattvas down to the appearance of the three Devatās) these latter are produced. There is next a sevenfold division. Parā-samvit or Paramaśiva is not technically accounted a Tattva, for the Supreme Experience is Tattvātīta. But if we include it as the transcendental aspect of the S'aiva-tattva from which the Ābhāsa proceeds, we get the number seven counting Puruṣa and Prakṛti as two.

The number seven is of frequent occurrence ; as in the case of the seven S'ivas, namely, Paras'iva, S'ambhu and the five Mahāpretas; the seven S'aktis of the Oṁkāra as given in the S'āradā-Tilaka ; the seven S'aktis, Unmanī and the rest as given in the Commentary of Kālicaraṇa on the Ṣatcakranirūpaṇa chapter of Pūrnā-nanda-S'vāmī's work entitled S'rītattva-cintāmaṇi (*The Serpent Power*) ; and the three and a half coils of Kuṇḍalinī of which the Kubjikā-Tantra speaks, namely Puruṣa, Prakṛti, Vikṛti, which it may be observed when uncoiled and divided by its diameter gives seven divisions.

The S'āradā speaks of six S'aktis which with Parames'vara who is Saccidānanda make seven, namely : S'iva, S'akti, Nāda, Bindu (Kāraṇa), Bindu (Kārya), Nāda (Kārya) and Bīja. The other seven S'aktis above mentioned are Unmanī (or Unmanā), Samanī (or Samanā), Āñjī, Mahānāda (or Nādānta), Nāda, Ardhacandra and Bindu. If in the first series we take Kārya-Nāda which is described as the Mithaḥ-Sama-vāya (mutual relation) of S'ivarūpakārya-Bindu and Bīja, which is Saktirūpa, as the correspondence in this scheme of the S'aiva S'uddhavidya-Tattva with its Samānādhikaraṇa, then this series represents all the S'aiva Tattvas up to and including Puruṣa-Prakṛti. The same remarks apply to the second series of S'aktis or causal forms (Kāraṇarūpa). The first is described by Kālicaraṇa as the state in which all-mindness (Manastva), that is ideation ceases. Here there is neither Kalā, nor Kāla, for it is "the sweet pure mouth of Rudra " (S'ivapada). The second is the cause of all causes (Sarvakāraṇakāraṇaṁ). The third which is also called by him Vyāpikā-S'akti appears in the beginning of creation. Mahānāda is the Kāraṇa-Nāda which is Kriyā-S'akti and the first appearance of Nāda. S'akti as Nāda is a development of the latter which is transformed into Ardhacandra and then Bindu.

These S'aktis (as well as two others with A U M, making altogether twelve) are explained according to S'aiva views in an account extracted from the Netra Tantra with Kṣemarāja's Commentary and from the Tantrāloka. There the S'aktis are given as Unmanā, Samanā, Vyāpika, (or Vyāpinī), Añjanī, Mahānāda, Nāda, Nirodhinī, Ardhacandra, Bindu, Ma-kāra, U-kāra, A-kāra. The Sanskrit passages here given are the summary in his own language made for me by the Kashmirian Paṇḍit Harabhatta Sāstri of Srinagar.

"When the Supreme S'iva beyond whom there is nought, who is in the nature of unchanged and unchangeable illumination moves forth by His will, such (willing movement as) S'akti, though in fact inseparable from Him, is called Unmanā ; Her place is the S'iva-Tattva" (*Anuttara-paramaśiva avicalaprakāsātmā yadā svecchayā prasarati sā śaktih śivād abhinnaiva Unmanā ityucyate ; tatsthānaṁ śiva-tattvaṁ iti*).

"When the Unmanā-S'akti displays Herself in the form of the universe beginning with the S'ūnya and ending with Dharā, formulates as mere thought the thinkable, then She is called Samanā as well as S'akti-tattva" (*Yadā unmana-śaktir ātmānam kṣobhayati śūnyadinā dharāntena jagat-ātmanā sphurati mantavyam mananamātreṇa āsūtrayati, tadā Samanā ityucyate S'akti-tattvam iti ca*).

"This Samanā-Sakti Herself is called Vyāpinī when She operates as the Power which withdraws into Herself all thinkables which are Her creation. She resides in the S'akti-tattva" (*Samanā śaktir eva svamantavye samhāra-pradhānatvena Vyāpinī ityucyate, eṣā S'akti-tattva-tiṣṭhati*).

"It is again the same Samanā Herself who is called
Śakti when her operation is chiefly creative in regard
to her own thinkables. She resides in the Śakti-tattva
and is also called Āñjanī because of Her being associated with the thinkable" (*Samanaiva svamantavya sṛṣṭipra-
dhānatvena śaktirityucyate eṣā Śakti-tattva tiṣṭhati mantavyo-
paraktatvāc ca Āñjanī ityapi ucyate*) "When Śabda-brahman moves forth with great strength from Its Śiva
form then the very first sound (produced thereby) like
the vibration produced by a sounding bell is called
Nādānta (*i.e.* Mahānāda). It resides in the Sadāśiva-
tattva." (*Yadā śabdabrahma śiva-rūpad ativegena prasarati
tadā prathamataraṁ ghantānuraṇātmā śabdo Nādānta
ityucyate, sa Sabdā-śiva-tattve tiṣṭhati*). When Śakti fills
up the whole universe with Nādānta then She is called
Nāda. And this also is the Sadāśiva-Tattva because of
the equality therein of the "I" and the "This"
(*Nādāntena yadā viśvam āpūrayati tadā Nāda ityucyate, sa ca
ahamte-damtayoh samānādhiharaṇyena Sadāśiva-tattvamiti*".
Samānādhikarana in its technical sense is the function of the later developed Śuddhavidyā-Tattva.
Apparently its original is here represented to be the
function of the earlier Sadāśiva-Tattva in which the
duality of the Aham and Idam first manifests.

"When Nāda, after having ceased to operate in its
universal scope, does so limitedly (or particularly) then
it is called Nirodhinī This Śakti rests in the Sadāśiva-
Tattva" (*Nādo yadā aśeṣavyāptim nimajjya adharam
vyāptim unmajjayati tadā Nirodhinī ityucyate sā Sadāśivātatt-
vam ālambate*). "When Nāda is slightly operative
towards the creation of the "speakable," it is called
Ardhacandra which is Īśvara-Tattva." (*Nādo yadā
iṣadvācyonmeṣaṁ śrayati tadā Ardhacandra ityucate Īśvara-
tattve*). Then "Parā-Śakti Herself is called Bindu

when She is in the nature of inseparate illumination in regard to the whole range of the speakable" (*Paraiva śaktih yadā samastavācye abheda-prakāśa-rupatām gṛhṇāti tadā Bindur ityucyate, sa Īśvara-tattve tiṣṭhati*).

Ma-kāra or Rudra-Devatā is defined : "When Bindu causes diversity to manifest it is called Makāra and It moves .in Māyā-Tattva" (*Yadā binduh pṛthag-bhāvam ābhāsayati tadā Ma-kāra ityucyate, saca Māyātattve*). When S'akti creates objects as separate existences then She is called U-kāra. It resides in the Prakṛti-Tattva " (*Yadā prameyaṁ pṛthag-bhāvena-unme-ṣayati, tadā U-kāra ityucyate, saca Prakṛti-tattve tiṣṭhati*). When the creation of the Tattvas has come to an end, then because objectivity is completely revealed, (Sakti as) Māntrī-Kalā (that is the creative art or process considered as "Sound" or Mantra) is called A-kāra " (*Tattvasargasya nivṛttīr yadā jāyate, tadā prameyasya pūrṇa-tayā prakāśanat A-kāra iti Māntrī-kalā ucyate*).

The extra five S'aktis enumerated in this account are due firstly to the inclusion of A U M; secondly to counting Vyāpinī and Āñjanī separately instead of as being the Nimeṣa and Unmeṣa aspects of one S'akti ; and thirdly the sevenfold series would appear to include Nirodhinī, also called Nirodhikā, in Nāda of which it is a more particularised development. Nāda would appear in the fuller series to represent Sāmānya-spanda of the sound emanation. For just as in the region of ideation the evolution is from infinite consciousness to the general and thence to particular ideas ; so from the corresponding objective or Mantra aspect, which is that of S'āktopāyayoga, motion commences from the unextended point first as general, then as particular movement, at length developing into the clearly defined

particularity of speech and of the objects which speech
denotes.   The rhythmic vibration of objects is the same
as that of the mind which perceives them, since both
are aspects of the one S'akti which thus divides itself.

Namaste ravatvena tattvābhidhāne

CHAPTER XX

THE KALĀS

KALĀ is a common term in Tāntrik literature for
which it is difficult to find an appropriate English
rendering. S'iva has two aspects Niṣkalā (Nirguṇa)
and Sakalā (Saguṇa) The former is therefore without
Kalā. The latter is with Kalā. S'iva is never without
S'akti, for the two are one and the same, and S'akti in
Herself, according to Her proper nature (S'akti-
Svarūpa), is Consciousness or Caitanya (Caitanyarū-
piṇī). Thus there are said to be no Kalās in Unmani
which is in the S'iva-Tattva. Thereafter with Samani
in S'akti-Tattva the Kalās appear. Thus in S'ri-Netra-
Tantra (Ch. 22) seven Kalās are assigned to Samani.
The S'akti of a Devatā is divided into sixteen Kalās or
" parts " of power. That aspect of Devatā which has
full power is called Pūrṇa-Kalāmūrti. One sixteenth
of that or any part of the whole (Pūrṇa) is Kalāmūrti.
A fraction again of that is Amśamūrti and a fraction of
Amśamūrti is Amśāmśa-mūrti. S'iva is partless. S'akti
has parts (Kalā). But parts as we know them do not
exist until after the universe has evolved from
Prakṛti : that is, parts in the literal sense of the Māyik
world. When therefore mention is made of Kalā in
connection with so high a S'akti as S'amani or any other
S'akti which precedes Prakṛti, what is meant is something which may be best expressed by modes or aspects

of S'akti. Kalā, in short, is a particular display of Power or Vibhūti. Kalā is also one of the Kañcukas which go to the making of the Puruṣa consciousness and is the product of higher S'aktis and Kalās. The Kañcukas or enveloping S'aktis cut down the natural perfections as they exist in the Supreme Self and thus constitute the evolved Self or Puruṣa. The four Kalās called Nivṛtti, Pratiṣṭhā, Vidyā, S'ānti are specific modes of S'akti well defined. These are explained later. As regards the other Kalās there is greater difficulty. In the first place the texts are not consonant. This may be either due to innaccuracy in the MSS. or real variances or to both. Then explanations of the terms are in general wanting though sometimes they are given by the commentators. The Sanskritist will however perceive that these latter Kalās are variant aspects (like Āvaraṇa-Devatās of worship), descriptive of the nature and functions of the S'akti whose Kalās they are and as such may have been set forth for Upāsanā ; the lengthy lists being in conformity with the taste of the age in which these S'astras were promulgated. Thus Kalās have been called Jyotsnā (moonlight) and the like on account of their Sarvajñata-dharma, that is, Prakāśa-rūpatā-dharma ; that which being in the nature of manifestation is white and brilliant as moonlight. So again Indhikā (kindling) Kalā is so called because it is Jñānarūpā or in the nature of knowledge ; and Rundhani is so called because of its opposing or staying quality as explained later. This great elaboration of S'aktis is also in conformity with a psychological principle on which Tāntrik Upāsanā is based into which I cannot enter here.

The above remarks are illustrated by the lengthy list of Kalās of the Varṇas and Praṇava given in

Ch. III of the Prapañcasāra-Tantra. The Kalās of Nāda,
Bindu, A U M are there given and I will not repeat
them here; but I will relate instead an account obtained
from the Kashmirian Paṇḍit Hara-Bhatta S'āstrī and
taken by him from S'rī-Netra-Tantra which has not
been published. The reader of the Prapañcasāra will
observe that the accounts vary both as to the names and
numbers of the Kalās. In S'rī-Netra-Tantra seven
Kalās are given of Samanī-S'akti, *viz.*, Sarvajña,
Sarvagā, Durgā, Savarṇā, Spṛhaṇā, Dhṛti, Samanā;
five of Āñjanī. *viz.*, Sūkṣmā, Susūkṣma, Amṛtā, Amṛta-
sambhavā, Vyāpinī; one of Mahānāda *viz.*, Ūrddhva-
gāminī; four of Nāda, *viz.*, Indhikā, Dīpikā, Rocikā,
Mocikā. Some texts speak of Recikā. Nirodhinī-S'akti
has five Kalās called Ruudhinī, Rodhinī, Raudrī, Jñānabodhā, Tamo'pahā. The Ṣatcakra-nirūpaṇa (V. 38)
speaks of Bandhatī, Bodhinī, Bodhā. Rodhinī and
Rundhanī, which mean "opposing," indicate the
opposition encountered by lower Experiencers such as
Brahmā and other Devas attempting to enter into the
higher state of Nāda. These S'aktis (like the "Dwellers
on the Threshold" of Western occult literature) oppose
all those to whom they do not extend their grace
(Anugraha) by the Kalās Jñānabodhā (Wisdom) and
Tamo'pahā (Dispeller of darkness). These Kalās are
therefore called Sarvadeva-nirodhikā, that is, they
oppose entrance into the higher state of consciousness
and they oppose the fall therefrom of such Devas as
have attained thereto. Of Ardhacandra there are five
Kalās, *viz.*, Jyotsnā, Jyotsnāvatī, Kānti, Suprabhā
and Vimalā, which are said to be Sarvajña-pada-
samsthitā. For She is Knower of all. If one can
remain in Ardhacandrapada then all things are
known—past, present and future. I am informed

that according to Sri-Netra-Tantra (Ch. 22) and Svacchandra-Tantra (Ch. 20), the four Kalās of Bindu are the very important ones Nivṛtti, Pratiṣṭā, Vidyā, Sānti; which however are said in Prapañcasāra to be Kalās of Nāda, the four Kalās of Bindu being there given as Pītā, S'vetā, Aruṇā and Asitā. These five modes of Sakti are described later. The number and names of the Kalās of A U M differ in these several texts. According to the former the Kālas of the Destructive Rudra are Tamomohā, Kṣudhā, Nidrā, Mṛityu, Māyā, Bhayā, Jaḍā; of the Protective Viṣṇu the Kalās are Rajas, Rakṣā, Rati, Pālyā, Kāmyā, Buddhi, Māyā, Nādi, Bhrāmaṇī, Mohini, Tṛṣṇā, Mati, Kriyā; and of the Creative Brahmā there are Siddhi, Ṛddhi, Dyuti, Lakṣmī, Medhā, Kānti, Dhṛti, Sudhā. The three Bindus of the differentiating Parabindu form the Kāmakāla. The Kalās Nivṛtti and the rest are the generalities (Sāmānya) of the Tattvas issuing from Prakṛti; that is the Tattvas are subdivisions or differentiations of these four Kalās. Nivṛtti-Kalā is the working force and essential element in the Pṛthivī-Tattva or Solidity; and is so called because here the stream of tendency is stopped and the manifesting energy turned upwards. When Pṛthivī has been reached by process of evolution, Sakti becomes Kuṇḍali (coiled; at rest). Her next movement which is that of Yoga is upwards by involution retracing the steps of descent. The Pṛthivī Aṇu or point of solidity is inexhaustible potentiality in, and as a physical, that is, sensible manifestation, of, the Spiraline Power welling up from and coiling round the S'iva-bindu. This aspect of the Power supplies (as a friend learned in S'iva literature informs me) the curving and circular motion which manifests as the rounding and spherical skin and flesh with which all Prāṇis are supplied. According to the same view Pratiṣṭhā which is the same force in all the Tattvas from Ap to Prakṛti (Tantrāloka Ahn. 10) is so called, because whilst Nivṛtti supplies the outer covering, Pratiṣṭhā, as its name indicates supplies the basis and inner framework on which the outer physical universe is laid. Vidyā-Kalā, which is so called because it is limited knowledge, is the dominant Kalā in the Tattvas from Puruṣa upwards together with five Kañcukas to Māyā. These are related to the Śaktis Vāmā, Jyeṣṭhā and Raudrī which manifest as the three motions which go to make the universe, which in terms of consciousness are the movements of the Antahkaraṇa towards the objects (Viṣaya) of its experience, such objects being the combination of lines on various planes, in curves and circles. The three-dimensional framework affords the basis (Pratiṣṭhā) for the outer solid covering (Nivṛtti) supplied by the spiraline Śaktis as the manifested sensible and physical. Beyond Māyā there is the consciousness which is peace (Śānti), for it is free of the duality which is the source of sorrow. The last Kalā is therefore called Śāntā and is dominant in the glorious experience of the Tattvas from Sadvidyā to Śakti-Tattva. Thus the Tattvas are only the manifestations of Śakti as three typical forms of movement starting from the kinetic state. It is these moving forces as the Kalās which are the inner life and secret of them. The Kalās are not dead forces; for the universe does not proceed from such. They are realised in direct experience as Devatās in and beyond all natural manifestations and may be made to serve the purpose of Sādhana. As Divine Beings they are modes of the one Divine Mother worshipped diagrammatically in Yantras. As the inner forces in the Tattvas the Kalās group together the latter into four great "Eggs" (Aṇḍa), that is, Spheroids comprising those Tattvas only of which a Kalā is the common dominant feature and inner force. These are the Brahmāṇḍa comprising Pṛthivī-Tattva in which all others are involved, the bounding principle or envelope of which is ether (Ākāśa) ; Prakṛtyaṇḍa or Mūlāṇḍa and Śaktyaṇḍa of which the envelopes are Prakṛti, Māyā and Śakti respectively. Beyond all these in the centre thereof and pervading all is the Śiva-Tattva in regard to which the Divine Śakti as a Kalā is an utter negation (Śūnyāti-śūnya), an empty space-giving or vacuity-producing power (Avakāśadā), which is the negative pole of the conjoint Śiva-Śakti-Tattvas. The Śiva-Tattva is thus the Paramaśiva or parāsamvit, the great Bhairava experience with its supreme experience of the universe negatived.

Regarding then this ultimate Śakti also, in so far as it is a manifestation, as a Kalā or moving Power, the thirtysix Tattvas of which the universe consists are but manifestations of five forces (Śakti) or Kalās into which the one partless Divine Śakti differentiates Herself in an infinite variety of permutations so as to produce the universe with parts : namely, Śāntātītā or Avakāśadā, Śāntā, Vidyā, Pratiṣṭhā, Nivṛtti.

According to the account given in the Ṣatcakra-nirūpaṇa (*The Serpent Power*) and the Commentaries of Kālīcaraṇa and Viśvanātha, there is a Śakti called Nirvāṇa-Śakti with two Kalās, which are Nirvāṇa-Kalā and Amā Kalā, known as the seventeenth and sixteenth Kalās respectively. Unmanī is Śivapada which is beyond Kāla and Kalā. In Śakti-Tattva these have their source. The highest Śakti in this Tattva is

Samanī; Nirvāṇa-S'akti is, according to Viśvanātha, Samanāpada or Samanī, the life and origin of all being (Sarveṣāṁ yonirūpiṇī). According to Kālīcaraṇa, Nirvāṇa-S'akti is Unmanī. S'akti as seventeenth Kalā is Cinmātrā and is called Nirvāṇa-Kalā. Viśvanātha identifies it with Vyāpinī-Tattva which is S'akti-svarūpā and above (Parātparā) the sixteenth Kalā. It is Antargatā of, that is, included within, Amākala, just as Nirvāṇa-S'akti is Antargatā of Nirvāṇa-Kalā. Kālīcaraṇa identifies it with Samanāpada. Amā is the sixteenth Kalā. She is the receptacle of the nectar which flows from the union of Para (Bindurūpa S'iva) and Parā (S'akti). Viśvanātha cites the Yoginīhṛdaya-Tantra to show that Amā is Vyāpikā-S'akti. Kālīcaraṇa agrees as to this. But it has been said by Viśvanātha that Nirvāṇa-Kalā is Vyāpinī-Tattva. We must take it then that according to this view Nirvāṇa-Kalā and Amā-Kalā are the two aspects, supreme and creative, of Vyāpinī-Tattva as Vyāpikā and Āñjanī. Beyond or more excellent than Amā-Kalā is Nirvāṇa-Kala, and then this last, Nirvāṇa-S'akti or Samanī in S'akti-Tattva wherein is bondage (Pāśajāla). Thus Nirvāṇa-Kala is the Cinmātra-svabhāvā or pure consciousness aspect of what in the creative aspect is called Amā, the receptacle of nectar, that is, the blissful current which flows from the union of S'iva and S'akti. This is the rapture of creation which is known to us also. The same S'akti is in differing aspect Amṛtākārarūpiṇī as the seventeenth and the receptacle of Amṛtā as the sixteenth Kalā. Amā is both Sṛṣṭyunmukhī (looking towards creation) and Ūrddhva-śaktirūpā (looking upwards, that is towards Liberation). The former is the meaning of the expression " downward-turned-mouth " (Adhomukhī.) This is the position of the Petals before Kuṇḍalinī ascends.

This is my reading of Texts which are not devoid of discussion. Thus apart from difficulties in the Texts cited I was informed in Kashmir that S'akti is called the seventeenth Kalā or Amā when Cinmātrasvabhāvā; and Amṛta-Kalā when Puruṣa is with the sixteen Kalās, which in this case are said to be the Jñānendriya, Karmendriya, Tanmātra and Manas (which includes Ahaṁkāra and Buddhi). This may be a difference of terminology only. What seems clear is that in S'akti-Tattva (of the thirty-six Tattvas) there are two Kalās which represent the supreme and creative modes of S'akti whether we call them Nirvāṇa and Amā or Amṛtākārā and Amṛta-Kalā. The sixteenth is the creative S'akti and the Kalā which is in the nature of ever-existent changeless Cit (Cinmātrasvabhāvā) is the seventeenth.

To sum up. Paramaśiva (Parā-saṁvit) in His aspects as S'iva-Tattvas is the S'ūnyāti-śūnya, so called because in His experience there is not the slightest trace of objectivity whatever. Both these aspects are S'āntātīta. S'akti then gradually unveils again the universe for the consciousness of S'iva who is Prakāśa or the Illuminating Consciousness which is the subjective aspect of things; and the experience which is summed up as S'āntā-Kalā arises, extending from S'akti-Tattva to Sadvidya, with the S'aktis, Saminī, Vyāpinī, Āñjani and their Kalās; and the S'aktis of the Nadā and Bindu groups with their Kalās. This is the Spheroid of S'akti (S'aktyaṇḍa) which is the abode of those glorious Beings who are called Mantra-māheśvara, Mantreśvara, Mantra and Vidyeśvara. The Vijñāna-kalās who are below S'uddha-vidyā are also above Māyā. From the unfolding of Bindu the other Spheroids emanate, which manifest the three principal forms of movement which go to the making of the universe. Next, in concentric circles arise the Spheroid of Māyāṇḍa, the field of operation of Vidyā-kalā, which is the S'akti producing the limited dual consciousness of all experiencers (Pralayākala, Sakala) below Sad-vidyā and in or below Māyā. Lastly, the Spheroids of Prakṛti and Brahmā, provide the vehicles in which the Experiencer called Sakala functions. These Experiencers comprise all things from Brahmā downwards who are not liberated. Brahmā, Viṣṇu and Rudra are the Lords of the spheres from Pṛthivī to Māyā ; Īśa and Anāśṛta S'iva of higher Tattvas ; and lastly S'iva of S'iva-Tattva, which is the ultimate source of, but is Itself beyond, all Kalās.

CHAPTER XXI

THE GARLAND OF LETTERS OR VARNAMĀLĀ

WE now speak of "Vāk" — "The Word" —a great concept of the S'āstras. S'ruti says: "Four are the steps measured by Vāk. The wise Brāhmaṇa knows them. Three being hidden in the cave do not issue. The fourth is spoken by men in their speech."

The Para-bindu is the S'abda-brahman: for on its differentiation arises the " unmanifest sound " (Avyak-tarava), the Hidden Word from which all manifested speech and the objects which it denotes are derived. This is the state of Supreme S'abda (Para-śabda), the evolution of which (Para-śabda Sṛṣṭi) has been shown in the previous Chapters. In its further development the existence of mind and body is assumed. This has been discussed in the account of the evolution of the objects (Arthasṛṣṭi) which man thinks and in uttered speech names. This S'abdabrahman as appearing in bodies is Kuṇḍalinī-S'akti (Kuṇḍalinī śabdabrahma-mayī). The S'āradā-Tilaka says (1-108, 109) :

Sā prasūte Kuṇḍalinī śabdabrahmamayī vibhuh
S'aktiṁ tato dhvanis tasmān nādas tasmān nirodhikā
Tato' ṛdhendus tato bindus tasmād āsīt parā iatah

" She who is Kuṇḍalinī, all-pervading S'abda-brahman, produces S'akti. From this came Dhvani;

from Dhvani, Nāda; from Nāda, Nirodhikā; from Nirodhikā, Ardhendu; from Ardhendu, Bindu; and then comes Parā."

It will be observed that just as there is a sevenfold cosmic development, it is repeated here in the case of individual bodies. Kuṇḍalinī is S'abdabrahman, an aspect of Caitanya or Consciousness (Cit). By S'akti is here meant Cit entered into by Sattva (Sattva-praviṣṭā), which is the Paramākāsāvastha. By Dhvani is meant that same Cit when entered into by Sattva (Sattvapraviṣṭā), penetrated by Rajas (Rajo'nuviddhā), which is Akṣarāvasthā. By Nāda is meant the same Cit penetrated by Tamas (Tamo'nuviddhā) or Avyak-tāvasthā. By Nirodhikā is denoted that same Cit with abundance of Tamas (Tamah-prācuryā); by Ardhendu the same with abundance of Sattva (Sattvaprācuryā). By the term Bindu is denoted that same Cit when in it there is a combination of the two (Tadubhayasamyogāt). This development appears to indicate the gradual process whereby S'akti passes through subtle to more gross forms of potency until it reaches that full potency for manifestation which is the Ghanāvasthā State or Bindu in which Kriyā exists in full creative perfection. So it is said. "Moved by the strength of Icchā-śakti (Icchā-śakti-balākṛṣṭah), illumined by Jñāna-śaktī (Jñāna-śakti-pradīpitah)," that S'akti (Sā śaktih) in male form (Pumrūpiṇī) who is the Lord (Prabhu) puts forth Her who is called Action (Kriyākhyā) that is, Kriyā-śakti.

The S'āradā then continues :

Paśyantī madhyamā vāci vaikharī śabda-janmabhūh.
Icchājñānakriyātmā'sau tejorūpa guṇātmikā.
Krameṇānena sṛjati Kuṇḍalī varṇamālikāṁ.

" (Then Parā) and then came Paśyantī, Madhyamā and Vaikharī-S'abda. In this order Kuṇḍalī who is Will (Icchā), Knowledge (Jñāna) and Action (Kriyā), who is both Light (Tejorūpā) and Cidrūpā (in Herself Consciousness) and in the form of the Guṇas (Guṇātmikā, that is, Prakṛti) creates the Garland of Letters."

Parā is S'abda as Para-bindu and is motionless (Niṣpanda). This as already explained becomes threefold and the threefold aspects from the S'abda standpoint are Paśyantī, Madhyamā, Vaikharī. Each of these is a manifested form of the Unmanifested Parabindu or S'abda-brahman. It is, as Rāghava says, by shifting to another place in Her (*Asyām eva binduh sthānānta-ragatah*) that Bindu which is Parā when unmanifested and motionless is called Paśyantī, Madhyamā and Vaikharī speech (Vāk). Parā is in the Mūlādhāra cakra, Paśyantī in Svādhiṣṭhāna (and upwards), Madhyamā in Anāhata (and upwards), and Vaikharī in the throat. In Kuṇḍalī, S'akti is subtle (Sūkṣmā) and in the form of mere light (*Jyotirmātrātmarūpi*) and not an object of hearing (Aśrotra-viṣayā). Thence She goes upward (Urddhvagāminī) and becomes Paśyantī, self-manifesting (Svayaṁprakāśā) in the Suṣumnā-Nāḍī (Suṣumnām āśritā). She again becomes Madhyamā as a form of Nāda (Nādarūpiṇī) when reaching the Heart Lotus (Anāhata). Then She goes upward as a mere undifferentiated " hum " (*Saṁjalpamātrā avibhaktā*). It is She who appearing at the chest, throat, teeth, nose, palate and head assumes the form of all letters (Varṇa) issuing from the root of the tongue and lips, and thus becomes Vaikharī, the Mother of all sounds, audible to the sense of hearing (Rāghava-Bhatta). The same commentator then says, citing the Kādimata section of Tantrarājā, " Under the influence of one's own will

(*Svatmecchāśaktighātena*) a high (Uttama) form of the
Nāda called Para generates in the Mūlādhāra as
Prāṇavāyu (*Prāṇavāyusvarūpatah*). This when carried up
by will (Icchā) and made to appear in the Svādhiṣthāna
is called Paśyanti associated with Manas. Gradually led
up by Her it is called Madhyamā associated with
Buddhi in the Anāhata. Carried still further upward
it is called Vaikhari in the Viśuddha in the region of
the throat. Thence it is generated as the Letters from
A to Kṣa through its presence at the head, throat,
palate, lips, teeth, tongue (root, tip and back), nose,
palate and throat (together), lips and teeth (together),
and throat and lips (together). Their letter-hood
(Akṣaratva) is said to be due to their being divided into
different parts beginning with the letter A and ending
with Kṣa."

It is Cit-S'akti which is called Parā, that is to say,
it is Para-Vāk not moved to vibration by the Māyā
which reveals (*Parāprakāśikā Māyā niṣpandā*) on account
of its bearing the reflection of Caitanya (*Caitanyābhā-
saviśiṣtatayā*). The vibratory states are Paśyanti and
the other two (*Saspandāvasthāh paśyantyādyāh*). Paśyanti
which is in the nature of Bindu (*Bindutattvātmikā*) is the
form of a general (that is, not particularised) motion
(*Sāmānya-praspanda-prakāśarūpiṇi*), which is manifested in
the region between the Mūlādhāra and the Navel
(*Mūlādhārādi-nābhyantara-vyaktisthānā*). It is called Paśyanti because of its being Jñāna (*Jñānātmakatvāt*). It is
associated with Manas. Madhyamā is in the form of
the internal and external instruments (*Bāhyāntahkaraṇāt-
mikā*) and manifests as Nādabindu (*Nādabindumayi*).
Hiraṇyagarbha sound (*Hiraṇyagarbharūpiṇi*) is in the
region extending from the navel to the heart (*Nābhādi-
hṛdayāntābhivyaktisthānā*). It is associated with the

Tattvas of specific ideation and so forth (*Viśeṣasaṁkāl-pādisatattvā.*) She is Madhyamā when Buddhi is Madhyamā. Madhyamā is middle, that is, "in the midst" between Paśyantī which is "Seeing" (Īkṣaṇa) and Vaikharī which is utterance. She is neither like Paśyantī nor does She proceed outward like Vaikharī with articulation fully developed. But She is in the middle between these two. Vaikharī is a form of Bīja (*Bijātmikā*) as Madhyamā is of Nāda (*Nādarūpiṇī*), and as Paśyantī is of Bindu (*Bindvātmika*). Vaikharī is manifested in the region from the heart to the mouth (*Hṛdayādhyāsyāntābhivyaktisthānā*). It is called Vaikharī according to Rāghava on account of its particular (Viśeṣa) hardness (Kharatva). Bhāskararāya (Lalitā v. 81) derives it from Vai = very; Khara = hard. According to the Saubhāgya-Sudhodaya, Vai = certainly; Kha = cavity (of the ear): R = to go or enter. But according to the Yogaśāstras the Devī who is in the form of Vaikharī (*Vaikharirūpā*) is so called because She was produced by the Prāṇa called Vikhara. This is Virātśabda, that is, the manifested letters which singly, or in combination, make certain sounds which are called Mantras. Strictly speaking all uttered sounds are Mantras, all uttered speech having a common origin or development: but in the more usual sense, Mantra means those letters or combination of letters which are used in Upāsanā and Mantrayoga and are the Mantras of the Devatās of Śāstrik worship. The Arthasṛṣṭi of Kuṇḍalinī are the Kalās which arise from the letters such as the Rudra and Viṣṇu Mūrtis, their Śaktis and so forth.

The root "Man" means "to think" and the suffix "tra" indicates the saving character of Mantra. I have elsewhere spoken of Mantra as "thought-movement vehicled by and expressed in speech " and as being a " power in the form of idea clothed with sound." I find that this has led to misunderstanding. I will therefore make my meaning clearer. The one supreme S'akti appears in dual aspects as the Word, the Sense by which as uttered sound it is heard, and as the Object or Artha which the word denotes. The child is taught the meaning of words. Such and such an object is pointed out as being indicated by a word. But a Mantra *is* the Devatā. The Sādhaka is taught who that Devatā is. He does not however at once see that Devatā. At this stage the Devatā exists for him clothed with or as an audible sound, which evokes a particular thought-movement or transformation of mental substance The next stage is by Mantra-Sādhanā to realise that Devatā ; to know it not only as a word and its mental counterpart, but as a form of that Power of which they are but a faint reflection in the world of mind and matter. That Power is infinitely greater than either, and the Mantra is a particular form of Devatā vehicled as all else in the world by mind and matter. The power by which the Devatā is realised is also S'akti, that is, Sādhana-S'akti, that is again the power of the individual Sādhaka to realise by Sādhanā. The Devatā whom he is taught to realise is infinitely greater than that. All is S'akti, but what is sought to be realised is S'akti Herself presented to the Sādhaka in the Mantra form. Brahman *is* of course in all things as their substance and all forms of *becoming* are without exception S'akti. But these forms are only S'akti as such. As such limited forms we realise them at once. For this we require mind, senses, and attention only in their functioning. But the Devatā, which the Mantra is, cannot be realised in

this way only, since in Itself (that is other than as
the sound heard, and the idea it evokes) it is not an
object in the ordinary material universe. The
Sādhaka has to pierce through the vehicle of the
audible S'abda and realise the Devata whose form
the Mantra is. He is enabled to do this by the
co-operation of the Mantra-S'akti with his own
Sādhana-S'akti. The latter gives to those who exert
their own power (Sādhana-S'akti) the ability to
achieve. At length and by striving, the Consciousness which manifests as Sādhana-S'akti unites
both, and the Consciousness, which is the Devatā,
is thus realised and in this sense appears to the
Sādhaka. This is the Saguṇa or Vācaka form of
Devatā, and this when realised at length procures
for the Sādhaka a realisation of the Vācyā-S'akti which
the Saguṇa-Devatā indicates. In short the Devi or
Supreme S'akti has two "forms", Her gross (Sthūla)
Saguṇa form as Mantra (Mantramayī) and Her subtle
(Sūkṣma) form as "light" (Jyotirmayī). Realisation
is the passage from that indirect knowing, through word
and its mental counterpart, to that direct knowledge
which is union with the Devatā whose form a particular
Mantra is.

S'abdabrahman is all-prevading, undifferentiated
S'akti, and Mantra is Its particular manifestation. It is
Varṇātmaka-śabda (Lettered sound) manifested by
Ākāśa caused by the contact of the surrounding air
with the vocal organs, the formation of which in speech
is in response to the mental movement or idea, which
by the will thus seeks outward expression as audible
sound. All S'abda has its corresponding Artha, for
neither can be dissociated from the other. The word
"Artha" comes from the root "Ri" which means to

get, to know, to enjoy. Artha is that which is denoted by Śabda and is that which is known and enjoyed. This Artha is either subtle (Sūkṣma) or gross (Sthūla). The latter is the outer physical object which speech denotes and the former is the Vṛtti (modification) of the mind which corresponds to the gross Artha ; for as an object is perceived the mind forms itself into a Vṛtti which is the exact mental counterpart of the object perceived. The mind has thus two aspects, in one of which it is the perceiver (Grāhaka) and in the other the perceived (Grāhya) in the shape of the mental impression. That aspect of the mind which cognises is called Śabda or Nāma (name) and that aspect in which it is its own or cognised is called Artha and Rūpa (Form), Śabda being associated with all mental operations. In the evolution of the universe the undifferentiated Śabda divides itself into subtle Śabda and subtle Artha which then evolve into gross Śabda and gross Artha. For the Cosmic Mind projects its subtle Artha on the sensuous plane which is then a physical gross Artha named in spoken speech. Thus the subtle Śabda associated with cognition is called Mātṛkā and the subtle Artha is the mental impression ; whilst the gross Śabdas are the uttered letters (Varṇa) denoting the gross outer physical object (Sthūla-Artha).

Just as the body is causal, subtle, gross, and as there are three cosmic and individual states, dreamless sleep, dreaming, waking ; Prājña, Taijasa, Viśva ; Īśvara, Hiraṇyagarbha, Vaiśvānara or Virāt; and a fourth transcendent state or Turīya ; so there are three states (Bhāva) of sound Paśyantī, Madhyamā, Vaikharī developed from a fourth supreme and undifferentiated state (Parā). This last and Paśyantī represent the causal aspect of Śabda, for Paśyantī is the actual moving aspect of the unmoving Parā. Madhyamā is Hiraṇyagarbhaśabda. This Sūkṣma-śabda and its corresponding Artha belong to the subtle body (Liṅga-Śarira). In creation the Cosmic Mind first develops Paśyanti-śabda and Artha, and then projects this subtle Artha into the world of sensuous experience and names it in spoken speech developed in the throat and issuing from the mouth. Vaikhari is Virāt-śabda belonging, as well as the physical objects it denotes, to the gross body (Sthūla-Śarira). This last Gross Śabda is language, that is, sentences (Vākya), words (Pada) and letters (Varṇa) which are the expressions of ideas and Mantra. Paśyanti is characterised by non-particular general movement (Sāmānyaspanda), the first undefined push of the Vāyu towards manifestation ; Madhyamā is specific movement (Viśeṣaspanda), the Vāyu commencing to differentiate ; and Vaikhari is Spaṣṭatara-spanda, that is, the clear separate movements of articulate speech. Mental Artha is a Samskāra, an impression left on the subtle body by previous experience and which is recalled when the Jiva re-awakes to world-experience and re-collects the experience temporarily lost in the cosmic dreamless state (Suṣupti) which is dissolution (Pralaya). The Cause (Kāraṇa) which arouses this Samskāra is the Śabda or Nāma, subtle or gross, corresponding to that particular Artha. There is thus a double line of creation from the Śabda-brahman, namely, language expressive of ideas and the objects which these denote. Uttered speech is a manifestation of the inner " naming " or thought which is similar in men of all races. Possibly for this reason a thought-reader whose cerebral centre is *en rapport* with that of another may read the hidden " speech, " that is, the thought of one whose spoken

speech he cannot understand. Vaikharī-śabda however
differs in various races owing to racial and climatic
conditions, the physical formation of the vocal organs
and so forth. But for each particular man speaking
any particular language, the uttered name of any
object is the gross expression of his inner thought movement. It evokes that movement and again expresses it.
It evokes the idea and that idea is consciousness as
mental operation. That operation can be so intensified
as to make itself creative. This is Mantra-caitanya
when thought is not only in the outer husk but is
vitalised through its conscious centre.

The above is but the Mantra way of saying that
the homogeneous Consciousness differentiates as Śakti
and appears as subject (Śabda) and object (Artha), at
first in the subtle form of mind and its contents generated by the Samskāra and then in the gross form of
language as the expression of ideas and of physical
objects (Artha), which the creative or Cosmic Mind
projects into the world of sensuous experience to be the
source of impressions to the individual experiencer
therein. The natural name of anything is the sound
which is produced by the action of the moving forces
which constitute it. He therefore, it is said, who
mentally or vocally utters with creative force the
natural name of anything brings into being the thing
which bears that name. Thus " Ram " is the Bīja of
fire ; and is said to be the expression in gross sound
(Vaikharī-śabda) of the subtle sound produced by the
activity of, and which is, the subtle fire-force. The
mere utterance however of " Ram " or any other
Mantra is nothing but a movement of the two lips.
When however the Mantra is awakened (Prabuddha),
that is, when there is Mantra-caitanya, then the

Sādhaka can make the Mantra work. However this may be, in all cases it is the creative thought which ensouls the uttered sound which works now in man's small magic, just as it first worked in the grand magical display of the World-Creator. His thought was the aggregate, with creative power, of all thought. Each man is S'iva and can attain His power to the degree of his ability to consciously realise himself as such. Mantra and Devāta are one and the same. By Japa the presence of the latter is invoked. Japa or repetition of Mantra is compared to the action of a man shaking a sleeper to wake him up. The two lips are S'iva and S'akti. Their movement is the coition (Maithuna) of the two. S'abda which issues therefrom is in the nature of Bindu. The Devāta thus produced is as it were the son of the Sādhaka. It is not the Supreme Devatā (who is actionless) who appears, but in all cases an emanation produced by the Sādhaka for his benefit only. The boy-S'iva (Bāla-S'iva) who thus appears is then made strong by the nature which the Sādhaka gives to his creation. The occultist will understand all such symbolism to mean that the Devatā is a form of the consciousness of the pure Sādhaka, which the latter arouses and strengthens and gains good thereby. It is his consciousness which becomes Bāla-S'iva and which when strengthened is the full-grown Divine Power Itself. All Mantras are in the body as forms of consciousness (Vijñānarūpa). When the Mantra is fully practised, it enlivens the Samskāra and the Artha appears to the mind. Mantras are thus a form of the Samskāras of Jīvas—the Artha of which appears to the consciousness which is pure. The essence of all this is —concentrate and vitalise thought and will-power. But for such a purpose a method is necessary, namely, language and determined varieties of practice according to the end sought. These Mantra-vidyā (which explains what Mantra is) also enjoins. For thought in the sense previously stated, words (gross or subtle) are necessary. Mantra-vidyā is the science of thought and of its expression in language as evolved from the Logos or Sabda-brahman Itself.

It is in this sense that the universe is said to be composed of the Letters. It is the fifty (or as some count them fifty-one) letters of the Sanskrit alphabet which are denoted by the Garland of severed heads which the naked Mother Kālī, dark like a threatening rain-cloud, wears as She stands amidst bones and carrion, beasts and birds, in the burning ground, on the white corpse-like (Savarūpa) body of Siva. For it is She who "slaughters," that is, withdraws all speech and its objects into Herself at the time of the dissolution of all things (Mahāpralaya). From Her in Her aspect of Mahā-kundalī coiled round the Siva-bindu they are derived. Mahā-kundalī when with one coil is Bindu; with two Prakṛti Puruṣa ; with three Saktis (Icchā, Jñāna, Kriyā and the three Guṇas, Rajas, Sattva, Tamas) ; with three and a half She is then actually creative (Sṛṣṭyunmukhī) with Vikṛti. Then with four coils and so on to 51. She is according to the Sakti-samgama-Tantra (Utpatti-Khānda, Ullāsa 1) Ekajatā, Ugratārā, Siddhakālī, Kālasundarī, Bhūvaneśvarī, Candikeśvarī, Dasamahāvidyā (ten coils), Smaśāna-kālikā, Candabhairavī, Kāmatārā, Vasikaraṇa-kālikā, Pañcadaśī, Sodasī, Chinnamastā, Mahāmadhumatī, Mahāpadmāvatī, Ramā, Kāmasundarī, Dakṣiṇakālikā, Vidyeśī, Gāyatrī (24 coils), Pañcamī, Sasthī, Mahā-ratneśvarī, Mūlasañjīvanī, Paramākalā, Mahānīla-sarasvatī, Vasudhārā, Trailokyamohinī, Trailokyavijayā, Mahākāmatāriṇī, Aghorā, Samitamohinī, Bagalā, Arundhatī, Annapūrṇā, Nakulī, Trikaṇṭakī, Rājeśvarī, Trailokyākarśiṇī, Rājarājeśvarī, Kukkutī, Siddhavidyā, Mṛtyuhāriṇī, Mahābhagavatī, Vāsavī, Pheṭkarī, Mahāśrimātṛsundarī, and S'rimātṛkotpatti- sundarī (coils 51) respectively. Each coil is said to represent the Mātṛkā or subtle form of each of the letters (Varṇa) and to denote the number of Kūtas or divisions in the Mantras of each of these Devatās. Mahākuṇḍalī coiled round the S'iva-bindu, as it were a mathematical line without magnitude, makes with it one point. When the time for creation comes She un- coils Herself and creates the whole universe in the form of the Letters and the objects which they denote. Having so created it, She again rests as Kuṇḍalī in the root centre of the body (Mūlādhāra) of all living creatures from which She issues as Paśyantī, Madhyamā, and Vaikharī S'abda. Man's body is called in the Tantras a microcosm (Kṣudra-brahmāṇḍa), containing within itself all which is in the universe (Mahā-brahmāṇḍa) of which it is a part. The Yoginī- hṛdaya-Tantra (Chap. I. 36) says that, when S'akti first "sees" (that is, ideates), She is Paramākalā in the Mother form (Ambikārūpa) which is both supreme Peace (Paramā-S'āntā) and Supreme Speech (Parā-vāk). She sees the manifested S'abda from Paśyantī to Vaikharī. The Paśyantī state is that in which Will (Icchā-śakti) is about to display the universe then in seed (Bīja) form. This is the S'akti-Vāmā. Madhyamā- Vāk which is knowledge (Jñāna) is Jyeṣṭhā. Here there is the first assumption of form as the Mātṛkā (*Mātṛkātvaṁ-āpanna*), for here is particular motion (Viśeṣa-spanda). Vaikharī state is that of Kriyā-S'akti (action) whose form is that of the gross universe. As the former S'akti produces the subtle letters or Mātṛkā which are the Vāsanā, so the latter is the S'akti of the gross letters (Varṇa) of words and their objects. These letters form the Garland of the Mother (Varṇamālā), issuing from Her as Kuṇḍalī and absorbed by Her in the Yoga which bears Her name.

As the Yoga-kuṇḍalī-Upaniṣad says: "That Vāk (Power of speech or Logos) which sprouts in Parā, gives forth leaves in Paśyantī, buds in Madh-yamā, and blossoms in Vaikharī. By reversing the above order sound is absorbed. Whoever realises the great Lord of Vāk, the undifferentiated illu-mining Self is unaffected by any word (S'abda), be it what it may." As the Haṭha-yoga-pradīpikā (IV. 101-102) concisely says: "Whatever is heard in the form of sound is S'akti. The absorbed state (Laya) of the Tattvas (Prakṛti's evolutes) is that in which no sound exists. So long as there is the notion of Ether, so long is the sound (that is, vibration) heard. The soundless is called Parabrahman or Paramātmā." S'abda-brahman is thus the Brahman in its aspect as the cause of the manifested S'abdārtha. It is the ideating kinetic aspect of the undifferentiated Ether of Consciousness, the Cidākāśa of Philosophy and the Saguṇa-Brahman of worship. It is Cit-S'akti vehicled by undifferentiated Māyā-S'akti or the manifesting Godhead uncreated, unborn, eternal, evolving the changing worlds of name and form (Nāma-rūpa) by its wondrous and inscrutable Māyā. Therefore, as Caṇḍī says, "Reverence to Her Who is eternal, Raudrī, Gaurī, Dhātrī, reverence and again reverence; to Her who is the Consciousness in all beings, reverence and again reverence."

OM

THE ancient Hindu had an aptitude, much to be appreciated in these often verbose days, of saying a great deal in a few words. The Mantra " Om " is an instance. For this short syllable contains a whole philosophy which many volumes would not suffice to state—an Eastern philosophy I may add which is gaining increased support from Western science. These two will before long be reconciled when the latter has cast aside what a friend calls its " habit blinkers." The beneficial result will, it is hoped, be a science which is religious, and a religion which is scientific.

The Mantra " Om " is composed of three letters A, U, M,—of which the first two vowels coalesce into O. Over the Om is written the sign Candrabindu or Nāda and Bindu, shown as a crescent with a dot or point over it. Nāda and Bindu are two of many aspects of That which in India is called the Mother, or great Power (Mahāśakti), as it was by the near East called Magna Mater and by the Gnostics Megale Dunamis. This is both the efficient and material Cause of the universe which is Its form or body. Nāda, is the Mantra name for the first going forth of Power which gathers itself together in massive strength (Ghani-bhūta) as Bindu to create the universe, and which Bindu, as

so creating, differentiates into a Trinity of Energies
which are symbolised by A, U, M. Nāda and Bindu
thus represent the unmanifested " fourth " (Turīya)
state immediately before the manifestation of the
world, in which animate life exists in the three conditions of dreamless sleep, dream, and waking. Man
always anthropomorphises. In the West he calls the
Creator the Father. More aptly Supreme Creative
Being in the East and by the S'āktas is called the
Mother, for this Power conceives in Its Womb, which
is Consciousness, gives birth to and nourishes, the
Universe. The first Mantra into which a child is
initiated is Mā or Mother, for that is its first word, and
Mother is often the last word on the lips of the dying.
Reverence to the natural Mother is reverence to the
Mother of all and they who in life and at death drink
the milk of that Mother attain to Her. Moreover in
the world the Mother-aspect of Her who is Brahman is
alone fully manifested. What She is in Herself (Svarūpa)
is not known to mind or senses. The Yoginī-hṛdaya-
Tantra says : " What man knows the heart of a woman ?
Only S'iva knows the Heart of Yoginī." This is the
Cosmic Heart of the universe whose systole and diastole
is the going forth and return of millions of worlds. This
process Brahmanism called Pravṛtti and Nivṛtti and
Taoism (which is perhaps a Chinese adaptation of the
doctrine of the Upaniṣads) names it Yang and Yinn.
Relatively to man's knowledge the Supreme Power is
said to be in Itself Being (Sat), Consciousness (Cit) and
Bliss (Ānanda). The Primordial Power or Ādyā S'akti
is inconceivably beyond manifested personality, for
this is limited experience hedged in by mind and matter.
Though not in Itself a Person as we understand that
term, It is ever *personalizing* in the form of all indivi-

dual (Vyaṣṭi) things in the world. It is also a Person as the aggregate (Samaṣṭi) of all such personalities. Whilst infinite, it contains in Itself the sum of all human and other experience. Whilst the Power (Mahā-śakti) is in Itself beyond mind and senses in that darkness (as man thinks it to be) which is the body of Mahākālī, its manifestations are seen. It is with refer-ence to such manifestation inferred to be the Radical Vital Potential which is, as it were, the thread (Sūtrātmā) of the whole series of beings, which form one Vital Continuity, a principle on which Indian Monistic philosophy is based. Nothing has an absolute commencement or end. All is transformed. Birth and death are modes thereof. Each existence is as it were a knot tied in an infinite rope which knot is made at birth and untied at death. Something does not come from nothing, and something never becomes nothing. An absolute beginning or end is inconceiv-able. Particular universes come into being and go. Birth, life and death are modes of the universal trans-formation governing all organic life " from a blade of grass to Brahmā Himself ". The divine infinitude is ever such, but appears as limited function and its effects, and as apparently discontinuous, because of the limita-tion of the senses which perceive its workings. The whole Fact is never present to consciousness, but only that section to which pragmatic attention is for the moment given, and which therefore appears localised and in succession of time. Nevertheless there is an infinite Vital Continuity stretching from the Radical Potential to its actualisation as the crust of matter, which is but an infinitesimal portion of the effect produced by the function of Substance relative to the whole universal efficiency. For ether (Ākāśa) is more

continuous than matter which is but the outer crust of
the Central Power. Ether is continuous and all-
pervading and is said to be more than a thousand times
denser than gross ponderable matter. The visible earth
is therefore but a microscopic point evolved by the
Vital Power (Sakti) of Substance (Siva) in the midst of
the invisible, perpetually active, but in its own nature
(Svarūpa) unaffected Divine Substance pervading all
space. Therein nothing truly exists independently of
another, but all are transformations of the one Power.
And as that Power is Itself vital and creative, its
products or rather transformations of Itself are that.
As It is Being with the potentialities of all life in form,
none of its manifestations is "dead," though in common
parlance we concede "life" only to that which displays
evolutionary growth. The search therefore for the
origin of life is futile, since life is eternal and had no
beginning.

All things are part of the one Mother who is Life
itself. It displays itself in innumerable forms, but the
vastest generalisation of Its working discloses three
movements of creative upbuilding, of destructive
disintegration and the holding of these two opposing
forces in equilibrium. Nāda-bindu differentiates into
the Trinity of Will (Icchā), Knowledge (Jñāna) and
Action (Kriyā), "Sun," "Moon," and "Fire," and
this self-explicating Power manifest in matter in
the threefold manner described. These three Powers
are A, U, M, or the Devatās Brahmā, Viṣṇu, Rudra.
These are not "Gods." There is only one God. They
are Devas or "Shining ones," being aspects and specific
manifestations of the One Divine Power whose Feet (in
the words of Sāstra) even Brahmā, Viṣṇu and Rudra
worship. They are scientific concepts deified, and

rightly so, for their content refers to aspects of the Supreme Power which is God. Scientifically they stand for the three functions of Vital Substance. It is incorrect to suppose that God in his aspect as Brahmā created the world some millions of years ago and has since done nothing, or that He in His form as Rudra has as yet had no opportunity of displaying His Power of dissolution. Brahmā is always creating and recreating the elements of manifested substance which Rudra is ever breaking down. Throughout Nature there are these twin forces upbuilding and destroying forms, integrating and disintegrating, anabolism and cata- bolism, tending to change and conservation of tissues and so on. The three aspects A, U, M, of the Primordial Power (Nāda-bindu) are always operating. Whilst Rudra is, by chemical destruction, breaking down the combinations of matter and thus working towards the final dissolution of things, that is the dis- integration of forms into either its more general elements (mahābhūta) or into the formless substance (Prakṛti) the material Cause of all, Brahmā creates it anew by His ever rejuvenescent molecular activity, thus rescuing organised vitality from the processes which are ever at work to consume its forms. Viṣṇu again is the power which stabilises matter in the midst of these conflicting forces and thus maintains all Existences. Things only possess relative stability. So it is that the Power of Rudra works its purpose at the end. Matter itself is only a relatively stable form of Energy from which as Supreme Will it appears and into which, on the attainment of its terminal state, it again merges. It is Viṣṇu who holds it together in equilibrium. Again leaving individual existences and looking at the sum total of manifested Energy, Viṣṇu, the Maintainer, throughout Space and Time, is a theological statement of the general Conservation of Energy. To these intuited laws and truths objective science is giving increasing support. In this sense "Om" is the Pratika or representative of the Radical Vital Potential of the Universe and of the Trinity of Energies by which It actualises and materialises Itself as the five forms of "matter" (though Ether is not ponderable matter), namely ethereal (Ākāśa), aerial (Vāyu), fiery (Agni), liquid (Ap) and solid (Pṛthivī). Through worship of and meditation on this Pratika, with all its implications, man, according to Advaita-Vedānta, realises himself as the one vital S'akti who is the Mother of all.

CHAPTER XXIII

THE NECKLACE OF KĀLĪ

THE world has never been altogether without the
Wisdom—the Mūla Veda nor its Teachers. The degree
and manner in which it has been imparted have,
however, necessarily varied according to the capacities
of men to receive it. So also have the symbols by
which it has been conveyed. These symbols further
have varying significance according to the spiritual
advancement of the worshipper. This question of
degree and variety of presentation has led to the
superficial view that difference in beliefs negatives the
existence of any commonly established Truth. But if
the matter be regarded more deeply, it will be seen that
whilst there is one essential Wisdom, its revelation has
been more or less complete according to symbols
evolved by, and, therefore, fitting to, particular racial
temperaments and characters. Symbols are naturally
misunderstood by those to whom the beliefs they typify
are unfamiliar, and who differ in temperament from
those who have evolved them. To the ordinary Western
mind the symbols of Hinduism are often repulsive and
absurd. It must not, however, be forgotten that some
of the symbols of Western Faiths have the same effect
on the Hindu. From the picture of the "Slain Lamb,"
and other symbols in terms of blood and death, he
naturally shrinks in disgust. The same effect on the

other hand is not seldom produced in the Western at the sight of the terrible forms in which India has embodied Her vision of the undoubted Terrors which exist in and around us. All is not smiling in this world. Even amongst persons of the same race and indeed of the same faith we may observe such differences. Before the Catholic Cultus of the " Sacred Heart " had overcome the opposition which it at first encountered, and for a considerable time after, its imagery was regarded with aversion by some who spoke of it in terms which would be to-day counted as shocking irreverence. These differences are likely to exist so long as men vary in mental attitude and temperament, and until they reach the stage in which, having discovered the essential truths, they become indifferent to the mode in which they are presented. We must also in such matters distinguish between what a symbol may have meant and what it now means. Until quite recent times the English peasant folk and others danced around the flower-wreathed Maypole. That the pole originally (like other similar forms) represented the great Linga admits of as little doubt as that these folk, who in recent ages danced around it, were ignorant of that fact. The Bishop's mitre is said to be head of a fish worn by ancient near-eastern hierophants. But what of that ? It has no such associations now.

Let us illustrate these general remarks by a short study of one portion of the Kālī symbolism which affects so many, who are not Hindus, with disgust or horror. Kālī is the Deity in that aspect in which It withdraws all things which it had created into Itself. Kālī is so called because She devours Kāla (Time) and then resumes Her own dark formlessness.

The Mahānirvāṇa-Tantra says (IV. 30-34) of the Supreme Mother : " Thou the supreme Yoginī moved by His mere will doth create, maintain and withdraw the world with all that moves and is motionless therein. Mahā-kāla (Great Time) the Dissolver of the universe is Thy form. At the dissolution of things it is Kāla (Time) who will devour all and by reason of this He is called Mahā-kāla and since Thou devourest Mahā-kāla Himself it is Thou who art called the supreme Primordial Kālikā.

" Because Thou devourest Kāla, Thou art called Kālī and because Thou art the origin of and devourest all things Thou art called the Ādya-Kālī. Resuming after dissolution Thine own nature dark and formless, Thou alone remainest as One, Ineffable, and Inconceivable. Though appearing in form Thou art yet formless ; though Thyself without beginning, multiform by the Power of Māyā, Thou art the beginning of all, Creatrix. Protectress and Destructress that Thou art". From Her then, in Her nature one with S'iva, the state which is Aśabda, issue all letters and words (S'abda) and the world of things (Artha) which they denote. Into Her as Kālī they are dissolved.

The scene is laid in the cremation ground (S'maśāna) amidst white sun-dried bones and fragments of flesh, gnawed, and pecked at by carrion beasts and birds. Here the " heroic " (Vīra) worshipper (Sādhaka) performs at dead of night his awe-inspiring rituals. Kālī is set in such a scene for She is that aspect of the Great Power which withdraws all things into Herself at, and by, the dissolution of the universe. He alone worships without fear, who has abandoned all worldly desires, and seeks union with Her as the One Blissful and Perfect Experience. On the burning ground all worldly desires are burnt away. She is naked and dark like a threatening raincloud. She is dark, for She who is Herself beyond mind and speech, reduces all things into that worldly " nothingness," which as the Void (Sūnya) of all which we now know, is at the same time the All (Pūrṇa) which is Light and Peace. She is naked, being clothed in space alone (Digambarī), because the Great Power is unlimited ; further She is in Herself beyond Māyā (Māyātītā) ; that Power of Herself with which She covers Her own nature and so creates all universes. She stands upon the white corpse-like (S'avarūpa) body of S'iva. He is white, because He is the illuminating (Prakāśa) transcendental aspect of Consciousness. He is inert because He is the change-less aspect of the Supreme, and She the apparently changing aspect of the same. In truth She and He are one and the same, being twin aspects of the One who is changelessness in, and exists as, change. Much might be said in explanation of these and other symbols such as Her loosened hair, the lolling tongue, the thin stream of blood which trickles from the corners of the mouth, the position of Her feet, the apron of dead men's hands around Her waist, Her implements and so forth. Here I take only the garland of freshly-severed heads which hangs like a Varṇamālā low from Her neck.

Some have conjectured that Kālī was originally the Goddess of the dark-skinned inhabitants of the Vindhya Hills taken over by the Brāhmaṇas into their worship.

One of them has thought that She was a deified Princess of these folk, who fought against the white incoming Aryans. He pointed to the significant fact that the severed heads are those of white men. The Western may say that Kālī was an objectification of the Indian mind, making a Divinity of the Power of Death. An Eastern may reply that She is the Saṁketa (symbol) which is the effect of the impress of a Spiritual Power on the Indian mind. I do not pause to consider these matters here.

The question before us is, what does this imagery mean now, and what has it meant for centuries past to the initiate in Her symbolism? An esoteric explanation describes this Garland as made up of the heads of Demons, which She as a power of righteousness, has conquered. According to an inner explanation given in the Indian Tantra-S'āstra this string of heads is the Garland of Letters (Varṇamālā), that is the fifty, and as some count it, fifty-one letters of the Sanskrit Alphabet. The same interpretation is given in the Buddhist Demchog Tantra in respect of the Garland worn by the great Heruka. (See *S'ri Cakra Sāmbhara—A Buddhist Tantra*). These letters represent the universe of names and forms (Nāma-rūpa), that is Speech (S'abda) and its meaning or object (Artha). She the Devourer of all, "slaughters," that is, withdraws, both into Her undivided Consciousness at the Great dissolution of the Universe. She wears the letters which She as Creatrix, bore. She wears the Letters which, She, as the Dissolving Power, takes to Herself again. A very profound doctrine is connected with these Letters, which space prevents me from fully entering into here. I have set it out elsewhere in greater detail. The movements of Her creative projection are indicated by the Letters subtle and gross which exist on the Petals of the inner bodily centres or Lotuses.

Very shortly stated. S'abda which literally means Sound—here lettered sound—is in its causal state (Para-śabda) known as "Supreme Speech" (Parā-Vāk). This is the S'abda-brahman or Logos; that aspect of Reality or Consciousness (Cit) in which It is the immediate cause of creation, that is of the dichotomy in Consciousness which is "I" and "This", subject and object, mind and matter. This condition of causal S'abda is the Cosmic Dreamless State (Suṣupti). This Logos awakening from Its Causal Sleep "sees", that is, creatively ideates the universe, and is then known as Paśyantī-S'abda. As Consciousness "sees" or ideates, forms arise in the Creative Mind, which are themselves impressions (Samskāra) carried over from previous worlds, which ceased to exist as such when the universe entered the state of causal dreamless sleep on the previous dissolution. These re-arise as the formless Consciousness awakes to enjoy once again sensuous life in the world of forms.

The Cosmic Mind is at first itself both cognising subject (Grāhaka) and cognised object (Grāhya); for it has not yet projected its thought into the plane of Matter : the mind as subject-cogniser is S'abda and the mind as the object cognised, that is, the mind in the form of object is subtle Artha. This S'abda called Madhyamā-S'abda is an "Inner Naming" or "Hidden Speech". At this stage, that which answers to the spoken letters (Varṇa) are the "Little Mothers" or Mātrikā, the subtle forms of gross speech. There is at this stage a differentiation of Consciousness into subject and object but the latter is now within and forms part of the self. This is the state of Cosmic Dreaming (Svapna). The Cosmic Mind then projects these mental images on to the material plane and there they become materialised as gross physical objects (Sthūla Artha) which make impressions from without on the mind of the created consciousness. This is the cosmic waking stage (Jāgrat). At this last stage the thought-movement expresses itself through the vocal organs in contact with the air as uttered speech (Vaikharī Śabda) made up of letters, syllables and sentences. This lettered sound is manifested Śabda or Name (Nāma) and the physical objects denoted by speech are the gross Artha or Form (Rūpa).

This manifested speech varies in men, for their individual and racial characteristics and the conditions, such as country and climate in which they live, differ. There is a tradition that there was once a universal speech before the building of the Tower of Babel, signifying the confusion of tongues. Of these letters and names and their meaning or objects, that is concepts and concepts objectified the whole Universe is composed. When Kālī withdraws the world, that is the names and forms which the Letters signify, the dualism in consciousness, which is creation, vanishes. There is neither " I " (Aham) nor " This " (Idam) but the one non-dual Perfect Experience which Kālī in Her own true nature (Svarūpa) is. In this way Her Garland is understood.

" Surely " I hear it said " not by all. Does every Hindu worshipper think such profundities when he sees the figure of Mother Kālī ? " Of course not, no more than, (say) an ordinary Italian peasant knows of, or can understand, the subtleties of either the Catholic mystics or Doctors of theology. When how-ever, the Western undertakes to depict and explain Indian symbolism, he should, in the interest both of knowledge and fairness, understand what it means both to the high as well as to the humble worshipper. Salutation is thus made to Her from whom the mind and its thoughts proceed and the language (Vāk) in which they are expressed. Vāk is Prakāśa, the illuminating consciousness, and Artha is Vimarśa its object. Vāk is in the form of Varṇa (letters), Pada (syllables) Mantra. Artha is Kalā, Tattva, and Bhuvana the other so-called Adhvās. (See Ch. XXVII). Out of Vāk and Artha the whole world, consisting of six Adhvās (Ṣadadhvātmaka) originated. Round the neck of Kāli the letters (Varṇa) which make the syllables (Pada) and Mantra are hung. In Her they are dissolved in the fiery ending of the worlds.

CHAPTER XXIV

DHVANI

MOTION may be either produced or unproduced. The latter is the causal stress itself, and the former the effect of it. In the world, sound is produced by the contact of one thing with another—of (say) the hand and the drum in case of unlettered sound and the vocal organs and air in the case of uttered speech. Causal stress itself is uncreate, is self-produced and not caused by the striking of one thing against another. For this reason it is called Anāhata. This Anāhata-S'abda which is Brahman-movement is heard in the heart which It has produced and which It causes to pulse, a movement which we can feel and hear.

This uncreated self-existing S'abda as causal stress manifests in double form as unlettered sound or Dhvani and is thus called Dhvanyātmaka-S'abda and as lettered sound or Varṇa which is Varṇātmaka-S'abda. And so the Bhāṣā-pariccheda says (164, 165) :

S'abdo dhvanisca varṇasca mṛdaṅgādibhavo dhvanih'
Kaṇṭha-samyoga-janmāno-varṇāste kādayo matāh.

That is S'abda is of two kinds—Dhvani and Varṇa. The first is illustrated in the sound given forth by a drum and the like. In the production of the second the throat organ is exercised and it is manifested as Ka,

DHVANI   243

Kha, and the other letters of the Alphabet. That is in
certain sounds such as the beating of a drum, the roar
of thunder, the sounds of laughing, crying and so forth
no letters appear to be manifested (*Varṇaviśeṣāna-
bhivyañjaka*) but that in certain others, letters or Varṇas
are manifested as in the case of sounds of articulate
speech. The former class are called Dhvanis and the
latter Varṇas.

In both cases it is to be observed that sound is
produced by the clashing (Abhigāta) of two created
things, *viz.*, the drum and the hand or drumstick and
the vocal organs in contact with the circumambient air.

The distinction therefore between the two classes
does not depend upon this—(1) that whilst Varṇas are
produced by the mutual impact of the throat, air, and
the ear, the Dhvanis are produced by an assemblage of
conditions of which the throat is not one. In other
words the Vyāpāra or functioning of the vocal organ
does not constitute the distinction between Dhvanyāt-
maka and Varṇātmaka-S'abda. For the vocal organ is
exercised in laughing, crying, and so forth and also in
the cries of animals, but in them we hear no Varṇātmaka-S'abda or articulate speech. Thus Dhvanis may
be produced by the vocal organs. (2) Nor can it be
said that the exercise of the vocal organs is the *sine qua
non* of the Varṇātmaka-S'abda. Thus when we hear
articulate sounds over the telephone or from the gramo-
phone, the immediate cause of the sounds is not the
Vyāpāra of the vocal organ, though the non-immediate
cause may be so. (3) Nor again can we say that the
Varṇātmaka-S'abdas are in all cases significant or
expressive of meanings and that the Dhvanyātmakas
are in all cases insignificant. In a general sense this is

so, and thus, in common parlance, we speak of Varṇātmaka-S'abda as having a meaning and Dhvani as being without it. But this is not necessarily and always so. Doubtless to Īśvara every Dhvani has a meaning, and even to us unlettered sound may express a meaning. Again some Varṇātmaka-S'abdas may not. For even to a man who knows a particular languge *any* combination of letters or any combinations of words will not be expressive language—but only letters in certain order and combination. Thus the sound of laughter or crying is Dhvanyātmaka yet the sound may express a meaning in the sense that it is recognised at once from the sound that a particular person is happy or in trouble. Many of the Dhvanis of animals may be significant in this sense. The sound of a bell, bugle, or drum may be suggestive of meaning as in the case of the midday gun. On the other hand many Varṇāt-makas may not express a meaning. Thus the combina-tion M, A, N has a meaning and spells " man " in English but M, N, A and other combinations (except N, A, M which may have some sort of meaning) do not express meaning. Each letter separately may have a meaning. According to the Vyāsa-Bhāṣya on Yoga, each Varṇa is capable of expressing all Arthas or meanings. But any arbitrary combination of separate letters will not give a meaning. A special combination of Varṇas is necessary to express a special meaning. Electricity may be latent in all material objects but we require to make special combinations of such objects (*e.g.*, zinc, copper and sulphuric acid in a cell) to make such electricity patent. Any arbitrary combinations (*e.g.*, of wood, water, and oil) will not effect this. In an unsuitable combination of Varṇas, their S'aktis check the one the other.

The distinction between the two classes is therefore a distinction between sounds which manifest themselves as letters and others which do not. The former are usually produced by the throat (*Kaṇṭha-samyoga-janmānaḥ*) but not invariably. On the other hand, as we have seen, Dhvanis too may be so produced. Both Varṇas and Dhvanis again are momentary (Kṣaṇika). Both therefore are produced by the contact (Abhighāta) of two or more created things. Let the letter " Ka " be uttered a hundred times. Each time it is a different sound which is uttered. Again one person says ' Ka ' and then another says Ka. The sounds again are different. The sounds produced and heard in these cases are indeed different. Nevertheless we may still recognise that one Varṇa sound, *e.g.*, ' Ka ' is being uttered by oneself all those hundred times and by oneself and the other person. We recognise here oneness in the midst of all differences of the individual sounds produced and heard. The recognition (Pratyabhijñā) takes this from :

" It is the same ' Ka ' that I utter now and that I uttered a moment before. It is the same Ka that you have uttered and I have uttered." Western psychology may attempt an explanation of this recognition of Varṇa identity by comparison, abstraction and assimilation. Thus if Ka is uttered by one person ten times, actually different sounds are produced varying in pitch, softness, harshness and so on. If another person utters the same letter ten times, then each of them is a different sound and the sounds are also different from the sounds produced by the first person. But though all these Dhvanis are different in pitch, timbre and the like, it will be admitted that both persons have uttered the same letter. Western psychology would explain this as follows :

The Dhvanis *are* different but we make a rapid *comparison* of them and find that though they have differences in pitch, timbre, etc., still they have a *great deal* of *similarity.* The differences are then thought away or abstracted and then the twenty sounds are *assimilated* so as to give us a generic sound which we recognise as the Varṇa sound " Ka ". It is in this way also we form the generic notion of " Man " or " Book." The generic sound Ka is not something that actually exists apart from the twenty variations which either of the two persons mentioned have heard. On the contrary the variations are the actual phenomena. The type (the generic sound) is simply our mental construction through comparison, abstraction and assimilation. To a mind which cannot compare, abstract and assimilate, the sounds are different sounds and it cannot recognise any typal sound in their midst. The Indian theory on the subject is, on the other hand, as follows :

The Varṇas or letters have imperishable and in-variable (Nitya) forms. As the Paramāṇus or prime " atoms " of matter are imperishable so are the Varṇa-śabdas. " Nitya " however here means " imperishable " so long as the cosmic order itself lasts. (*Natu madhye varṇānāṁ, utpatti-vināśan.*"—Vedānta-Paribhāṣā). That is in the period of cosmic life beginning with Creation (Sṛṣṭi) and ending with Dissolution (Laya) the Varṇa sounds persist. They are compared to a jar in a dark room which cannot by reason of darkness be seen. (*Andhakārastha-ghaṭānupalambhavat* - Vedānta-Paribhāśā). Just as the jar existing in the dark may not be seen with the eyes, so the prime S'abdas or Varṇas, though always given, may not be always manifested as acoustic phenomena. To be thus manifested they require a manifestor (Abhivyañjaka) or vehicle of expression. This vehicle (Abhivyañjaka) through which an eternal existing letter becomes an acoustic phenomenon *now* and *then* is called Dhvani. The period of cosmic life (Madhye) is a 100 years of Brahmā when the world dissolves (Laya). The Varṇas persist during all these years of Brahmā—a time which is called Kalpa. In Laya they enter the germinal state as seeds of potency. This view is thus essentially different from that of ordinary western psychology. Plato's doctrine of ideal archetypes and their sensible variations comes nearer the Vedānta doctrine.

According to this the Varṇa-śabdas are always (*i.e.*, during a Kalpa) actually going on (Nitya and Anāhata *i.e.*, continuous and uninterrupted.)—produced by artificial means. But they are often unmanifest (Avyakta) to the gross perceptive organs. They become manifest (Vyakta) to gross sensibility through certain manifestors (Abhivyañjaka) which are the Dhvanis. Thus the S'abda "Om" is uninterruptedly going on, but this it is said, one can only hear in certain stages of Sādhanā, or in a quiet place particularly during night time when there is little promiscuous interference of the sound-waves. The Kālī-Mūrti is an eternal symbol of the world-process (involving Cit and the play of S'akti) and the Garland of Letters (Mātṛkās) on the breast of the Mother is also an eternal possession. Whether the Varṇas are uttered and heard or not, they are Anāhata sound-forms and according to Indian ideas they are more real and more actual than the variations (differing in pitch, timbre and so forth) which are uttered and heard. Thus the variations alone are not the actual phenomena as the ordinary western empiricist would hold.

Therefore a Dhvani as an acoustic manifestation of a Nitya S'abda is subject to all conditions of place, time and circumstance and is non-permanent (Anitya) and variable (Vikārī). This variableness and transitoriness which really pertain to the Abhivyañjaka-Dhvani are transferred by us (through association) to the manifested letter (Varṇa). Thus we say "Ka is now produced and is no more." But really that which comes to be or ceases to be is the vehicle (Dhvani) and not the Varṇa-S'abda. As the Vedānta-Paribhāṣā (Ch. IV) says :

Utpanno gakāra ityādipratyakṣatu so'yam gakāra ityādipratyabhijña-virodhād apramāṇaṁ. Varṇābhivyañjaka-dhvanigatotpatti-nirūpita-paramparā-sambandha-viṣayatvena pramāṇam vā. " The apprehension (Pratyakṣa) that " Ga " is now produced is not right apprehension because it conflicts with the recognition (Pratyābhijñā) of the present ' Ga ' (*i.e.*, at present uttered and heard by me) being identical with all other ' Ga ' (*i.e.*, those uttered and heard in the past). Or we may take it as a correct apprehension if we ascribe the idea of production to the Varṇas (which are manifested but not produced) seeing that the Dhvanis which manifest them are produced and using a characteristic which really belongs to the manifestor for the manifested.

S'aṁkarācārya discusses the theory of Varṇa and Sphota in his S'ārīraka-Bhāṣya (1-3-28). He describes Dhvani in these words :

" *Kaḥ punarayam dhvanir nāma, yo dūrād ākarṇayato varṇavivekam apartipadyamānasya karṇapatham avatarati, pratyasīdataśea mandatvapatutvādibhedaṁ varṇeṣvāsañjayati, tannibhandhanāścodattādayo viśeṣā na varṇasvarūpanibandhanāḥ, Varṇānāṁ pratyabhijñāyamānatvāt,* etc." By

Dhvani is to be understood that which is heard by a person listening from a distance without distinguishing the separate letters and which in the case of a person standing near-by affects the letters with its own distinctions of high and low pitch and so forth. It is on this Dhvani that all the distinctions of Udātta, Anudātta and the like depend and not on the intrinsic nature of the letters which are recognised to be the same whenever pronounced.

When a man is heard shouting from a great distance we do not catch his actual words and yet we can hear the pitch, modulation and so forth of his voice. When he speaks close to us we catch his words as well as the modulation, pitch, sweetness or otherwise and so forth of his voice. In both cases the pitch, etc., of the sound constitute its Dhvani. These qualities of pitch, sweetness and the like do not inhere in the Varṇas themselves but belong to their acoustic expression, the Dhvanis. Thus Dhvanis are (1) gross embodiments (Anitya, Vikārī) or Nitya, Avikārī Varṇa-S'abdas ; (2) other gross sounds (either produced in nature such as the sound of the storm or produced by ourselves such as laughter or the sound of musical instruments) which do not appear to us as embodying Varṇa-S'abdas. Those who believe (such as the Grammarians) in Sphota regard Dhvani as its Abhivyañjaka. S'amkara however contests the necessity of assuming Sphota or that which causes the apprehension of the sense of a word.

Dhvani however is used also in a sense different from that in which it is defined in Nyāya or Vedānta as expounded by S'amkara and different from Dhvani as conceived by those Grammarians who regard Dhvani as the manifestor (Vyañjaka) of the ideal sound called ' Sphota.'

In the Tantras Dhvani is a form of Causal S'abda. Thus we hear of the "sweet murmuring Dhvani of Kuṇḍalinī," the Creatrix of all S'abdas and Arthas.

The S'ārāda-Tilaka to which I have repeatedly referred (1, 108-109) says :

Sā prasūte Kuṇḍalinī *śabda-brahmamayī vibhuh.*
S'aktim *tato* Dhvanis *tasmān Nādas asmān* Nirodhika.
Tato'rdhendus *tato* Bindus *tatmādāsīt parātatah.*
Paśyantī Madhyamā vāci Vaikharī śabdajanmabhuh.

The words in roman type are various forms of S'akti, producing one another in the order in which they are mentioned in the verse. From Kuṇḍalinī issued S'akti, from S'akti, Dhvani and so on. From the order of evolution it will appear that Dhvani in such Sāstra is a subtle causal principle and not a gross manifestation of S'abda which is its ordinary sense. It is Vaikharī which is the gross manifestation of S'abda. Here the S'abda manifests from its subtle state as Madhyamā, which issued from the causal state as Parā, Paśyantī, through the Dhvani caused by the contact of the vocal organs and air. Parā and the rest are located in various Cakras and tracts of the bodily organism. Rāghava-Bhatta quoted by Vācaspatya (page 60) says—

Saivorah-kāṇṭha-tālusthā śiro-ghraṇa-radastitā.
Jihvā-mūloṣṭha-nisyūta-sarva-Varṇa-parigrahā.
S'abda-prapañca-jananī śrotra-grahyā tu vaikarī.

" She (Kuṇḍalinī) being in the heart, throat and palate and going through the passages of the head and nose and teeth and coming out from the base of the tongue and the lips becomes audible Vaikharī—the

Kuṇḍalinī who has invested Herself with the Varṇas and is the Mother of all varieties of S'abda. "

S'akti, Dhvani, Nāda and the rest are described as various aspects of Cit due to its varied association with the Guṇas—Sattva, Rajas and Tamas. Thus S'akti is defined as the Sattva-predominant (Sāttvika) condition of Cit; Dhvani as the Rājasik-Sattvik condition (Rajo'nu-viddha Sāttvika) of Cit, that is a Sāttvik condition in which there is also a trace of Rajas ; and Nāda a state of Causal śabda in which there is a trace of Tamas (Tamo'nuviddha). These are called Paramā-kāśāvasthā, Akṣarāvasthā, Avyaktāvastha. Whether then we have to deal with Dhvani in the sense of a form of causal S'abda or as a gross manifestation of S'abda depends upon the context.

CHAPTER XXV

SUN, MOON AND FIRE

THESE words do not refer to the heavenly lumina-
ries of Fire in the three worlds of Birth and Death, but
are technical terms of the Mantra-śāstra denoting the
creative Trinity.

In the Brahmasvarūpa is merged Vimarśa
(Antarlīnavimarśa). Śruti says that there was first
merely One without a second or Brahman. It became
inclined towards creation (Śṛṣṭi-mukha). The material
cause out of which the world is made is, according to
the Vaidik Text, " May I be many." Vimarśa is that
which is the object of experience as " This " (Idam)
and this Idam is the Universe. The " Idam " is thus
the world as object of experience (Prapañca-parāmarśa).
Vimarśa-Śakti is thus the Power which produces and
exists in the form of the universe. Before the world
existed it was in the Brahman in the form of Brahma-
Śakti. Then alone was the Light which is beyond Sun,
Moon and Stars which in the Āgama is known as the
imperishable Supreme World (Anapāyini, Parā-Vak).

She the supreme Vimarśa-Śakti is our Supreme
Lady (Parā-bhaṭṭārikā) Mahā-tripura-Sundarī, in
whom are all the 36 Tattvas beginning with Śiva
and ending with Kṣiti, who is in the form of all
worlds (Sarva-prapañcātmika) and also transcends

them (Taduttīrṇā). She is beyond the three S'aktis who are Sun, Moon and Fire. She is the causal seed of all, with whom S'iva unseparately is. For S'iva cannot create without S'akti nor S'akti without S'iva. As between moon and moonbeam there is no difference so there is none between S'iva and S'akti. The Svarūpa of S'iva is " I " (Aham), for it is said in the Kāma-kalā-vilāsa from which this account is, in general, taken (S'ivasya svarūpam aham-ityeva-mākāram). The Vimarśa of that is the experience of " I-ness." She the primordial Vimarśa-S'akti is the pure mirror which manifests that Experience (Tasya prakāśane nirmalādarśah). The work cited illustrates this as follows :

A handsome King looking at his reflection in a mirror which is before him knows " I am he who is thus reflected." So the Supreme Lord looking at His own Power within Himself knows His own Self as " I am all (Paripūrṇo'ham)," that is, the whole or Perfect " I ". This is the union of A = S'iva and Ha = S'akti, A + Ha = Aham or " I ". S'iva indicates Jñāna-S'akti, and S'akti, Kriyā-S'akti — Knowledge and Action. S'iva is illumination (Prakāśa). The Vimarśa mirror is composed of a mass of His rays and Vimarśa-S'akti is impulse (Visphuraṇa-S'akti) maturing in action. The Rays being reflected back on the foundation of Consciousness there is the Mahābindu. So when the Supreme Lord who is Illumination (Prakāśa) is connected with the mirror-like Vimarśa there shines forth the Parameś-vara as Pūrṇo'ham (The Lord Experience as "I am all.") The Supreme " I " is thus the massing together of S'iva and S'akti. This "I-ness" (Ahambhāva) arises upon the gaze of S'iva upon His own luminous S'akti or Power. So it has been said that in the notion of ' I ' Illumination rests in itself (Ātmaviśrānti). So

S'ruti (Svet. 4-1) says, " That which is letterless (Avarṇa) generates many letters (Varṇa)." This supreme " I " is Cittamaya.

We have spoken of the Aham or " I " and Idam or " This ". The first is known as the white (Sīta) Bindu or " Moon " and represents the S'iva aspect of this supreme " I," and the second is the red (S'oṇa) Bindu or " Fire," the S'akti aspect. They are in conjunction known as the Divine Husband and Wife (Kāmeśvara and Kāmeśvarī). The union of both is the Mixed (Miśra) Bindu or " Sun ". The " Sun " is Kāma and Kalā is " Moon " and " Fire," the three Bindus being known as the Kāmakalā. This mixed Bindu becomes creative and is the cause of the manifested Word (Vāk) and its meaning (Artha). From this Bindu issues Nāda-S'akti in seed form. The Bindu is the union of the letters A and Ha, which denote the union of Prakāśa and Vimarśa, that is, white and red Bindus.

Kāma is that which is desired (Kāmyate) by the great Yogīs who knew the Paramārtha as their self. Mahā-tripurasundarī, inseparable from Kāmeśvara, is the collectivity of the Bindus and Kāmakalā. The Bindu above is Her Face (Sun) and the two Bindus below are Her two breasts (Moon and Fire) and the Kalā below it, which is half of Ha, is Her womb (Yoni). Nāda which comes forth is the cause of the origin of all sounds. This Nāda is eventually divided into all the particular letters and words, their compounds and the subtle elements and all objects, their compounds. For both the world of speech and of objects have ultimately the same origin. A letter or word is the Brahman as such, just as an object denoted

by the word is the Brahman as such object. The two
Bindus are inseparate, that is, Prakāśa and Vimarśa.
For this reason it is said that S'iva and S'akti are one
Tattva. In the same way there is no difference
between Vidyā or Mantra as indicator (Vedaka,
Vācaka) and the Devatā thereby denoted (Vedya,
Vācya). Vāk and Artha are always united. This is
realised in Sādhanā when the Devatā, the Artha of the
Mantra, appears and leads the Sādhaka to a realization
of the Vācyā-S'akti, the Brahma-Svarūpa. So Natanā-
nandanātha in his Commentary on Punyānanda's
Kāma-kalā-vilāsa (VV. 6, 7) says that great Yogīs
worship the Mother Mahātripura-sundarī, who is
Kāmakalā, the collectivity of the three Bindus. For
" Pura " here means Bindu, the three (Tri) which are
Sun, Moon and Fire, which are Illumination and Bliss :
within whom is the Power (Vīrya), which is the endless
mass of letters (Anantākṣararāśi) and great Mantras.
In the worship of the great S'rīcakra-Yantra (figured in
my Edition of the Kāma-kalā-vilāsa) the gross letters,
in Vaikharī form, are in the outer Maṇḍalas, and
passing through the subtler forms of S'abda, the S'abda-
brahman and the S'ūnya are attained. He therefore
cites the Vijñāna-bhaṭṭāraka as saying : " By passing
through the different Maṇḍalas (of the S'rīcakra) where
the gross (Sthūla) letters (Varṇa) are, and rising up to
Ardhendu, Bindu, Nādānta and to the S'ūnya in the
Bindurūpacakra, one becomes S'iva." This is the
worship which a Missionary author describes as worship
of the *pudendum muliebre*. The Yantra is composed of
intersecting triangles, some upright and some inverted.
The latter only are symbolic of the Yoni, which is here
not the Yoni of any woman. Here it is the womb of
the Divine Mother of the world. Here is the seat of

the secret play of S'iva and S'akti as "Moon," "Fire" and as the "Sun" which is the union of both—the Divine Energy, whence proceeds the world of Name (Nāma = S'abda) and Forms (Rūpa = Artha).

CHAPTER XXVI

BĪJA-MANTRA

ACTION necessarily implies movement. Whenever therefore, there is action, there is Spanda or movement and therefore what to the perceiving subject (when heard) is called Sound. This may or may not be heard. One person may have a sharpened natural faculty of hearing ; so that he may hear what escapes the ear of another. There is Sound, though the latter may not hear it. Similarly, there is Sound which is not heard by any natural ear until assisted by the extension of the faculty procured by a material scientific instrument. Similarly again, there is Sound which cannot be heard by any material instrument, but which is apprehended by the Yogic Mind as part of its experience. In the beginning of things the natural Principle (Prakṛti) was in a state of equilibrium (Sāmyāvasthā). Then there was no Sound, for there was no movement of the objective world. The first Vibration which took place at the commencement of creation, that is, on the disturbance of equilibrium (Vaiṣamyāvasthā) was a general movement (Sāmānya-Spanda) in the whole mass of Prakṛti. This was the Praṇava-Dhvani of Om Sound. It is not that the Sound is represented as it is by the Sound of the letters Om. Om is only the *approximate* representation or gross utterance to gross ear of the Subtle Sound which is heard in Yoga experience of the

first movement which is continuously taking place, for
at each moment the creative movement is present.
From out of this general movement and Sound special
movements (Viśeṣa-Spanda) and Sounds arise. The
following apt illustration has been given (see "World's
Eternal Religion"). If a vessel of water is shaken,
there is first a general movement of the whole water in
the vessel. Next, there are particular movements in
every part of the water, now this way, now that So
the evenly balanced Guṇas or factors of Prakṛti equally
vibrate throughout their whole mass, and as the movement continues, the equilibrium is disturbed and the
Guṇas act and re-act on one another as in the second
state of the water in the illustration. Diverse vibratory
conditions being set up, diverse Sounds are given forth.
The first equally distributed motion throughout the
mass is Om, which is the great seed-mantra (Maha-
bīja), for it is the source of all others and of all compounded Sounds. Just as Om is the general Sound,
the other Bīja-Mantras are the particular Sounds which
are the letters of the alphabet. These are evolved out
of the general Sound which underlies all particular
Sounds. Both the Oṁkāra or Praṇava and the Bīja-
Mantras as pronounced by the mouth are thus the
articulate equivalents of the inarticulate primal Dhvani.
They become articulate at the last stage called Vaikharī
or Spaṣṭatara-Spanda of the four stages, known as
Parā (Rest passing into movement), Paśyantī (general
movement), Madhyamā or special movement of subtle
character heard by the subtle ear, and Vaikharī or
special movement which as speech is the fully articulat-
ed Sound heard by the gross ear. The Praṇava-Mantra
is thus the Sound Equivalent of Brahman and the
Bīja-Mantras are the various forms with attribute

(Saguṇarūpa) of the Devas and Devis. It is true that the approximate Sound Om is said to be constituted of the letters a, u, m. This is not to say that the primordial Dhvani was these letters or their combination. For these letters are the product of the primordial Dhvani which precedes them. What is meant is that Om as a gross Sound heard by the gross ear is the Saṁdhi or combination of these letters. A European Sanskritist told a friend of mine that *Om* said before a Mantra is simply the "clearing of the throat" before utterance; and I suppose he would have said—the clearing of the throat after utterance; for *Om* both precedes and follows a Mantra. Why however should one clear the throat then? *Om* has nothing to do with hawking sounds, or the throat. *Om* is, according to Indian belief, a sound actually heard by Yogīs as above described. If moreover, the learned man had ever heard the Mantra *Om* recited he would have felt that it could not be explained in so shallow and materialistic a way. For *Om* is sounded as from the navel with a deep rolling and continuous Sound ending at the upper part of the nostrils where the Candra-bindu is sounded. Moreover, how are we to account for the other Bīja Sounds on this hypothesis, such as Am, Ām, Em and so forth, except by supposing that the unpleasant and unmannerly act of clearing the throat had undergone an unaccountably varied development? Be the doctrine true or false, it is more profound than that.

Mantras are given various names according to the number of their syllables. A Bīja or Seed-mantra, is strictly speaking, a Mantra of a single letter such as Kam, which is composed of the letter K (Ka) together with Candrabindu which terminates all Mantras. Even here there is in a sense another letter. The

reason is that the vowel cannot be interminably pronounced and is therefore terminated by a consonant.
In fact, as Pāṇini says, the function of a consonant is to
interrupt a vowel sound. The consonant cannot be
pronounced without a vowel, which is hence known as
the S'akti of a consonant. Here the termination is M
in the form of the nasal breathing called Candrabindu
which is Nāda and Bindu. The M which ends the
Bīja is sounded nasally, high up in the bridge of the
nose, and never reaches the lips. In all the other
letters one or other of the five Bhūtas or forms of sensible
matter (Ākāśa, Vāyu, Agni, Ap, Pṛthivī) predominates.
For this reason, in the selection by the Guru of the
Mantra for his disciple the letters are chosen according
as an examination shows that there is an excess or deficiency of any particular Bhūta. Where there is excess
of a Bhūta, the letter in which it is predominant is said
with the outbreathing. Where there is deficiency it is
said with the inbreathing. M is chosen to end the Bīja
because here Bhūtas are said to be in equipoise Though
strictly the Bīja is of one letter as the seed from
which the Mantra springs, popularly other short
unetymological vocables such as Hrim, S'rim, Krim,
Hūm, Aim, Phat are called Bījas. In these there are
two or more letters, such as in the first H, R, I and
Candra-bindu. Thus a Mantra may or may not,
convey on its face its meaning. Bījas have no meaning
according to the ordinary use of language and for this
reason they have formed the subject of ridicule to
those ignorant of the Mantra-śāstra. The initiated
however know that their meaning is the own form
(Svarūpa) of the particular Devatās whose Mantra
they are, and that they are a form of the Subtle Power
as creative Dhvani which makes all letters sound and

which exists in all that we say or hear. Each Devatā
has His or Her Bīja. Thus the Devatās of Krīm, Hrīm
and Ram are Kālī, Māyā and Agni respectively. The
primary Mantra in the worship of any Deva or Devī is
known as the Root Mantra (Mūlamantra). Every letter,
syllable and Mantra is then a form (Rūpa) of the
Brahman, and so is the image and all the lines of the
Yantra and all objects in the universe. And so the
Śāstra says that they go to Hell who think that the
image is merely a stone and that the Mantra is merely
a letter of the alphabet. All letters are forms of S'akti
as sound-powers. The S'akti, of which they are a
manifestation, is the living Energy which projects
itself into the form of the universe. The Mantra of a
Devatā is the Devatā. The rhythmical vibrations of its
sounds not merely regulate the unsteady vibrations of
the sheaths of the worshipper, thus transforming him,
but through the power of striving (Sādhana-śakti) of
the worshipper, there arises the form of the Devatā
which it is. And thus the Bṛhad-gandharva-Tantra
(Ch. V) says :

Sṛṇu devī pravakṣyāmi bījānām deva-rūpatām.
Mantroccāraṇamātreṇā deva-rūpam prajāyate.

The Bījas thus have a meaning. They indicate the
Artha or Devatā which they are. What that Devatā is,
is taught to the Sādhaka, just as the child learns that
rose means a particular flower, and that rice and milk
are the names for particular forms of food and drink
which he takes.

The Bījas of the five Bhūtas, that is, of the Devatās
of the four forms of sensible mater, are Ha, Ya, Ra,
La, Va, with Candra-bindu. Where there is more than

one letter, each has its meaning. As examples I here select twelve Bīja-mantras (in their popular sense), the meanings of which are given in the 6th Chapter of the Varadā-Tantra as quoted in the well-known Bengali compendium known as the Prāṇatoṣiṇī. I may here observe that the meaning of individual letters is given in the Bījakośas, such as the Tantrābhidhāna. The Varadā-Tantra, Ch. 6, says :

Haum

Śivavācī *ha*kārastu *au*kārah syāt Sadāśivah.
Śūnyam duhkhaharārtham tu tasmāttena Śivam yajet.

That is,

Ha means Śiva. Au is Sadāśiva. The *Śūnya* is that which dispels sorrow. Hence with that Śiva should be worshipped.

Dum

Da durgāvācakam devī *u*kāraścāpi rakṣaṇe.
Viśvamātā *nāda*rūpā kurvartho *bindu*rūpakah.
Tenaiva Kālikādevīm pūjayedduhkhaśāntaye.

That is,

Da, O Devī, means Durgā. U also means to save. *Nāda* is the mother of the Universe. *Bindu* means (pray) do.

Krim

Ka Kālī brahma *ra* proktam Mahāmāyārthakaśca ī.
Viśvamātārthako *nādo bindu*rduhkhaharārthakah.

That is,

Ka is Kālī. Ra is said to be Brahma. Ī means Mahāmāyā. *Nāda* means Mother of the universe. *Bindu*

means Dispeller of sorrow. With that Devī Kālika
should be worshipped for cessation of sorrow.

Hrīm

*Ha*kārāh śivavācī syād *rephah* prakṛtirucyate.
Mahāmāyārtha *ī*-śabda *nādo* viśvaprasūh smṛtah.
Duhkhaharārthako *bindu*bhuvanām tena pūjayet.

That is,

Ha means S'iva. *Ra* is said to be Prakṛti. *I* means
Mahāmāyā. *Nāda* is said to be mother of the universe.
Bindu means dispeller of sorrow. With that Bhuvaneś-
varī should be worshipped.

S'rīm

Mahālakṣmyārthakah *S'ah* syād dhanārtho *repha* ucyate.
I tuṣtyartho' paro*nādo bindu*rduhkhaharārthakah.
Lakṣmīdevyā bījam etat tena devīm prapūjayet.

That is,

S'a means Mahālakṣmī. *Ra* is said to mean wealth.
I means satisfaction. *Nāda* is Apara (which may mean
Aparabrahma or Īśvara). *Bindu* means Dispeller of
sorrow. This is the Bīja of Devī Lakṣmī. With it the
Devī should be worshipped.

Aim

Sarasvatyārtha *ai*-śabdo *bindu*rduhkhaharārthakah.
Sarasvatyā bījam etat tena Vāṇim prapūjayet.

That is,

Ai means Sarasvatī. *Bindu* means Dispeller of
sorrow. This is the Bīja of Sarasvatī. With it Vāṇī or
Sarasvatī should be worshipped.

Klīm

Kah Kāmadeva uddiṣṭo' pyathavā Kṛṣṇa ucyate.
La Indra ī tuṣṭivācī sukhaduhkhapradā ca *am*.
Kāmabījārtha uktaste tave snehān maheśvarī.

That is,

Ka refers to Kāmadeva, or according to some to Kṛṣṇa. *La* means Indra. *I* means contentment. *Am* is that which grants happiness and sorrow. Thus, O Maheśvari, the meaning of Kāmabīja is spoken unto Thee out of my love for Thee.

Hūm

Ha śivah kathito devi *ū* Bhairava ihocyate.
Parārtho *nāda* śabdastu *Bindu*rduhkhaharārthakah.
Varmabījatrayo hyatra kathitas tava yatnatah.

That this,

Ha, O Devī, is said to be S'iva. *Ū* is said to be Bhairava. *Nāda* means Para, Supreme. *Bindu* means Dispeller of sorrow. Here the three composing the Varmabīja (armour-bija) are spoken unto Thee owing to Thy solicitation.

Gam

Ganeśārthe *ga* uktas te *Bindu*rduhkhaharārthakah.
Gaṁbījārtham tu kathitam tava snehān maheśvarī.

That is,

Ga, I speak unto Thee, means Ganeśa. *Bindu* means Dispeller of sorrow. Thus, O Maheśvari, the meaning of Gam-bīja is spoken unto Thee out of love for Thee.

Glaum

Ga Ganeśo vyāpakārtho *la*kārasteja *au* matah.
Duhkhaharārthako *bindu*rganeśaṁ tena pūjayet.

That is,

Ga is Ganeśa, *La* means what pervades. *Au* means tejas. *Bindu* means Dispeller of sorrow. With it Ganeśa should be worshipped.

Kṣraum

Kṣa, Nṛsimho Brahma *ra*śca ūrdhvadantārthakaśca
au.
Duhkhaharārthako *bindu*rNṛsimham tena pūjayet.

That is,

Kṣa is Nṛsimha and *Ra* is Brahma. *Au* means teeth pointing upwards, *Bindu* means Dispeller of sorrow. With it Nṛsimha should be worshipped.

Strīm

Durgottāraṇavācyah *sa* tārakārtha*sta*kārakah.
Muktyārtho *repha* ukto'tra mahāmāyārtnakaśca *i.*
Viśvamātārthako *nādo Bindu*rduhkhaharārthakah.
Vadhūbījartha ukto'tra tava snehān maheśvarī.

That is,

Sa means deliverance from difficulties. *Ta* means Saviour. *Ra* here means salvation or liberation. *I* means Mahāmāyā. *Nāda* means Mother of the universe. *Bindu* means Dispeller of sorrow. Thus the meaning of Vadhūbīja is spoken unto Thee, O Maheśvarī, out of love for Thee.

A close examination of the above may raise some difficulties, but must, in connection with what is elsewhere written, remove the charge that the Bija is a meaningless saying to the worshipper. It is full of meaning to him.

ṢADADHVĀS

ADHVĀ means a path, and Mantrādhvā is all knowledge relating to Mantra. The Six (Ṣat) Adhvās are, on the Śabda side, the three Varṇa (letter), Pada (syllable) and Mantra (combination of syllables), each being dependent on one another, Pada on Varṇa, and Mantra on Pada, which are said, in the work from which I take the following table, to be 51, 81, 11 respectively. On the Artha side the three other Adhvās are Kalā (5), Tattva (36) and Bhuvana (224), each similarly dependent. The science of the Ṣadadhvās is referred to in both Śaiva and Śākta works, but seems peculiarly characteristic of the Śāmbhava-Darśana in which Śaiva and Śākta Darśanas are synthetised. The Śākta doubtless worships Śiva as well as Śakti with emphasis on the latter aspect. The ordinary Śaiva worships Śakti as well as Śiva with emphasis on the latter aspect. In Śāmbhava Darśana both are raised into a higher synthesis. In the same way Kulā = Śakti and Akula = Śiva, ānd therefore Kulīna means one who worships the two in one.

Kalā means Śakti either generally in its higher aspect and more commonly some specific aspect and function of Śakti. The five chief Kalās which sum up in themselves groups of Tattvas are Śāntyātītā-kalā, Śāntikalā, Vidyā-kalā, Pratiṣṭā-kalā, Nivṛtti-kalā.

These have been already referred to. These are the Powers of certain Tattvas or Principles, and two stages in the emanative process. They (the Tattvas) are 36 in number and are divided into 3 classes, *viz.*, Pure (S'uddha-tāttva), Pure-Impure (S'uddhāśuddha-tattva) and Impure (Aśuddha-tattva). Three groups of tattvas are also called S'iva, Vidyā, Ātma Tattvas. The first as stated in the Siddānta-Sārāvali and other works comprise the S'iva-Tattva and S'akti Tattva ; the Second the Tattvas from Sadāśiva-Tattva to S'uddha-vidya-Tattva ; and the third the Tattvas from Māyā to Pṛthivi.

The Word Bhuvana means world or region. Bhuvana = *Asmāt bhavati iti bhuvanam,* or "what comes from this," that is, "what is produced" is Bhuvana. These Bhuvanas or Regional Bodies are also Pure, Pure-Impure, and Impure. These are shown with the corresponding Kalā and Tattva in the accompanying table which I have extracted with the permission of the owner of the copyright from pp. 392-367 of Part II, Vol. II of the late T. A. Gopīnātha Rao's " Elements of Hindu Iconography " where they are conveniently tabulated. I have made one or two verbal corrections.

Kalās	Tattvas	No. of Bhuvanas	Names of the Bhuvanas
(a) Śāntyātita-kalā	i. Śuddha-tattvas.		
	1. Śiva-tattva ..	10	Anāśrita, Anātha, Ananta, Vyomarūpini. Vyāpini, Ūrdhvagāmini, Mōcikā, Rocikā, Dipikā, and Indhikā—(Five of these are śākta—bhuvanas and the remaining five Nādorddhva-bhuvanas.)
	2. Śakti-tattva ..	5	Śāntyatitā, Śānti, Vidyā, Pratiṣṭhā and Nivṛtti—(These are called the Baindavapuras).
	Total ..	15	
(b) Śānta-kalā	3. Sadāśiva-tattva ..	1	Sadāśivabhuvana.
	4. Īśvara-tattva ..	8	Śikhandi, Śrikaṇṭhā, Trimūrti, Ekaruda, Ekanétra, Śivottama, Sūkṣma and Ananta.
	5. Śuddhavidyā-tattva ..	9	Manonmani, Sarvabhūta-damani, Balapramathani, Balavikaraṇi, Kāli, Raudri, Jyeṣṭhā and Vāmā.
	Total ..	18	

Kalās	Tattvas	No. of Bhuvanas	Names of the Bhuvanas
	ii. S'uddhāśuddhā-tattvas		
(c) Vidyā-kalā	6. Māyā	8	Anguṣṭhamātra, Īśānta, Ekekṣaṇa, Ekapingala, Udbhava, Bhava, Vāmadeva and Mahādyuti.
	7. Kāla	2	S'ikheśa and Ekavīra.
	8. Kalā	2	Pañcāntaka and Sūra.
	9. Vidyā	2	Pinga and Jyoti.
	10. Niyati	2	Samvarta and Krodha,
	11. Rāga	5	Ekaśva, Amanta, Aja, Umāpati and Pracaṇḍa.
	12. Puruṣa	6	Ekavīra, Īśāna, Bhava, Īśa, Ugra, Bhima and Vāma.
	Total	27	
	iii. Aśuddha-tattvas.		
(d) Pratiṣṭhā-kalā	13. Prakṛti	8	S'rikantha, Auma, Kaumāra, Vaiṣṇava, Brahma, Bhairava, Kṛta and Akṛta.
	14. Buddhi	8	Brahma, Prajeśa, Saumya, Aindra, Gandharva, Yakṣa, Rākṣa, Rākṣasa and Pisāśca.
	15. Ahamkāra	1	Sthaleśvara.
	16. Manas		
	17. Śrotra		
	18. Tvak	1	Sthūleśvara.
	19. Cakṣus		
	20. Jihva		

Kalās	Tattvas	No. of Bhuvanas	Names of the Bhuvanas
(d) Pratiṣṭhā-kalā	21. Nāsā	1	Śankukarṇa
	22. Vāk		
	23. Pāni		
	24. Pāda		
	25. Pāyu		
	26. Upastha		
	27. Śabda		
	28. Sparśa		
	29. Rūpa	5	Kālañjara, Mandaleśvara, Mākota, Drāvinda and Cakalaṇḍa.
	30. Rasa		
	31. Gandha		
	32. Ākāśa	8	Sthāṇu, Svarnākṣa, Bhadrakarṇa, Gokarṇa, Mahālaya, Avimukta, Rudrakoṭi and Vastrapāda.
	33. Vāyu	8	Bhimeśvara, Mahendra, Attahāsa, Vimaleśa, Nala, Nākala, Kurukṣetra and Gayā.
	34. Tejas	8	Bhairava, Kedāra, Mahākāla, Madhyameśa, Amra-tāka, Jalpeśa, Śriśaila and Hariścandra.
	35. Jala	8	Lakuliśā, Pārabhūti, Diṇḍi, Muṇḍi, Vidhi, Puṣkara, Naimiṣa, Prabhāsa, and Amareśa.
	Total	56	

Kalās	Tattvas	No. of Bhuvanas	Names of the Bhuvanas
e) Nivṛtti-kalā	{ 36. Pṛthivī ...	108	From Bhadrakāli to Kālāgni.
	Grand Total ...	224	

Thus to take the first and highest or S'iva-tattva and the associated S'akti-tattva, the Bhuvanas are Anāśrita, the Region or Bhuvana without support and self-sustaining, Anātha or Lordless because there is no higher Lord here, Ananta or endless, Vyomarūpiṇī in the form of the all-spreading Ether, Vyāpinī all-spreading, Ūrddhva-gāminī upward going, Mocikā freed of all bonds, Rocikā Beautiful or source of Beauty, Dīpikā illuminating, Indhikā destroyer of all impurity. Such are the Bhuvanas of the Kalā S'āntyātītā (Beyond even the high abode of Peace) and the conjoined S'iva and S'akti-Tattvas. Five of these are called S'ākta and the remaining five Nādorddhva (above Nāda) Bhuvanas. The rest are various other divine bodies named after their divine residents. All these regions have been created by Parama-śiva for the enjoyment of the Beings therein ; there being an immense variety of beings in an ascending hierarchy from man up to the supreme Lord and Lady of all. The beings in the Pure regions are wholly Pure and the others Pure-Impure or Impure. Impurity or Mala is ignorance and is of three kinds, namely, Mala, Māyā and Karma. There are thus three classes of Paśus or created beings, namely, Vijñānakalās enveloped by that ignorance which is called Mala, Pralaya-kalās enveloped in both Mala and Māyā, and Sakalās or those surrounded by the three forms of ignorance Mala, Māyā and Karma. Above the Vijñāna-kalā are the beings called Mantras. The Mala envelope when in the stage at which it is about to leave the being is said to have undergone Paripāka. The Vijñāna-kalās, whose Mala is in a high state of Paripāka, are the eight Vidyeśvaras. They are eight in number and are variously coloured as in the following table, for which I am indebted to the same work.

THE GARLAND OF LETTERS

No.	Name	Colour
1.	Ananteśa	Blood-red
2.	Sūkṣma	White
3.	S'ivottama	Blue
4.	Ekanetra	Yellow
5.	Ekarudra	Black
6.	Trimūrti	Crimson
7.	S'rikaṇṭha	Red
8.	S'ikhaṇḍī	Dark-brown

The author cited refers to several southern Āgamas, such as Pūrva-Kāraṇa, Aṃśuma-bhedāgama, Kāmilka and other works for their Dhyāna. From these it would appear that the colours and so forth are not always given in the same way.

These Vidyeśvaras are higher spiritual Entities, by whose aid the lower orders of beings attain the higher stages of spiritual evolution. Next to the Vidyeśvaras come the Mantreśvaras. Having been given pure bodies (Tanu), instrument (Karaṇa), regions (Bhuvana) and enjoyment (Bhoga), these gradually get rid of all Mala. Above the Mantreśvaras are the Mantra-maheśvaras and beyond these are the Eternal and unproduced S'iva-Tattva and S'akti-Tattva.

In the Vimarśinī on Īśvara-pratyabhijñā (III) Sadāśiva-Tattva is described as that particular specialisation (Cid-viśeṣatvam) which consists in the experience of that Bhāvarāśi or mass of ideation belonging to the collectivity. (Varga) of Caitanya called Mantra-maheś-vara. Of the Vidyeśvaras it is said (cf. III, 1-6) that whilst the Ego-side is pure, yet unlike the experience of higher states they perceive the object as different from themselves in the same way as the Īśvaras, as recognised by the Dvaitavādins, perceive theirs. The various locations of the Jīvas in the various Tattvas is given as follows: Mantramaheśvara in Sadākhya-Tattva, Maheśvara in Īśvara-Tattva, Mantras in Śuddhavidyā-Tattva (the eight Vidyeśvaras Ananta and the rest are different from the Mantras), Vijñānakalās below Śuddhavidyā but above Māyā, Pralayā-kalās in Māyā, and Sakalas include all other beings from Brahmā downwards who are not Mukta.

The whole of the Śāmbhava-Darśana rests on a principle of the specialisation of Consciousness, stages of descent from Pure Cit to the consciousness of the gross material world. Each stage is more bound in ignorance than the former until gross matter is reached. The Śāstra speaks of the eight called Cit, Citi, Citta, Caitanya, Cetanā, Indriyakarma, Deha and Kalā. The first is consciousness in the pointed or Bindu state, the second out-spreading (Vyāpinī), the third with inward and outward activity, the fourth the Bodha or experience which is from outwards inwards, the fifth is the retention (Dhāraṇā) of that Bodha, the sixth is experience through action of the senses, and the seventh and eighth are the Body and its inherent subtle moving forces such as the 38 Kalās of Moon, Sun and Fire. In moon Sattva is dominant and in Fire Tamas. The Rājasik activity of the Sun mediates between these opposites. The Lords of the Tattvas proceeding from "Earth" (Pṛthivī) upwards are Brahmā from Pṛthivī to Pradhāna (Prakṛti), Viṣṇu from Puruṣa to Kalā, Rudra in Māyā, Īśa in the regions extending to Sadā-khya-Tattva. Then follow Anāśrita Śiva and Paraśiva.

MANTRA-SĀDHANA

In the Gāyatrī-Tantra it is said—"that is called Mantra, by the meditation (Manana) on which the Jīva acquires freedom from sin, enjoyment of heaven and Liberation and by the aid of which he attains in full the four-fold fruit (Catur-varga)." Elsewhere it is said "Mantra is so called because it is achieved by mental process". "*Man*" of "Mantra" comes from the first syllable of *Manana* or thinking and "*tra*" from Trāṇa or liberation from the bondage of the Samsāra or phenomenal world. By the combination of "*man*" and "*tra*" that is called Mantra which "calls forth" (Amantraṇa) the four aims of being (Caturvarga).

A Mantra is composed of letters. Letters and their combinations as syllables and words are all forms of manifested S'abda, that is, Brahman-forms. They are each and all forms of the Creative Stress as uttered by the mouth, heard by the ear, and apprehended by the mind; but what are ordinarily called Mantras are those particular sounds which are used in worship and practice (Sādhana) which consist of certain letters, or arranged in a definite sequence of sounds of which the letters are the representative signs. The relations of Varṇa, Nāda, Bindu, vowel and consonant in a Mantra constitute the Devatā in varying forms. Certain

Vibhūti or aspects of the Devatā are inherent in certain Varṇas. The Mantra of a Devatā is that letter or combination of letters which reveals the Devatā to the consciousness of the Sādhaka, who has evoked it by Sādhana-śakti. The form of a particular Devatā therefore appears out of the particular Mantra of which that Devatā is the Adhiṣṭhātri-Devatā. The Mantra is intoned in the proper way according to letter (Varṇa) and rhythm (Svara). For these reasons a Mantra, when translated ceases to be a Mantra, that is, the sounds heard and uttered in the translation are not the body of and do not evoke, the Devatā. We are then not dealing with the same sound, but with a translation in another language, with other sounds giving the meaning to the intellect of the Sanskrit Mantra. This shows that Mantra is not mere individual thinking but a particular sound-body of consciousness.

A particular Mantra therefore (such as the Gāyatrī) is not a mere collocation of words. Though to a non-believer it may seem but a string of mere letters bearing on their face a particular meaning or in the case of Bīja Mantras apparently no meaning at all, to the Sādhaka it is a very mass of radiant *Tejas* or energy. An ordinary collection of words is something gross. These as all else, are forms of S'akti. But the Mantra of which we speak is the Devatā Himself or Herself in Mantra-body. Mantra is thus a mass of radiant Energy. Sayings give information and advice to men of the world, whilst Mantras awaken super-human power or S'akti. A mere saying is therefore, like a Jīva, subject to birth and death, whilst a Mantra is directly Brahman in sound-body, unwasting and undecaying. A Mantra again is not the same thing as prayer or self-dedication (Ātma-nivedana). Prayer is conveyed in what words the worshipper chooses and bears its meaning on its face. It is only ignorance of Śāstrik principles (See " Principles of Tantra " as to what precedes and follows) which supposes that Mantra is merely the name for the words in which one expresses what one has to say to the Divinity. If it were, the Sādhaka might choose his own language without recourse to the eternal and determined sounds of Śāstra.

Śabda is Śakti. The Viśvasāra-Tantra (Ch. II) says that Śabda-brahman which is Mantra (Mantra-maya) exists in the body of Jīva and is the subtle aspect of the Jīva's vital Śakti. As the Prapañcasāra-Tantra states, the Brahmāṇḍa spheroid (universe) is pervaded by Śakti as Dhvani, called Nāda, Prāṇa and the like. The manifestation of the gross (Sthūla) form of Śabda would not be possible unless Śabda existed also in a subtle (Sūkṣma) form.

Śabda is the Guṇa of Ākāśa, but is not produced by it. It manifests in it; and Śabda-svarūpa is the Brahman. In the same way, however, as in outer space waves of sound are produced by movements of air (Vāyu), so in the space within the Jīva's body, waves of sound are produced according to the movements of the vital air (Prāṇavāyu) and the process of inhalation and exhalation. The Śabda which first appears in the Mūlādhāra (See *The Serpent Power*) is in fact the Śakti which gives life to the Jīva. The Jīva who inbreathes and outbreathes utters a great Mantra. This is the Ajapā-Mantra or Hamsah, called " Ajapā ", because it repeats itself naturally without any effort on the part of the Jīva. It is the heaving of the Dhvani which causes alternate inspiration and expiration. Śakti

it is who is the Cause of the sweet, indistinct and murmuring Dhvani (See Ch. XXIV) which sounds like the
humming of black bees. This sound is Parā, and then
Paśyantī, which becomes subtle as Madhyamā and
gross as Vaikharī. Kuṇḍalinī, who is Varṇamayī and
Dhvanimayī, is the manifestation in bodies of the
Paramātmā. So the substance of all Mantra is Cit,
manifested as letters, syllables, words and their
sentences. In fact the letters of the alphabet which are
known as Akṣara are nothing but the Yantra of the
Akṣara or imperishable Brahman. It is the gross or
Sthūla form of Kuṇḍalinī, appearing in different aspects
as different Devatās, which is the presiding Devatā
(Adhiṣṭhātrī) of all Mantra, though it is the subtle
(Sūkṣma) form at which all Sādhakas aim. For in
every Mantra there are two S'aktis. The Vācya-S'akti
and the Vācaka-S'akti. The Devatā who is indicated
(Pratipādya-Devatā) as the ultimate Svarūpa is the
Vācya-S'akti, and the Devatā who is that Mantra
(Mantramayī-Devatā) is the Vācaka-S'akti. Thus if
Durgā is the Devatā of a Mantra, then Mahāmāyā is
the Vācyā-S'akti. The latter is without attribute and
Vācaka-S'akti is with attribute. The latter is the
object of worship and is a support and means whereby
the Vācya-S'akti is realised. For worship assumes as
its object some form. When the S'akti with attribute,
resident in and as the Mantra, is by dint of Sādhana
awakened, then She opens the gate of monistic truth,
revealing the true nature and essence of the universe.

There are thus two S'aktis, *viz.*, the Mantra-S'akti
and the Sādhana-S'akti, that is the S'akti of the Sādhaka
generated by Sādhana. It is the uniting of these two
S'aktis which accomplishes the fruit of Mantra-sādhana.
How ? The Saguṇa-S'akti is awakened by Sādhana

and worshipped. This Saguṇa-Devatā is the Presiding Deity (Adhiṣṭhātrī-Devatā) of the Mantra as the Nirguṇa (formless) Īśvara or Īśvarī is the Vācya-Śakti. Both are one; but the Jīva by the laws of his nature and its three guṇas must first meditate on the gross (Sthūla) form before he can realise the subtle (Sūkṣma) form which is liberation.

The utterance of a Mantra without knowledge of its meaning or of the Mantra method is a mere movement of the lips and nothing more. The Mantra sleeps. There are various processes preliminary to, and involved in, its right utterance, which processes again consist of purification of the mouth (*Mukha-śodhana*), (See Chapter X, Śārada-Tilaka, *Japa* of *praṇava* or the mantra *Om* varies with the Devatā—*e.g.*, Om Hsau for Bhairava), purification of the tongue, *Jihva-śodhana*, (seven *Japa* of one-lettered *Bīja* triplicated, *Praṇava* triplicated, then one-lettered *Bīja* triplicated) and of *Aśauca-bhaṅga*, *Japa* of *Mūla-mantra* preceded and followed by *Praṇava*. As to the " birth " and " death " defilements of a *mantra*, see Tantra-sāra 75. *et seq.*, *Kulluka*, see Śāradā, *loc cit*. Thus *Kulluka*, which is done over the head of Kālikā is Māyā, (see Puraścaraṇa-Bodhinī., p. 48, and Tantra-sāra); *Nirvāṇa Japa* of *Mūla* and *Mātṛkā-bīja* in the *Maṇipūra*, *Setu* (Generally the Mahāmantra *Om* or *Māyābīja* Hrīm, but it also varies. Thus *Setu* of Kāli is her own *Bīja Krīm*, of Tārā, *Kūrca* etc.) ; *Nidrā-bhaṅga*, awakening of mantra (*Japa* of the *Mantra* preceded and followed by *Īm* seven times); *Mantra-caitanya*, or giving of life or vitality to the *mantra* (Japa of *Mūlamantra* in *Maṇi-pūra* preceded and followed by Mātṛkā-*bīja*. Meditating on the *Mūla-mantra* in the *Sahasrārā*, *Anāhāta*, *Mūlādhāra*, with *Hūm*, and again in Sahasrāra. The *Mūla* is the principal *mantra*,

such as the *Pañcadaśī*) ; *mantrārtha-bhāvana*, forming of a
mental image of the Divinity (Lit., thinking of meaning
of *mantra* or thinking of the *mātṛkā* in the *mantra* which
constitutes the Devatā from foot to head). There are
also ten *Saṃskāras* of the *mantra* (See Tantrasāra, p. 90).
Dīpanī is seven *Japa* of the *bīja*, preceded and followed by
Om. Where *Hrīm* is employed instead of *Om* it is Prāṇa-
yoga. Yonī-mudrā is meditation on the *Guru* in the
head and on the Iṣṭadevatā in the heart, and then on
the *Yonī-rūpa Bhagavati* from the head to the *Mūlādhāra*,
and from the *Mūlādhāra* to the head, making *japa* of
the *Yonī Bīja* (*Em*) ten times (See Purohitadarpaṇam.)

The Mantra itself is Devatā, that is, the Supreme
Consciousness (Cit-śakti) manifesting in that form.
The Mantra is awakened from its sleep (Mantra-
caitanya) through the Sādhana S'akti of the mantrin.
It is at base one and the same S'akti which appears as
Sādhana-Sakti and Mantra-śakti, the latter however
being the more powerful manifestation. The consciousness of the Sādhaka becomes *en rapport* and in union
with the Consciousness in the form of the Mantra ;
and the Devatā who is the Artha of the Mantra appears
to the Sādhaka, whose mind has been cleansed and
illumined by devotion. Though the substance of the
Mantra is Consciousness, that fact is not realised without the union of the Sādhaka's S'akti derived from
Sādhana with Mantra-śakti. The Devatā is then
revealed. In the case of Pūja, Dhyāna and other
Sādhanās, it is only the Sādhakā's Sādhana-S'akti which
operates, whilst in the case of Mantra-sādhana,
Sādhana-śakti works in conjunction with Mantra-śakti
which is all-powerful and re-inforces Sādhana-śakti
which is imperfect and meets with obstacles. The
individual S'akti is like fire. Just as waves of air,

when struck and restruck by flames of fire, set up a
blaze with redoubled force, so the Sādhaka's individual
S'akti when struck by Mantra-śakti is rapidly developed,
and then a strong active individual S'akti unites with
Mantra-śakti to make the latter doubly powerful. It is
because Mantra possesses this wonderful power that a
Jīva can, it is said accomplish that which appears
impossible. Otherwise a Jīva could not achieve by his
own effort the treasure which is worshipped even by
S'iva. The Jaivī-S'akti or S'akti of a Jīva (as such)
is transformed by the aid of Mantra into the Daivī-
S'akti or the S'akti of a Deva (as such). With this
S'akti he can accomplish that which a Deva can.
Mantra is thus an aspect of the Divine Mother appear-
ing through Mantra-sādhana with devotion to Her.
It has been thus said (Tantra-Tattva II, 45): " The
string of fifty letters from A to Kṣa which are the
Mātṛkās is Eternal, unbeginning and unending and
Brahman itself. " This great saying is the first of all
Tantras. The realization of this Mantra-consciousness
is Mantra-siddhi. If a Sādhaka attains perfect Siddhi
in even a single Mantra he becomes possessed of the
spiritual knowledge which is acquired by learning all
Vedas. For Veda is the Pariṇāma or evolution of the
Dhvani of Kula-Kuṇḍalinī in the body of Īśvara, and
the Pariṇāma of the same in the body of the Jīva is
S'abda. For Veda is Dhvani uttered by Brahma and
S'abda is Dhvani uttered by the Jīva. In that S'abda
is every form of Mantra which, is that which gives
vitality to the Jīva. It is this Dhvani too which
evolves into gross S'abda as uttered sound, the body of
the Devatā. Siddhi in such Mantra is not gained so
long as such Mantra is not awakened. It may be that
the appearance of the Devatā is a fact or it is not a fact.

But it cannot be said that the mere utterance of a Mantra is superstitiously supposed to effect any result, or that Japa of the Mantra is done with no other object than a mere vain and senseless repetition. The particular Mantra suitable for a Sādhaka is a matter determined by Cakra and other calculations.

CHAPTER XXIX

THE GĀYATRĪ-MANTRA

The Gāyatrī is the most sacred of all Vaidika *mantras*. In it the Veda lies embodied as in its seed. It runs: *Om. Bhūr bhuvah svah : tat savitur varenyam bhargo devasya dhīmahi : dhiyo yo nah pracodayāt. Om.* " Om. The earthly, atmospheric and celestial spheres. Let us contemplate the wondrous Solar Spirit of the Divine Creator (Sāvitri). May He direct our minds (that is, towards the attainment of *Dharma, Artha, Kāma,* and *Mokṣa*). Om."

The Gāyatrī-Vyākaraṇa of Yogī Yājñavalkhya thus explains the following words: *Tat*, means *that*. (*Tat* is apparently here treated as in the objective case, agreeing with *varenyam*, etc., but others holding that the *vyāhṛti—Bhūr bhuvah svah—*forms part of, and should be linked with, the rest of the Gāyatrī treat *that* as part of a genitive compound connected with the previous *vyāhṛti*, in which case it is *teshām*). The word *yat*, " which," is to be understood. (It may, however, be said that *yat* is there in *Yo nah*). *Savituh* is the possessive case of *Sāvitri*, derived from the root *sū*, " to bring forth." Sāvitri is, therefore, the Bringer-forth of all that exists. Bringing forth and creating all things, it is called Sāvitri. The Bhaviṣya-Purāṇa says : " Sūrya is the visible Devatā. He is the eye of the world and the Maker of the day. There is no other Devatā eternal like unto Him. This universe has emanated

from, and will be again absorbed into Him. Time is
of and in Him. The planets, stars, the Vasus, Rudras,
Vāyu, Agni, and the rest are but parts of Him." By
Bhargah is meant the Āditya-devatā, dwelling in the
region of the Sun (*Sūrya-maṇḍala*) in all His might and
glory. He is to the Sun what our spirit (*Ātmā*) is to our
body. Though He is in the region of the Sun, in the
outer or material sphere, He also dwells in our inner
selves. He is the light of the light in the solar circle,
and is the light of the lives of all beings. As he is in
the outer ether, so also is He in the ethereal region of
the heart. In the outer ether He is the Sun (Sūrya),
and in the inner ether He is the wonderful Light which
is the Smokeless Fire. In short, that Being whom the
Sādhaka realizes in the region of his heart is the Āditya
in the heavenly firmament. The two are one. The
word is derived in two ways: (1) from the root *Bhrij*,
"to ripen, mature, destroy, reveal, shine." In this
derivation Sūrya is He who matures and transforms all
things. He Himself shines and reveals all things by
His Light. And it is He who at the final Dissolution
(*Pralaya*) will in His form of destructive Fire (*Kālāgni*)
destroy all things. (2) From *bha* = dividing all things
into different classes ; *ra* = colour, for He produces the
colour of all created objects ; *ga* = constantly going and
returning. The Sun divides all things, produces the
different colours of all things and is constantly going
and returning. As the Brāhmaṇa-sarvasva says : " The
Bharga is the *Ātmā* of all that exists, whether moving or
motionless, in the three *Lokas* (*Bhūr Bhuvah Svah*). There
is nothing which exists apart from it."

Devasya is the genitive of Deva, agreeing with
Savituh. Deva is the radiant and playful (*Līlāmaya*) one.
Sūrya is in constant play with creation (*Sṛṣṭi*), existence

(*Sthiti*), and destruction (*Pralaya*), and by His radiance pleases all. (*Lila*, as applied to the Brahman, is the equivalent of *Māyā*). *Vareṇyam = varaṇiyam* or adorable. He should be meditated upon and adored that we may be relieved of the misery of birth and death. Those who fear rebirth, who desire freedom from death and seek Liberation and who strive to escape the three kinds of pain (*tāpa-traya*), which are *Ādhyātmikā*, *Ādhidaivika*, and *Ādhibhautika*, meditate upon and adore the *Bharga*, who, dwelling in the region of the Sun, has in Himself the three regions called *Bhūr-loka*, *Bhuvar-loka* and *Svar-loka*. *Dhīmahi = dhyāyema* (from the root *dhyai*), we meditate upon, or let us meditate upon.

Pracodayāt = may He direct. The Gāyatrī does not so expressly state, but it is understood that such direction is along the *Catur-varga*, or four-fold path which is *Dharma*, *Artha*, *Kāma*, and *Mokṣa* (piety, wealth, desire and its fulfilment, and Liberation). The Bhargah is ever directing our inner faculties (*Buddhi-vṛtti*) along these paths.

The above is the *Vaidiki-Gāyatrī*, which, according to the Vaidika system, none but the twice-born may utter. To the S'ūdra, whether man or woman and to women of all other castes it is forbidden. The The Tantra-S'āstra, which has a Gāyatrī-Mantra of its own, shows no such exclusiveness; Chapter III, verses 109-111, of the the Mahānirvāṇā-Tantra gives the *Brahma-gāyatrī* for worshippers of the Brahman: "*Parameśvarāya vidmahe para-tattvāya dhīmahi : tan no Brahma pracodayāt*" (May we know the Supreme Loid. Let us contemplate the Supreme Reality. And may that Brahman direct us.)

CHAPTER XXX

THE GĀYATRĪ-MANTRA

AS AN EXERCISE OF REASONING

THE Society [1] is called "Rationalistic." If its formation was meant to be merely a homage to one form of modern western thought, the title may be fairly correct. I think however that you had no intention of adding to the volume of imitativeness in this country, but by your action you wished to affirm the necessity of such reasonable thinking and practice as characteristic of the Ārya-Dharma, rightly understood and cleansed of all bad and useless accretion. There is always a difficulty, when English verbal labels are used to describe Indian philosophical and religious theories and practices. In fact such labels are a fertile source of confusion. I hear of a good suggestion to call it *Satyajñāna-Sabha* or a similar name.

Rationalism, in the sense of its technical opposition to Sensationalism, has no meaning in this country for those who believe that a child is born with his *samskāras*.

"Rationalism" in its more general sense involves, it has been said, the following beliefs: (1) Reason is the chief source and final criterion of knowledge.

---

1 This Chapter reproduces a lecture given to the Rationalistic Society, Calcutta.

(2) Each individual must investigate and gain knowledge for himself, and must not merely submit himself to to external authority. In other words he must do his own thinking. (3) As a result of this it is said that a rationalist must reject any alleged knowledge, the truth of which cannot be rationally demonstrated.

Upon such a statement a Vedāntist (I speak throughout of the Advaita-Vedānta) would ask what is the "knowledge" here mentioned? If worldly (Laukika) knowledge is meant, then the Rationalist and Vedāntist are at one. Worldly knowledge is apprehended through the senses (Indriya). In its own sphere, reason is the chief source of knowledge and final criterion. So much is this so, that S'aṁkarācārya says that if even Veda were to contradict what is the subject of worldly proof (Laukika-Pramāṇa) it would not be Veda. In this sphere it is not a Pramāṇa, which overrides the testimony of the senses and inferences therefrom. The Yoga-Vāsiṣṭha (Bk. 2—Ch. 18, vv. 2-3) says :

> *Api pauruṣam ādeyam śāṣtram ced yuktibodhakam*
> *Anyat tvārṣam api tyājyam bhāvyam nyāyyaikasevinā.*
> *Yuktiyuktum upādeyam vacanam bālakād api.*
> *Anyat tṛṇam iva tyājyam apyuktam Padmajanmanā.*

That is, " Even a S'āstra of purely human authorship should be accepted if conformable to reason. Anything else (which is unreasonable) even though it the word of a Ṛṣi, should be rejected by one who follows reason. The word of a boy if reasonable should be accepted. Anything unreasonable should be rejected as of no more count than a blade of grass, even if it be uttered by the Lotus-born (Brahmā) Himself." On this subject read the whole of the 14th Chapter of

Book II of the Mumukṣu-Khāṇḍa of this work which is
a glorification of Vicāra or reasoning.

But there is more than what is seen with the eyes.
The mind admittedly exists, but it is not seen by the
senses (Atindriya). Again as to objects, scientific
instruments enable the sense to perceive more than is
presented to them in their natural state. These instruments thus effect a material extension of natural faculty.
Then there are Psychic Powers (*Siddhi*), the subject of
much study to-day in the West, but matters of long
familiar practice in this country. Here the mind
may operate independently of the gross bodily
organs of sense, as also occurs in some cases of Hypnosis.
These psychic powers are again extensions of natural
faculty. They are not supernatural, except in the sense
that they are supernormal. They may, in any one
individual, be natural or produced, but we do not
reason ourselves into them. We can reason only upon
whether they exist, and what they are and indicate.
That is, we reason about them. In themselves they are
peculiar mental faculties, by which the mind sees
things or imposes itself upon and controls, or affects,
others such as Clairvoyance, Clairaudience, Hypnosis,
Thought-reading, Telepathy and so forth. There is
nothing unreasonable in all this. On the contrary
an affirmation of their existence is reasonable and
in accordance with the Vedāntic theory of Being
upon which this paper proceeds. The only question
about them is one of fact or proof. Do they exist or
not? Nothing is more unscientific than to pronounce
a priori against them and without investigation into the
facts. Notwithstanding scientific bigotry (for there is
a bigotry of science as of religion) psychical research is
coming to be recognised as a useful form of enquiry.

Lastly, there is what is called spiritual or religious experience, which is of varying degrees and kinds, and is a knowledge of the nature (through an actual participation in Its Being) of the excelling and infinite Principle which lies behind and manifests all phenomena. Professor James's celebrated work " Varieties of Experience " is one of the first essays in a field, which is only now commencing to be cultivated extensively. The possibility or fact of such experience cannot be said to be unreasonable. Such experience has been affirmed by all the great Religions, and by some of the great philosophies. If it is unreasonable, then the bulk of Humanity has been lacking in reason in all the past and in the present times. The question again here is one of fact and proof. Have such experiences taken place in fact? Are they real experiences or mere hallucinations? In the latter case why should they occur? The only direct and certain proof is the having of such an experience oneself. Probable proof may be had in various ways, such as the persistence and universality of such experiences, the nature of the truths said to be revealed by them, and, in particular the extraordinary effect which they have produced on the individuals who have had such experience, and (in the case of the greater experiences) the effect that they have produced on the world at large. To my mind it is a very shallow view which regards the effect produced on millions of past and present Humanity, by the Ṛṣis and S'ākya-Muni of India, by Laotze, Jesus and Mahommed, as the outcome of the hallucination of the *Mahātmās* named and others. Which of these experiences, it may be asked, is true, or which one is truer than the others? This is too vast a question to be answered here. Let me however say this, that those who read these experiences with knowledge will find elements common to all together with some elements which seem to vary. As to these last let it be noted that just as in our ordinary life one man sees and knows more than another, so it is with spiritual experience, of which there are many grades. If two men are approaching a mountain, is the experience which one man has of it 50 miles distant untrue, because it differs from the experience of the other man who sees it at its foot? Do we not say that both are true, considering the position of each experiencer?

In India spiritual experience is called Veda, from the root " *Vid* " to know. It is experience in the limit, of which all others are gradual and partial reproductions. This may be primary, that is, an individual may himself have the experience, or he may accept the authority of those who have had such experience, for reasons I have slightly indicated but cannot develop here.

The Vedānta says that Reason is supreme in wordly (*Laukika*) matters open to our senses. By reasoning we may establish Laukika truth, but as regards what is not seen, such as the being of one Supreme Cause of which the Universe is an effect, unaided reason can only establish probabilities and not certainty. Thus one may, with reasonableness, argue for or against Monism, Dualism, Pluralism and so forth. In this way mere reasoning may lead to contrary conclusions. And in fact what is more contradictory than the conclusions of Western philosophy with Realism (old style and new as propounded by Mr. Bertrand Russell), Idealism (objective and subjective), Monism, Pluralism, Panpsychism, Humanism, Pragmatism and the many other systems which jostle for men's custom in this Philosophical Fair ? It is a matter of doubt whether modern metaphysic is any real advance on that of the greater among the ancients. In my opinion none is better constructed than the Six *Darśanas*. The advance has been made in Science. But even here there is dispute, both as to the facts observed and the theories based on them. For me, their greatest importance just lies in the fact, that the latest scientific inferences corroborate the intuitively derived teaching of the ancient sages. Thus present scientific conceptions of the constitution of matter, and notably the breakdown of the Atomic Theory, support the notions of Māyā, a single material basis of the Universe, and the existence of Ether which, as Ākāśa, was accepted in India when Europe had not passed beyond the so-called " four elements." Both science and Indian beliefs posit an evolution of beings from the inorganic to the organic, and, in the latter division, from plant to animal and animal to man. In India it has always been held that there are no partitions or gulfs between the various forms of existence, and that, for instance, the difference between man and animal is not a difference of kind but of degree. Again from the new Psychology and Psychical Research, Vedānta gains support, as from theories touching the nature of mind as a material force (as Herbert Spencer teaches) and as a power (the predominant idea in " New Thought " literature), the extension of the field of Consciousness, dual personalities and various forms of psychical phenomena.

Nevertheless, so far as ultimates are concerned, neither Metaphysics nor Science can establish more than a high degree of probability ; they may lead to the door of the shrine, but they do not directly and

unaided place the enquirer within. The Brahman or
all-Pervader cannot be established by reason, because
it is never an object of knowledge. The Sāstra says,
one can only know Brahman by *being* Brahman and
that is by spiritual experience. Its being and nature
are taught by revelation. Revelation is not the speaking
of any voice, divine or otherwise, from without. It is
self-knowledge in its deepest sense and nothing more.
The Vedāntist affirms that we can know ourselves, not
only in our gross or physical aspect as being fair or
dark, short or tall and so on, or in our subtle or mental
aspect as perceiv'ng and reasoning beings, but in our
innermost essence as that of which both body and mind
are manifestations. It may be the fact or it may not
be the fact, but there is nothing unreasonable in the
proposition as such. It is this Self-knowledge, attained
by oneself in varying degrees, or accepted as the
experience of others (Sruti), whose testimony we may,
for reasons satisfying to ourselves, accept, which renders
certain that which to reason is only probable. Once
Sruti is accepted, Reason can follow its teaching without violence to its own principles. What was before
reasonable and probable is now both reasonable and
certain. This must be so, unless we assume what is
impossible, namely a divorce between rational and
spiritual truth. Truth however is one and what is
unreasonable must be rejected, whoever says it, " even
if He be the Lotus-born."

It is not India who has denied the rights of Reason.
It is Europe who in the past has done so. But Europe
has now, after fierce contest against Church tyranny
and oppression (aided by the State) with its imprison-
ment, torture and burning at the stake, largely achieved
in the present the right of free-thinking. Had India

been so opposed She might have been to-day more intellectually active. In the same way the political activity of Europe has been stimulated by the oppressive governance of its peoples. We westerners have had to fight for all the things of worth we have won.

Nowhere however has intellectual liberty been so authoritatively, and for such a length of time, recognised as in India. The word " Man " is derived from the root *Man,* which in Sanskrit means " to think ". Man is *Manu.* Therefore man is " *The Thinker* ". He is thus distinguished from the rest of the world by his *thinking.* What greater definition than this of our Aryan forefathers can be found? In no country in the whole world has there been more thinking than in India, which has been indeed a very hot-bed of speculation and divergent beliefs and practices : such as the Materialism of Chārvāka and the Lokāyatas, true atheists, men of the type of Ajitakeśakambali, the opponent of Sakya-Mūni, who denied that any Brāhmaṇa, or any one else, had discovered any truth concerning any other life than this, who said that man was made of the four elements and dissolved into the elements at death and had gone for ever ; such again as the Sānkhyas, dualists and realists, affirming the existence of Spirit, but holding a God as Governor of the universe unproved (Nirīśvara-Darśana) ; the Nyāyavaiśeṣikas, Pluralists, Realists affirming the existence of the Supreme Lord ; Buddhist idealism (Vijñānavāda) and so called " Nihilists " (Sūnyavādins) ; Vedāntic Monism, qualified Monism, and Dualism in various theistic forms, Mimāṃsakas, Jainas and every shade of thought imaginable.

In Vedāntic Sādhana, Reasoning or *Manana* occupies, with *S'ravaṇa* and *Nididhyasana*, a principal place. All the *Darśanas* particularly perhaps the Nyāya, are written to serve *Manana* or reasoning, and the Brahmasūtras, which the Vedāntic systems expound, are known as Vaiyāsikanyāyamālā.

As regards science, India has had its own great achievements which you will find recorded in part in Professors Brojendranath Seal's and Binoy-kumar Sirkar's works on the subject. Up to the modern period India was more than the equal in this field of any other country. But undoubtedly, since that period, the palm for scientific thinking and experiment must be given to the West. Those who however imagine, that reasoning and freedom of thought are a distinctive appanage of the West are very ignorant of the history of their country. If one had to make the comparison, and one did make it over a period, extending from say (to go no further) 2000 B.C., the statement must be reversed in favour of India. No country has honoured Reason more, or given it greater freedom than India. The cultural restrictions in this country have been of a different kind, consisting in the social ordering of life, and in later times exclusion from knowledge by reason of artificial distinctions of caste. But those, to whom the book of knowledge was open, have always been able to think freely enough. When Europe was under ecclesiastical domination, the attempt was made to make every one think the same way in the manner laid down by Church authority. It is against this that European Rationalism protested.

I at first found a difficulty in choosing a subject to address to you out of the many which presented themselves, and I had practically written a paper, with which I was not satisfied, because I could not put before you (as indeed I cannot even now) what I wished to say within the limits available to me, when, by something more than chance, I found amongst my old papers a note sent me some years ago on the Gāyatrī-Mantra, the holiest expression of the thought of India. I therefore restate its argument more summarily in words, and with some further additions of my own.

The Mantra opens and ends with the *Praṇava* or *Om.* This refers in the first place to the threefold aspect of the World-Cause in manifestation. That there is a cause (Mahāśakti) which, as the universal Self, contains the universe within Itself, is dealt with in the meditation which follows. Here both the Cause and Its manifestation are the object of thought. The Nādabindu indicates that causal state of the World-Power, prior to its threefold differentiation as represented by the letters A, U, M, which coalesce into *Om.* These letters stand for its working which is observable by all. For the first and second refer to present activities, as well as those in the past and future, of the *Mahāśakti*, as the Radical Vital Potential. M or Rudra as so observed is chemical action breaking down the combinations of matter. This is the disintegration of form. A (Brahmā) is the force which creates it anew by its ever rejuvenescent molecular activity, thus rescuing organised vitality from the processes which are ever at work to consume (as " M ") its forms. U (Viṣṇu) is the maintaining power which stabilizes matter which is only a relatively stable condition of energy, from which it appears, and into which it, at length, merges. Looking at the sum total of manifested energy,

Viṣṇu as Maintainer, through space and time, is a
theological statement of the doctrine of the general conservation of energy. The Mahāśakti, in Herself Perfect
Consciousness (Cidrūpiṇī), is the threefold Powers
of Will, Knowledge and Action and manifests in the
building up, maintenance and disintegration of forms.
What follows, as all else, is contained in *Om*, but some
of its implications are developed in the rest of the
Gāyatrī-Mantra. *Om* considered as a sound (*Dhvani*)
is the approximate natural name of the first undifferentiated movement (*Sāmānya-Spanda*) of the stressing
material cause (Prakṛti) of the universe. The primordial " Sound " or Stress is the primordial functioning
of the Brahma-S'akti.

Then follow the three *Vyāhṛtis—Bhuh, Bhuvah,
Svah*, which are *Lakṣaṇa* of, that is, stand for, all the
fourteen Lokas, though now in the (Vyāvahārika) world
we are only concerned with the first three ; Bhūh for
Bhūh and the seven nether Talas, Bhuvah for itself,
and Svah for Svah and the remaining upper regions up
to Satya. The Lokas represent states of consciousness.
Bhūrloka or earth is the state of normal experience.
The Lokas above it are states of supernormal consciousness, and the Talas below are conditions of sub-normal
experience. Objectively considered, matter becomes
more and more dense as one descends from the highest
to the lowest Loka and thence to the Talas ; and as the
veil of matter is more or less dense, so the state of
consciousness varies. The first five Lokas, from and
including Earth, are those of the five forms of sensible
matter, the sixth is that of Mind ; and the seventh is the
causal state of both Mind and Matter. Earth and the
nether states are the gross body, the Lokas from Bhuvah
to Tapah are the subtle body, and Satya is the causal

body of the great Puruṣa referred to in the Gāyatrī and worshipped in the Sun-circle (*Āditya-maṇḍala*). The *Vyāhṛtis* indicate that the Great Self which is indicated in *Om* pervades all the regions of the universe. How then do we get the notion of that Self and then experience it ?

In our ordinary condition of consciousness, the outer world is completely objective and stable and independent of it. It lies " over there " in the outer space entirely external to us, having, apparently its existence in itself and of itself. This state of consciousness is indicated by the first *Vyāhṛti* " *Bhūh.* " This is our normal state. Our mind is Here. It is one thing— *Aham* or I. The object, the *Idam* or " This, " the Vimarśa-Śakti, is there. It is another. But a little reflection reveals that these seemingly independent objects are for us bundles of certain qualities, which are so, only because they are sensed by the Senses which are constituted in a particular way. It is obvious that if our senses were not there, or if they were not seizing the object, there would be no sensation and no object. Again if the senses themselves were modified, the sense perceptions would also change. In that case the objects, which at first sight exist independently of our perceptions, would become something different from what they formerly were, as they would exhibit a different set of qualities. Thus the objective world is not really independent as we first thought, and the form it presents to us is due to the action of some objective force acting upon the subjectively sensuous character of the beings who perceive it. With such reflections the notion of objective stability wears off, and the world first assumes a mobile condition, in so far as it is seen that the objects, which at first seem to possess the qualities which characterise them, do so not only of themselves but also of ourselves. The condition of mind in which this notion is firmly held is the second of the seven divisions or stages of the Pārthiva consciousness. All materially-minded thinkers, who look upon the objective world as independent of a subjective perceiver, are in the Bhūrloka.

The second condition of consciousness in which the subjectivity of the self first asserts itself, and the objective world loses its absolute and independent character and appears as dependent upon, influenced and modified by the subjective factor, is expressed in some forms of idealism. In such cases though the subjective element is recognised, it is not ideal in the sense that it has its root wholly in itself, but it is objectively actual in the sense that it has its existence at least mainly in the external. The seer, seeing, and seen, are localised, in the outer space. As we proceed upwards, whilst the seen (*Jñeya*) remains external to us, the seeing (*Jñāna*) is localised internally, until at length the seer (*Jñātā*), seeing (*Jñāna*), and seen (*Jñeya*) are all internalised, subjectified and unified. This *Jñāna-svarūpa* of the Supreme Consciousness is opposed to *Jñānavṛtti* or the limited and differentiated consciousness.

After the attainment of this second stage we pass to the third. We then ask, what lies behind the senses, wherein to a great extent the appearance of the external world depends ? We then perceive that the senses do not apprehend objects unless attention, in the form of *Manas* is bestowed upon them. The whole world, open at any moment to the senses, is impinging on them at every moment, but only that is perceived to which we pay attention. The Bṛhadāraṇyaka Upaniṣad gives good psychology when it says, "I did not hear. My mind was elsewhere." But attention must be directed and willed. We learn then that behind the Senses there is some Self which directs its attention to a particular object, and so perceives it by the medium of the senses. There is thus no sense-perception without the co-operation of the attention of the Self. Therefore the world (considered apart from what it may possibly be in itself) is dependent both upon the senses and attentive mind of the self which is behind them. The attainment and habit of this thought is the third ascending stage of the Pārthiva consciousness.

We have thus attained a knowledge of the self. We next reflect upon its nature. To the ordinary consciousness of the first two states, the self either did not appear important, or seemed to be limited to the body and restricted within its scope. But reflection has now shown that not only is it unconditioned by the senses, but actually conditions them, giving them effective operation through its power of attention. The self then appears uncontrolled by the physical body, self-luminous and overlapping the bounds of the physical senses. When this notion is reached the fourth stage of consciousness is attained.

The next question is—what is the relation of the self, the senses and the objects? Are they each independent in their origin the one of the other, or is one the cause of the other two? They cannot be independent of each other, for this would mean that either they had no relation to each other, or if there is any relation it is due to some fourth thing external to the others, which is the basis of their relation and apart from which they cannot be in relation. It is obvious that they are in relation

to each other, and, as such the ground of their relation
must be either in, or outside, themselves. It is sufficient
to say here that no fourth principle capable of holding
them together and bringing them into relation is perceived. But logically the same result can be established,
for if a fourth principle bringing them into relation
were assumed, which was dependent on some one or
other of them, the causal element would be still to seek,
whereas if it were independent and still in relation to
the three, then the ground of this relation would have
to be sought for in some fifth element, and so on with
regressio ad infinitum. We must then confine ourselves
to the three and examine the nature of this relation.

The relation can be grounded only in that element
out of the three which is independent of the others, for
a dependent entity cannot have the ground of its
relation to others within itself. The perceived objects
are not independent. For they require the senses to be
perceived as objects of that character according
to which we perceive them. The senses are not
independent, for sense-perception requires attention of
the Self. Objects in order to be objects must be
perceived by the senses. Without the senses they are
not objects for us. The senses are not operative senses
without the attention of the Self behind them, On the
other hand the Self does not cease to be the Self, when
it is not attentively perceiving objects through the
senses, as we see in the case of dream. The Self in
dream is cut off from the senses. Indeed it evolves both
objects and senses. The Self in dream is cut off from
the objective world, having nothing in it but ideas
thereto. Yet it transforms for itself those ideas into
outer objects and the sense which perceives them.
What we see in dream is real while it lasts. Thus the

Self is independent of the other two and has within itself the ground of the causal relation by which it evolves them. The firm and lasting consciousness which realises this is the fifth step in the ascending consciousness.

What then is the nature of the relation between the cause producing the objective world and the effect so produced ? Is it a cause material in its nature, producing an effect external to itself, or an ideal cause working ideally upon itself to produce an effect ? The cause cannot produce an effect which is really external to itself. Were this so, the dream-world of which we are creators would be external to the self which produces it. In that case it would not vanish with that state of consciousness which lies at the root of it. The objective world can only be ideally connected with its cause. Gradually the notion that the objective world is produced by a cause external to it is rejected, and the notion is accepted that the cause has the effect lying ideally within it, which is projected and externalised in the course of cosmic evolution. For when mind and matter are evolved, each has equal reality and (in the sense of impermanence) unreality. In its highest sense Reality = Persistence = Deathlessness (Amṛtatva) = Ānanda, which is living unimpeded in the fullest measure, which is Ātmā. And so Herbert Spencer on biological principles defines " pleasure " as the index of the unimpeded flow of vitality. What fully persists and is therefore fully " real " is the self. The firm establishment of this experience is the sixth consciousness. Just as the dream-world lies within the consciousness of the dreamer, who projects it into fancied objectivity, so the objective world of common (*Vyavahārika*) experience lies within, and is projected by, the Consciousness of the so-called World-dreamer, who sums up in Himself all experiences. Is the world or its cause necessarily thus by virtue of the nature of the cause itself, or on account of some external fact? There is no material other then itself outside the cause which it takes within, works upon, and puts forth. It might be thought that there was ideal connection with the objective world on the causal side, but that the root of the objective world upon which it operates was something lying elsewhere than in its inner being. But this is not so as the effect, the objective world, must necessarily be within the cause, otherwise it is not possible that it should be ideally connected with it. If the connection with the cause were something other than the constitution of the cause itself, there must be an indication of what that something is and the nature of its connection with the cause. Moreover if that something lies outside the cause, we must suppose some medium connecting that something with the cause itself. And again the question would arise whether this connection was natural and necessary, or adventitious. If the latter, then what is it which brings about the connection? In this way we have a *regressio ad infinitum* unless we suppose the connection to be natural and necessary. It is reasonable then to hold that the objective world lies necessarily in its root the cause. Moreover, having arrived at the consciousness that the effect is ideally connected with the cause, it is more reasonable to hold that this connection is due to the constitution of the cause itself. When the entire objective world is viewed as necessarily lying within the cause, the seventh, or what we may call the Satya stage of the *Pārthiva* consciousness, is attained.

Up to this we have only dealt with the sub-divisions of the *Pārthiva* or earth consciousness, that is, experience as beings in the *Pārthiva* state elaborated by reflection to its highest point. By such reflection we reach the standpoint from which the whole universe is viewed as lying in a seed (*Bija*) form, ideally and potentially within its cause which is nothing but the Self.

Thus one aspect of the grandeur of the Self as the potential cause of the entire universe is revealed. The *S'ādhaka* has thus passed through higher and higher stages of the *Pārthiva* consciousness to the indwelling Spirit within it. His thus expanded consciousness brings forth the exclamation which is the Gāyatrī-Mantra, in which homage is made to the Supreme Power, which manifests in this and all other forms of experience and its objects in the Universe. Hence the word by which the *Sādhaka* denotes this indwelling Spirit is *Savitā*, or the Projector of the Universe from out of Its own thought, without external material or aid. It is however to be remembered that the strength of the force of the externality-notion which commenced at the stage of Ether (*Ākāśa*) reached its greatest power in the earth-principle (*Pṛthivī-Tattva*) of solid, ponderable, three dimensioned matter and in the *Pārthiva* consciousness. Therefore it is that *Savitā* the Producer, though really the Inner Self, is itself, externalised as something placed out in space and hence we find it designated by *Tat* or That. This " Thatness " will, as we proceed, meet in one unity the Supremeness of the last stage. But it is the characteristic of the *Pārthiva* consciousness that it always tends to locate both the Seer and the Seen in outer space. The devotee to whose mental gaze the indwelling Spirit reveals itself,

bursts forth into the Mantra : " Let us meditate on the
adorable darkness-dispelling Spirit of the self-luminous
all-producing *Savitā*," with the prayer that It may
inspire and illumine our inward Reason. It is through
this illumination of the Reason by the source of Reason,
that the inner Reason which is our inner being sees and
understands the entire universe and its principles. This
Savitā produces the universe in accordance with the
principles of Reason which are at base His own inner
being (*Vicāracamatkritih paramātmamayi*), and this production of His is revealed to us and realised by us in
participation with the Divine Reason of His being.   As
we are, in our deepest ground, the Spirit which, in its
outer aspect, is our limited selves and what is not ourselves ; as our reason is an efflorescence of Its own
eternal all-knowingness, so our outer reasoning is in
conformity with the truth in its own sphere, and is
illumined to pass beyond reasoning upon the objective
world to an understanding of the rational vesture of
the Spirit, and then to the intuitive realisation of the
Spirit Itself. This union of ours with the universal is
shown by the fact that we, as so many individuals, if
we were to remain confined within our individuality,
could never perceive the universe as common to us all.
This common perception of the universe could not be
achieved by us as individuals, but only as being one
with the universal. And therefore in so far as we are
the common perceivers of the universe, we are not
individual but universal. Our individuality consists
in our perception of the universe in so far as it differs
from that of others. Thus difference of perception,
which individualises us, is not based upon any inherent
differentiating condition in our essential being, but
upon the externalising limitations, the result of

particular Karma, which make it impossible for all to perceive everything at the same time to the same extent. This perception of the difference of the many, due to limitation, differentiates each individual from the other, but it does not, and cannot, differentiate him from the Indwelling Universal (here *Pārthivā*) which is the common ground of all. Thus the *Sādhaka* says that it is this *Savitā* or Indwelling Universal, which inspires the Reason of us all, both as individual and as universal, and it is through the Self-luminous Consciousness of this Most Glorious Self (known not only in *Samādhi*, but in and through every act of reasoning, its mental embodiment) that we are enabled to learn and understand the Truth (*Satyam*). For it is *Satya* or the Persistent Self Itself. The relation between the individual and the universal being thus grasped, and it being realised that the individuality of the individual is only through the universal, we should then proceed to see what is the nature of this Universal which makes it project the universe as we see it around us.

Here we pass beyond the Gāyatrī Sādhana into the subtle Ātma-sādhana. The Vedāntist says that to such as truly see, whether with the eye of reason or intuition, the whole universe is perceived as originating from its source, as the Gangā from the Himālayas, and at length returning thereto. Its source is in the Power of the Perfect Consciousness which is S'iva, which means the Auspicious and Good, the Brahman or all-Pervading. All which exist are Its varying forms, existing in happiness so long as they are in Harmony with Him who is Bliss (Ānanda) itself. Power and Harmony—let us repeat these words day by day. Think continuously the Thought of Power and be powerful. Individual Power is a small thing, but when

it links itself to, or identifies itself with, the Supreme
Power, it shows its mightiness according to the degree
of such harmony and union. Power however does not
merely mean material force. The latter is only Power
translated to the material plane. Power is also mental,
moral, spiritual. Love is Power—the greatest of Powers.
Everything in fact which exists is Power, which is the
Mother (Ambikā).

We may intellectually conceive this. But how to
realise it? Here the Vedāntic practice (Sādhana) is as
profound as its theory. It says that man as body,
mind and spirit is one whole. If one would understand and realise the Pure, one must be that, both in
body and mind (Suddhātmā). In the West it is commonly supposed that a man may arrive at or at any
rate is competent to seek for, the truth by reason alone.
Mere reason however is insufficient. A man may be
deemed a philosopher in the West, and yet lack in
character and morals. This is not so in Vedānta which
says that its doctrine cannot be perfectly understood,
much less realised, unless the body and mind are made
pure enough to approach the Purity which that doctrine
teaches. The whole being must be brought into harmony,
so far as may be, with it. Thus is it understood and at
length realised. The pure mind and body naturally
think the thoughts which link man's mind with the
Universal Mind and the Universal Self of which it is the
subtle form. Sādhana varies according to the stages of
development and therefore competency (Adhikāra) of
man. But the highest of Sādhanas is Karuṇā or compassion. I took up recently an English novel, curiously
enough called " The Rationalist. " There I found the
phrase " this new thing appearing on the horizon—the
phenomenon of Compassion which is now beginning to

express itself in action. " This " new thing " is as old here as the Vedas and the Buddha Gotama who ceaselessly taught it. Avoid giving pain. Allay it where it is. Yet the application of this principle is not so simple as is sometimes thought. The truly great of our race need no other power nor effort than to be themselves. By the mere fact of their own self-redemption, they redeem others. Others must at least strive to hold in view the ideal in the midst of the struggles into which their nature and circumstances may lead them. Mere apathy however is not Yoga. Yoga is unity with the Lord in the forms of His Power as one's family, friends, people and the world at large. He is *Jagadbandhu*, that is Friend of the World. We can each make effort to follow this Supreme Law and to extricate ourselves from the morass of merely selfish struggle. And as we successfully, according to our varying opportunity and capacity, do so, we will find that we make individual advance, and that the power to impose our will on others increases. If each will, according to his capacity, so order his life that he does not cause pain to, and relieves the suffering of this great Body of the Lord which is the Universe, of which each is an infinitesimal part, then they will commence to really *understand*. The greatest cloud upon understanding is selfishness. The mass of men are still mere candidates for Humanity and must raise themselves to it. The meaning of Evolution is the liberation of the Spirit or Inner Self from all which obscures its essential freedom. This liberation is taking place in the gradual ascent from inorganic to organic being and the advance of organism culminating, for the present, in man as we know him. The highest humanity is that in which it and Divinity meet. In man the I principle is still being developed in present humanity. The end is perfection of the present " I, " and then by stages its identification with the Universal " I ", the *Pūrṇāham* which is the Infinite Self. The *Sādhaka* thinks of this ascending or return movement repeatedly for *Japa* on the Gāyatrī is necessary to correct the natural objective tendencies of thought. This is the true performance of *Sandhyā*, which literally means perfect *Dhyāna* or meditation, of which the Gāyatrī-Mantra is the soul.

Those who have not learnt the goal of evolution do not realise the necessity of Sandhyā. They have before their eyes only the present powers and capacities of man and think that his present possibilities on the lower plane should alone be realised. They think only of the fulfilment of desires, shutting their eyes to the purpose for which man exists in the world, namely, first harmony with the Active (Viśvātma-Śakti) and then union with the Unchanging Brahman (Cidrūpiṇī-Śakti). They fail to realise that the Reality, which underlies all phenomena, must also be in the deepest nature of man, and unless that Reality is known the deepest aspirations of Humanity cannot be fulfilled. From the earliest beginnings all earnest minds have sought the solution of the riddle of the universe. All types of thinkers whether materialists, idealists, or spiritualists, have supposed that there is some Reality, call it Matter, Mind, Spirit, Brahman, God, Allah, what they will, which whilst eluding their mental grasp, is all the same there, though it cannot be comprehended by the mind in its fullness. It cannot only be there, but it must be *here* within the inmost nature of all, as one with the deepest inmost self. If so, man must not only study the objective universe, which he should do to gain knowledge of the external Śakti-aspect of this reality, but he must plunge deep into his own nature, for he can only realise It within and not without the self. Man's present existence is a mode of consciousness, ordinarily in the spiritual *Bhūh* Consciousness, or in the forms of a *Tala* Consciousness. The search is to find out the universal principle. Beings in the lower order of evolution have not the " I " principle evolved to the level of *Vijñāna* or *Buddhi*, and therefore the reason and understanding must be developed. The greater portion of the work of evolution must be done by the individual himself, under the guidance of the divine principle of Reason, and if we do not wish to be left behind in the general progressive movement, we must give up all lethargy and the contentment which the animal (whether as beast or man) has with his present powers and capacities and their external environment. Man must seek to understand the meaning of life and its end, and looking beyond by the Eye of Divine Wisdom (*Jñāna-cakṣu*) endeavour to first intellectually grasp, and then to realise, that which is the Beginning, the Maintainer and the End of all— the *Vacyā-śakti* of the Gāyatrī-Mantra.

CHAPTER XXXI

ĀTMA - SĀDHANA

(YOGA BY REASONING)

I HAVE in the previous article shortly indicated a form of Gāyatrī-Sādhana given to me some years ago. Here follows the Ātma-Sādhana which is taken up at the point at which the Gāyatrī-Sādhana ends.

Duality is inherent in the constitution of all manifested being. Therefore until man realises the whole (Pūrṇa-brahman), that is, the Universe as one with its both immanent and transcending Root, there is an object whether the same is apparently wholly outside, and different from, and independent of the Self, or whether it is experienced internally as a mode of the latter's subjective existence. But the experience is of varying grades. For just as matter, objectively considered, becomes more and more gross from its first ethereal (Ākāśa) form to scientific, that is, ponderable matter, so when in the upward ascent of consciousness Matter has been withdrawn into itself and exists there as a mode of being, that mode becomes a more and more subtle expression of the principle whence all objectivity, whether externally sensed or internally experienced, is derived. At the stage of complete manifestation, that is, ordinary *Bhūh* experience, the object or "This" (Idam) is wholly outside, and independent of, the Self, the two being mutually exclusive the one of the other. Matter is then in the form in which we ordinarily sense it. We may remain at this stage which is that of objective science or go within and to the Root of all experience. If that Root is within, then introspection can alone discover it. How? That which carries upwards or inwards is the will-to-know of a nature ever more and more purifying itself and thus gaining strength by its approach to the Almighty *Savitā* of all. This is Prayer in its highest form. At each moment of attainment and advance we naturally render homage to the glory of the All-pervading Being, who gradually reveals His infinite Self, just as Linnaeus the great botanist fell on his knees when he first saw Its objective expression in the form of the golden beauty of the flower of the wild Gorse. But the object, though it persists in experience until the attainment of the perfect Consciousness (Brahma-Svarūpa), is yet diversely realised as we proceed innerwards. In the first place it is brought from without to within the Self, and there experienced not as something different from the Self but as a mode of its own existence. Next as such it becomes less and less pointed and more diffused and is brought into closer and closer touch with the subjective being. This is effected by an intense and penetrating meditation at each stage of advance with a view to realise the subjective root of that stage. When the objective tendencies of thought are held in check, Consciousness of Itself more and more purely manifests.

In the Pārthiva consciousness, matter is in a fully pointed condition outside the Self until the Satya stage is reached. Even the Self appears as a concentrated objective point in space. At the Satya stage the notion is gained through reasoning that the entire universe must lie within the Self as its cause. Acting on this suggestion of the Reason, the Pārthiva consciousness turns back into itself, and for the first time as *Antarmukhī* is conscious of something within itself lying there in a pointed form. The pointedness remains, but the world is carried within the Self, where it is grasped as a mode of its own existence. The peculiar consciousness is *Rasa*, which is the subjective root of what objectively appears to the Pārthiva consciousness as *Ap*. The external particularised location disappears. If the point is located outside, there is *Gandha*—experience of matter in its Pṛthivī condition. Gandha, Rasa, Rūpa, Sparśa, Sabdha are the various kinds of consciousness, which in the evolutionary process are the subjective root of sensible matter and which on the full externalisation of such matter are the five different ways in which it affects the senses as smell, taste, sight, touch, and hearing.

In *Rasa* experience the object is brought in closer relation with the Self, both by reason of its being placed therein, and of a lessened intensity of its pointedness to the self as compared with Gandha or Bhūh experience. With a lessening intensity of the Rasa experience, the latter is shifted from the inner to the outer and seems to be coming from outside less in the form of feeling than of intellection in the shape of general unqualitative and undifferentiated form. There is then the idea of something there all round the Self, affecting the subjective being by way of a superficially, instead of interiorly, felt experience. This is *Rūpa* experience, the subjective root of Agni who is the builder of forms. This is the last of the form (Mūrtta) division of Tattvas. The lessened intensity of the Rasa-feeling has necessarily the effect of setting consciousness on the surface of subjective being, and as the idea of space or co-existing externality-points is already there, this weakened Rasa experience, being externally localised, spreads itself over the space and becomes the subjective root of the Rūpa consciousness. The Rūpa experience, when closely looked into and allowed to come very close to the subjective being, is experienced as Touch or *Sparśa*, the subjective root as Vāyu. This is not the touch produced by specialised form, for this is a sensation had only after the production of Agni. The experience may be compared to the perception in ordinary life of the thermal quality of objects. The subjective intensification of Rūpa, with its surface expansion, when concentrated into a point of the inner subjective being, produced the Rasa feeling, which one located outwards was, as Gandha, the subjective root of the externalised objectivity of daily life. Rūpa affects the surface subjective being, whilst Sparśa again shifts experience into the inner, as the whole subjective being then responds to Sparśa as a whole. This Sparśa Consciousness, which is objectively Vāyu, is when closely examined found to consist of externality idea-points spread over the surface of the subjective being, receding away as mere hints of outsideness, as compared with the something which is outside of Rūpa experience. This is Śabda experience, the subjective root of Ākāśa, the seed of all externalised or externally located world-phenomena. It persists as the deathless basis (Amṛta) of all manifestation downwards or outwards; into which all phenomena are resolved in their upward or inward course. The realisation of this is the Śabda consciousness.

The root of externality-consciousness refers back to its origin the inner mind (which projects the idea of mere outerness and which is its counterpart), the root from which the notion of externality arises as the tree from its seed. This internal-root which grows into Akāśa is the Brahma-consciousness as the internal root-will (corresponding on the Pārthiva plane to the Manas) which lies at the root of all manifestation. Behind this is the " I am myself ", which subjectifying itself as the " I am myself I " becomes the Cosmic Will. The former is Cit as the objectified self-consciousness. And from the fact that it is the starting point and internal correspondence of the objective world it may be called the Bhūh Consciousness of the internal ideal, the subjective region as distinguished from the Bhūh consciousness of the external, actual objective region, the first Vyāhṛti in the ascending scale. But this Supreme Bhūh, being the terminating point of objectivity in the form of the Self as Universe cannot stand by itself. It must be the result of some assertion of consciousness which is not that of any other than Self-Being, as all other assertions or Vyāhṛtis of the external world are here transcended. Thus this assertion as " I am " may be called the *Bhuvah* of the supreme objective region as distinguished from the Bhuvah of the objective region lower down. And behind this assertion of self-existence as its root is the eternal subjective " I " (Aham) of the supreme *Svah* as distinguished from the external objective " I " or individuality in the Svah lower down. This completes the field of assertion of self-consciousness behind which lies the entire Consciousness (Cit) Itself, that is, Conciousness (Cit) *per se*, which whilst itself ever unchanged and unconditioned, is the source of All the changing forms of experience mentioned which again merge into it. This is Bliss itself (Ānanda) or Joy, of which the world is an expression in time and space, the Joy by which it is maintained and the Joy into which the world re-enters, the Universal Mother (like the earthly mother) clasping the child which She has produced to Her breast.

The " I " or Aham here spoken of is not the limited " I " of Ahangkāra which is only a gross and particularised reflection of the former. In the Kāmakalā-vilāsa, the Supreme I (Aham) is very beautifully explained as the union (Sāmarasya) of its own infinite Self as Prakāśa with itself as Vimarśa-Śakti, which is a pure mirror (Darpaṇa) made of a mass of the Prakāśa Śiva's own rays. These are reflected back and the Pūrṇāhambhāva or the experience of the " I " as being all arises. That is the notion of Self had by reference to the Self which is then the Enjoyer of Bliss. There is no other but the Self in the fullest purity and un-limitedness of both and is thus the supreme Aham. From this root " I ", which is Kāma, the will to create and the collectivity (Samaṣṭi) of all the powers which constitute all manifested things, there burgeons forth the trunk, the branches, the leaves and fruit of the great Aśvattha tree which is the universe.

It is only when this Supreme Universal " I " is reached that it is possible to realise its eternal inward-ness as Mahāśūnya, which is the Great Void in the sense that it is nothing which thought can conceive or words utter. None of the higher stages can be realised until the next lower one is grasped. Before the universal " I " is reached, it is not possible to realise the " I-less " Cit or consciousness, as the veil of matter covers (though with decreasing thickness as we ascend) its Glorious Face. It requires a strong effort of subjective penetration to pass though this covering, dense as ponderable matter at its lowest end, and to reach the Consciousness which lies behind, of which all forms are Its assertions. At the time of meditation, the entire thick veil of material (Pārthiva) existence must be gradually thinned by moving inwards according to the stages described ; by reducing the crude and thicker form of consciousness into the subtle and more refined, till by gradual inner progress the subtlest point of the universal " I " which is the Lord (Īśvara) of Vedānta is reached. After this That which is the eternal and changeless ground of even this is realised and then there is Kaivalya Mokṣa the ultimate Basis of all the Forms which have arisen out of Its self-assertion —the Will to be many of which the Veda speaks. This is the great Self of the Vedānta. This is the Perfect Experience which is called the Supreme Love (*Niratiśayapremāspadatvam ānandatvam*).

These forms of the Self can be broadly classified into the actual, objective or external which is the waking state (Jāgrat avasthā) ; the ideal, the subjective or internal, the assertional or the state of dream (Svapna) ; and the third the state of dreamless slumber (Suṣupti) which is the bare subjective standing by, itself not yet in active assertion, but having passed the equilibrium point about to assert itself, but for the time being having the assertion latent in it, lying there unperceived, but ready to shoot forth into assertion, at first qualitative, and then into perception, by reason of both qualitative and external manifestation. Herein all ideas become merged and latent and thence project themselves into the Ideal and thence again into the Actual in the course of the involution of the Self into the Māyik covering which is the universe. The Perfect

Consciousness, as realising all these three stages with all their differences and similarities, lies beyond them all, though it is one with all, supporting them by Its own essential Being and Power (S'akti). They are Its forms —the forms of that Consciousness which It is. It runs through all (Sūtrātmā) and unifies them all, but remains in Itself unlimited and unconditioned, giving them both their separate existence, yet summing them up into Its own Life and Being, which comprehending all yet transcends them from the standpoint of its own Being in itself or Svarūpa. It is beyond all because it is infinite. It comprehends all in its supremely rich experience because It is the whole (Pūrṇa). It is Love because It is the Love of the Self for the Self. It is Joy because all Love is that; but it is perfect also. It is the Perfect Experience (Jñānasvarūpa) which thought achieves by a pure mind in a pure body. It is thus the Supreme Siddhi of all Sādhana and Yoga.

Om Tat Sat